THE SEX IMPERATIVE

THE SEX IMPERATIVE

Mwalimu K. Bomani Baruti
(formerly Larry D. Crawford)

ISBN: 0-9678943-5-2

Akoben House
P.O. Box 10786
Atlanta, Georgia 30310

Printed in the USA by
Morris Publishing
3212 East Highway 30
Kearney, NE 68847
800-650-7888

TO

Yaa Mawusi, my complement

Acknowledgments

Madasi pa to Odumankoma, the Abosom, the Nananom Nsamanfo, the millions upon millions of Afrikans who embodied traditional Afrikan values of whom we are the culmination, and my immediate ancestors who safely brought me back from the insanity of this Western cultural wasteland.

Madasi to my queen, editor, soulmate, counsel, motivator, inspiration, guide, Yaa Mawusi, who knew who I was before I did and replaced my bottle with Afrikan books, my anger with passion and my selfish individualism with our daughter. These thoughts are as much hers as mine. Adwoa Foluke, our daughter, has become my patience, vision, hope, voice, determination, primary researcher, on-call editor and victory. Madasi to my mother, Irene Loretta Chambers Crawford, and father, Frank Crawford, who reared me, tolerating me and suffered my confused rage New Europe. Appreciation also goes out to Mama Hill, who with patient persistence put me back in touch with the means to this end and my elder brother, Garry Jonathan, who served as my model for reading while defending me when I was young and dumb.

It was Ptah Hotep who uttered, "The wise man who ceases to learn ceases to be wise," and Erykah Badu who reiterated it in "the man who knows something knows that he knows nothing at all."[1] It is my students who continue to teach me what I need to know. On this project, I am especially indebted intellectually, emotionally and spiritually to Kwaw Andreas Woods, Obadele Kwame Kambon, Kwadwo Fodwo Gyase, Kwabena Ofosuhene, Fenyx, Yaw Theory Thompson, Sowande Mustakeem, Ijeoma Ananaba, Amika King, Kwame Hines, Ojo Harris, Adofo Axam, Chinua Woods, Tor Callahan, Simba Blackwell, Becktemba Charleston, Ata Charleston, Adjwoa Hogue, Adisa Mitchell, Malikah Mitchell and Joseph Brownlee. These thoughts have evolved over many years, so I would be remiss if I did not express a special appreciation to all the students from my *Men in Society* classes at Morehouse College, as well as the many others in the Atlanta University Center and beyond who chose to become and remain Afrikan and express their Afrikanity despite

---

[1] *Baduizm*, "On & On," 1997.

the machinations of negro/negroette[2] administrators, faculty and classmates. I thank each and every one of you for forcing me to define what it meant to be and become Afrikan.

Madasi to the collection of individuals who supported me over the years with their space, time, resources, thoughts and spirit, working to push and prod these ideas out of me even before I fully recognized their existence. For this I am greatly in debt to Marcus 3X, Dr. Afia Serwaa Zakia, Dr. Llaila O. Afrika, Marcus Kline, Jendayi O. Foluke, all the supporters of the Akobɛn Institute, the family of Mutana Health Café and last, but in no way least, the brothers who drum and sisters who dance in the Afrikan way at the Fihankra Cultural Center whose sounds and movements allowed Spirit to more easily guide my editing. I sincerely apologize to any Afrikans I may have overlooked for at no point could I claim this work as my own. Everyone I know feeds me.

---

[2] My usage of the term "negro" (and negroette) is detailed in the essay "negroes" in Larry D. Crawford (Mwalimu A. Bomani Baruti), *negroes and other essays* (Atlanta, GA: Ankoben Institute, 2000, pp.143-173). Also see Council of Black Internal Affairs, *The American Directory of Certified Uncle Toms*, NY: CBIA & DFS Publishing, 2002.

TABLE OF CONTENTS

Introduction by Dr. Llaila O. Afrika

This book makes a very complex subject transparent. It challenges the reader to re-define sex and create a holistic sex that reflects an African culture. Sex is a culture's non-verbal communication. The Chinese, Japanese and caucasians have different sex rituals and ceremonies because their cultures are different. Sex has to be consistent with a culture's norms (value system). Sex transmits and translates culture. Many words of a culture's language, as well as it's rituals and ceremonies, can not be translated from one culture to another. The same can be said for a culture's sex rituals and ceremonies. Nature fixes boundaries between races and cultures that can not be crossed. For example, if a lion (African) is made to perform a monkey's (caucasian's) sex rituals and ceremonies that does not make the lion a monkey. The lion would be performing out of its nature and performing a sexuality created by the monkey's mind. The lion would be sexually out of out of it's nature, out of its mind and culture. Sex speaks to a culture's value system. A caucasian sexuality speaks to a caucasian reality. It makes sense to them and them only. It is a foreign language that can not be holistically translated.

Caucasians have colonized the concept of sex and sexuality. They have attempted to universalize and globalize sex via movies and psychology. Nature will not and can not allow sex to be universalized or globalized. Sex is unique to a people's culture – it is not multicultural. For example, in nature there are many different types of grains (barley, wheat, rye, etc.) and not one universal strain. At one time the caucasians used one strain of cotton seed on southern cotton plantations. The boll weevil insect favored that type of cotton and attacked and basically destroyed the cotton industry. Nature will not allow universalization of seeds. The caucasians use military logic to universalize plants, people and sex. This is against nature.

Caucasians are colonizing sex and attempting to program their sexuality into Africans. Caucasian sexuality practiced by Africans puts the African in conflict with African culture and nature. It makes the African an enemy of their own culture. The caucasians are trying to change a lion's nature to that of a monkey. And this makes the African mentally ill and a sexual Uncle Tom. The purpose of African sex is to serve Maat (truth, justice, harmony, balance, etc.). African culture believes that the sex organs have two functions which are reproduction (ejaculation, conception) and regeneration (injaculation, orgasm without climax). African culture also believes that each act of sexual intercourse creates either a child, a spirit child or a thought. African sex is a spiritual activity and a way to serve God and usually a prayer is said before the act of sex or a ritual and/or ceremony is done to spiritualize the activity. Caucasian sex is based upon their lust, violence and gods alien to Africans.

Caucasian sex may seem perverted, freaky and abnormal to Africans. However, this book details its natural progression and history and its confinement within the caucasian culture. It shows that the confusion over its normalcy among caucasians is ours not theirs and that caucasians are united in their effort to turn the world into their sexually perverted playground.

The caucasian woman may seem like she is exploited and abused. However, she is a co-partner in sustaining, creating and recreating their sexuality. She is not running away from their sex rituals and ceremonies by moving their sex into another form. In their sex mythology sex is ruled by the planet Mars who is called the troublemaker, warmonger and rules the zodiac sign Aires. Mars is the planet of war, cruelty, violence and aggressive sex which is symbolized by the color red. Hence, the caucasian woman wears red lipstick, fingernail polish, ruby red underwear and wears thongs (military underwear of Greeks). Ruby is a derivative of the word rape, rapture, reptile (penis), ruthless, etc. However sick or abnormal an African may view caucasian sexuality – it is sicker than that. The caucasian woman has created a sexuality that keeps her man interested in her despite the fact that the caucasian man "believes a dog is his best friend." And, the caucasian male has created a sexuality that keeps his woman interested in him despite the fact that she believes "diamonds (power) are a girl's best friend." The author points out these and many more sexual icons that glue the caucasian male and female together in their sexuality. A female wolf, elephant or rat is just as dangerous as a male. The caucasian woman is just as sexually sick and sexually happy as her mate.

Do not be deceived by other culture's sex such as the Chinese, Japanese, Koreans, Arabs and Indian (from India) as they are just as sexually sick as the caucasian. They are not to be imitated or copied. The African culture's Maat sex is the highest sexuality for Africans. It allows us to reach our highest level of humanity while other's sex

ii

causes us to be inhuman (animal-like). This book over and over again points to the reality of our sexual situation and is a wake up call for us to either acculturate our African sexuality or lose it to the caucasians.

Introduction

To be unwilling or afraid to define and model morality for our children because it may make them different from the European norm, and therefore make their lives more difficult, is for Afrikans to react out of fear. Morality, like fear, is a group, not individual, definition and state. There are serious limitations to the ability to explain individual behavior outside the group complex. It would be extremely difficult, if not impossible, to underestimate

> the impact of the group on the cultural socialization of an individual's decisions. Isolating particular individual choices, as if individuals developed their desires, skills and personalities in a vacuum and not families, groups and society, and whether intentional or not, ignores the social conditioning individuals go through that fits them into the culture. All people are socialized. It is a lifelong process....Humans socialize humans...People become who they are through interacting with others, conforming their behavior to a cultural standard. They are educated through the rewards and punishments applied by significant others. All societies and groups socialize their members to conform to their cultural personality.[1]

And Europeans are the group out of which we are defining our children's morality.

If, as adults and their parents, we do not believe we have the right or knowledge to teach them right from wrong, or we believe the European way is moving all humanity in the direction of being correct or that it already has done so, then we are sacrificing our future to a lesser god. The ultimate statement of our perception of our ability to provide guidance and promote healthy, sane minds for our Afrikan future is in allowing those of extremely questionable moral orientation to teach our children without our interference. It is to accept having no future outside European culture. Silence *is* a choice. It *is* the making of a decision.

The question of who we are is bound to our understanding of what culture is. So our understanding of this concept should be clear. Culture is said to be everything man-made, material and nonmaterial, passed down from one generation to the next, that is specifically "designed to ensure the survival of a people, of a way of life, of a deliberate history."[2] Yet it is even more than that. For culture is also the foundational ideas out of which the material and nonmaterial aspects of the life of a people are created. And even though ideas are already included as a nonmaterial aspect of a people's culture, they are usually not thought of as those ideas upon which the culture originated; rather they serve as the unspoken guide to its material and nonmaterial development. These foundational ideas are a society's lifeblood.

Cultural creations, be they thoughts, words, deeds or things, are not arbitrary. They, as culture, have intent. And the intent is found only in the ideas and ideals that evolved in the minds of a people as unique to their original environment and circumstance. Culture is the living membrane through which individuals and groups interpret and create their reality. Cultural socialization is also the process by which individuals, from birth, become bona fide members of the group. It is the way in which they are taught to become citizens of a social contract and living examples of their cultural personality. The heart of every culture is shown through the historical evidence of what it and its human products have said and done. "Societies like people have their hearts."[3]

Moreover, culture takes on a life of its own, reproducing itself through the society it maintains. A cynic might even call culture a parasite, unable to survive without the society it manipulates so it can keep itself alive. But the people it guides and controls make choices which keep it alive. Moreover, culture can be good or bad. Whatever the opinion, it is intentional. It is deliberate in its selections of acceptable thought and behavior regardless of what individuals in other cultures may feel about the validity, logic or outcome of those choices. The Heike crab of Japan is a useful case in point for this arbitrary but intentional selection process.

Nearly 800 years ago, the Japanese people lost a large number of samurai warriors in battle. Soon afterward a crab was caught whose shell imprint, as designed by nature, resembled the scowling face of a samurai warrior. The people came to believe that these crabs were those warriors reincarnated. And, out of respect, they refused to eat these crabs, throwing them back into the sea whenever they were caught. The Heike crab has been left without human enemies for so long that they have overpopulated their seashore to the point where fishing has become nearly impossible there. Yet, the tradition of respect remains. The point, however, is that other than for the imprint on their shells, these crabs were physically/biologically no different than any other. But through the perception, definition and acceptance of their honored human origins, they gained cultural protection and immortality.[4]

Still, it is very important to distinguish those "foundational ideas out of which the material and nonmaterial aspects of the life of a people are created" from their normal and evolving day to day thoughts and behaviors. These "foundational ideas" we call the *asili*. A people's asili is their essence or reason for being. It is the "seed" – the source, the beginning. The asili is the voice of reason out of which a culture develops. But, in being so, it becomes inseparable from the culture it forces into an evolving creation. As the seed grows into a tree, the seed still remains. A people's reason evolves out of its identification and interpretation of universal laws that explain their physical environment and socially constructed world. As originally defined by Marimba Ani, the asili is

> ...the germinal principle of the being of a culture, its essence...[It] is like a template that carries within it the pattern or archtypical model for cultural development; we might say that it is the DNA of culture. At the same time it embodies the "logic" of the culture. The logic is an explanation of how it works, as well as, the principle of its development. Our assumption then is that the *asili* generates systematic development...it is ideological in that it gives direction to development...Cultural *asili*(s) are not made to be changed.[5]

No statement or action by a culture is independent of the asili within which it was born. So if the asili is not understood, the cause and effect of its culture will be misinterpreted. People may even become confused into working within a particular culture to change things which cannot be changed because they have been determined and are set at the asilic level. Yet, because the culture is born of the asili, and because there are ideas in culture, it is often difficult to tell where one begins and the other ends.

Nonetheless, we will use the terms "culture" and "asili" relatively interchangeably in this work. Technically, one is the other except in terms of original cause. Asilis cause cultures. Therefore, for the intents and purpose of this book, the distinction between asili and culture is not necessary, although theoretically the distinction is very important.

A related concern here will be with the use of *generalizations* to describe European as contrasted with Afrikan thought and behavior. Many, because they do not understand the method of the social sciences, will argue that making blanket statements about a people or group is inappropriate because there is almost always an exception to the rule. But those who understand that summary statements are not compromised by one or two oddities or abnormalities, and that we are seeking to understand the general or majority behavior of groups, will not have a problem with Afrikan and European generalizations because they eliminate historical confusion. Simply put, generalizations help Afrikans not to confuse that one or two "good" European they met with the history of the bloody relationship that has existed between Europeans and Afrikans over the last several thousand years and will continue into the future.

We must remain conscious of what sociologists call "statistical insignificance." When analyzing the thought and behavior of a large group of people, a small number of individuals deviating from what has been determined as normal for that group is not considered statistically significant or meaningful for deeply studied generalizations about them. When the statistically insignificant is emphasized, cultural politics are at work. For, in a population of millions, a few exceptions do not change the rule.

One other definition is important for our discussion because, as social creatures, individuals in a society must feel compelled to become members of the group. So there must be a model for them to follow and aspire to become. That group is usually the group in power and is called the *reference group*. An individual's reference group is that cultural group whose thoughts and behaviors s/he seeks to imitate and assimilate. It is that group in society, or the entire society, whose approval s/he endeavors to earn. Therefore, if a thought or behavior is normal and natural to an individual's reference group, it becomes (or is made) normal and natural to him/her. At the same time, though, it must be remembered that that relationship is mutually beneficial. For the reference group, "Imitation is the highest form of flattery." Specifically, for Europeans, exploitation is empowering. It is not news that Europeans are dependent on the acceptance and praise of others for their psychological well-being. And, for any people dependent on the approval of others for their self-esteem and self-validation, imitation tells them that whatever they do is what everybody else wants them to do and wants to do.

> Cultural conquest leads to the cultural inauthenticity of those who are invaded; they begin to respond to the values, the standards, and the goals of the invaders. In their passion to dominate, to mold others to their patterns and their way of life, the invaders desire to know how those they have invaded apprehend reality – but only so they can dominate the latter more effectively. In cultural invasion it is essential that those who are invaded come to see their reality with the outlook of the invaders rather than their own; for the more they mimic the invaders, the more stable the position of the latter becomes....For cultural invasion to succeed, it is essential that those invaded become convinced of their intrinsic inferiority. Since everything has its opposite, if those who are invaded consider themselves inferior, they must necessarily recognize the superiority of the invaders. The values of the latter thereby become the pattern of the former. The more invasion is accentuated and those invaded are alienated from the spirit of their own culture and from themselves, the more the latter want to be like the invaders: to walk like them, dress like them, talk like them.[6]

Moreover, this analysis is in no way limited to Afrikans in this society. The condition and fate of Afrikans in any society orchestrated by the Western agenda is the same globally. Make no mistake. This is a PanAfrikan nationalist book. We are approaching Afrikans as Afrikans and Europeans as Europeans at the global level because that is our historical and cultural reality.

We should not separate Europeans anywhere from Europeans everywhere. It is not necessary to divide them by geographical locale, dress, language or any other superficial abstraction because it confuses the issue to their advantage. Differences only indicate variations within a common cultural core. The same applies to Afrikans. As with Europeans, differences between people of Afrikan descent are ethnic not cultural. Therefore, throughout this work, these racial-cultural definitions and distinctions apply.

> ...Europe must be brought into focus as a cultural entity.
> By emphasizing the ideological function of culture, it is
> possible to make sense of the intimidating confusion and
> superficial complexity of the European experience.
> Understanding culture as ideology allows us to approach
> European culture in such a way as to make it a visible,
> extremely cohesive and well-integrated phenomenon, in a
> sense more "simple" than we might suppose. Beneath its
> deceptive heterogeneity lies a monolithic essence; an
> essence that accounts for the success of European
> imperialism.[7]

Culture must also be understood as race. Europeans actively practiced and perfected their way in isolation for over 18,000 years before coming in contact with others. That's 900 generations of cultural development and crystallization of distinct thought and behavior. Race produces culture through the social development of a people relative to their environment. In order for culture to be born, evolve and normalize among a population, people must have lived together for thousands of years, biologically, socially, intellectually and spiritually creating and recreating themselves in isolation from others.

Cheikh Anta Diop's "two cradle" theory explained this well enough. In *The Cultural Unity of Black Africa: The Domains of Patriarchy and of Matriarchy in Classical Antiquity*[8] we learn that there are qualitatively meaningful differences in the nature of the Afrikan and European asilis as evident in their historical habits and relationships with themselves and others. As Diop explains it, the social and cultural development of Afrikans and Europeans was originally forged by the radically different physical environments within which they originally defined themselves as people and nations. Europeans were born and raised in the cold harsh "northern cradle" where scarcity made violent aggression and intolerance a natural way of life. Family, especially dependent members such as children, the elderly and often women, were seen and acted on as liabilities because they could not, or could not as well as adult males, supply for their own needs.[9] What evolved into a nomadic lifestyle left little room for the development of surplus and advanced technological knowledge and, therefore, called for the continuous search for, when possible, the forcible, combative appropriation of others' physical and intellectual wealth. Afrikans, on the other hand, were brought up in the warm environment of the "southern cradle." This allowed for a sedentary, agrarian lifestyle and, in turn, the development of surplus. When people are able to settle in one place, we find they accumulate surplus and rapidly develop their intellectual faculties. Families, especially the wisdom of the elders, the procreative capacity of women and the importance of children for the extension of their nation through time, were equally if not more important than the men who provided much of the backbone for the physical development of Afrikan civilization. That primitive Europeans originally migrated from the Afrikan continent in the form of the Grimaldi Negroid does not negate these facts.[10] The point of the Afrikan origin of all humanity does not negate the fact that Europeans are culturally and historically anti-Afrikan.

Of course, naysayers will always try to push forth those one or two groups who appear to contradict Diop's theory. Yet, in their last ditch efforts to get around truth by highlighting insignificant trivia, they overlook the simple fact that there is an exception to every rule in human development. There is always the statistically insignificant minority that cannot be generalized into the human experience as seriously contradicting normal human development. And, as in the case of such an extraordinarily deep and thoroughly substantiated theory as this one, there are always sound reasons for the exceptions. [11]

We are then only left to conclude that race is culture. Biological and social endogamy, or inbreeding among a people, produce culture as race and race as culture. Because there are cultural distinctions, there are racial distinctions. Therefore, we will use the terms Afrikan and European to identify the two basic racial-cultural groups under consideration in this discussion. The word Afrikan will especially be hard on the eyes of those Afrikans who subconsciously and consciously see Afrika as a remote, powerless and undesirable place and past to which they refuse any but the most forced superficial and exploitative connection. The designation will be even harder on the psychology of those determined to be individual, raceless "Americans." As I have stated elsewhere,

> As a result of this confusion we have become so locked up in patriotism and loyalty to European nation-states that we forget that Afrikans are one people. I agree with Ayi Kwei Armah. "I prefer not to forget several thousand years of our common history because of a few centuries of separation." That twenty-six plus thousand years of Ta-Merrian, Saisian, Puntian, Alkebu-lanian, Nubian, Kushite, Ethiopian, Kemetic, Egyptian, Malian, Songhaian and Ghanaian community makes it imperative that we use the terms Afrikan and European to distinguish us from them. "A people's name is a powerful force." For those who find it necessary to visualize in terms of melanin, or lack thereof, Black is synonymous with Afrikan and white with European. For the more patriotic, African-American and American could be matched with Afrikan and European, respectively....The words chosen to identify the two groups in this work are no more limiting than the terms plant and animal. Realistically, as historical fact and future vision, Afrikan and European speak to race as culture.[12]

Cheikh Anta Diop reflected on this fundamental truth when addressing the biological similarities but cultural differences of humanity.

> But as one would expect, physical anthropology, using the latest findings of genetics, molecular biology, and linear analysis, denies race and admits only the reality of differing populations. It is sophisticated science strongly coated with ideology!...Certainly, the dilution of the human species' genes during prehistoric times is very

important; but from there to deny race, in the sense that it impacts on history and on social relations, meaning at the phenotypical level, which is of interest solely to the historian and to the sociologist, is a step that the daily facts of life prohibit anyone from taking.[13]

The fantasy individuality of Western culture is not reflected in the thrust of this book. What is being done to Afrikans by commercialism, crack and white supremacy in Chicago, Atlanta, D.C., Houston and L.A. is being done to Afrikans in London, Cape Town, Sydney, Montreal and Buenos Aires. Likewise, the privilege of Europeans to exploit and abuse others with impunity extends wherever they are found.

With this statement in mind, let us begin our study of the European sex imperative and its impact on the Afrikan spirit, mind and body.

1. A Sexual Framework

"He who is ruled by his appetite belongs to the enemy."

Ptah Hotep

People who have adjusted to and prize a life of sex are more easily and willingly exploited sexually in whatever way sexual predators wish to use them. There are few limits to what the human body and mind are capable of. People are easy, and often willing, prey. As this book will clearly show, European media have already revealed the extent to which the human body can be manipulated beyond its natural limits to service sexual organs as well as a multitude of other devices. And, serving as the primary models of what to almost everyone except them is new, Europeans themselves have already demonstrated how virtually any object, animal or human can be used in their game of sexual exploitation. People who have adjusted to and prize a life of sex are easy prey for those determined to turn the world into their personal orgy. There is no doubt that a human mind singularly focused on sexual conquest can be as effective and destructive as one obsessively bent on violence or consumption. And where there is no order, no moral or ethical guidelines based on the laws and conditions of the Universe, no conception of right and wrong as long as it makes me feel good and I am powerful enough to uncontestedly declare that it does not harm those minds and bodies I exploit, the unbridled pursuit of sexual pleasure can become the majority of individuals' all in all.

If the drives are permitted to rule the self, the person becomes only a physical pleasure-seeker. He is concerned only about what brings physical pleasure: food, sex, physical relaxation. If the drives are given free rein, they will drive the entire community to seek only pleasure. Fear can come to rule and the person is constantly nervous or anxious in his persistent drive to avoid pain.[1]

Europeans are psychologically driven by the pursuit of individual pleasure. And sex is seen as the cheapest and most gratifying means of controlling and reaching this constant, and constantly elusive, end. Because of this, they are the ultimate pleasure seekers. These are a constantly agitated, restless people, seeking an unattainable fulfillment. And the sexual mindfield is full of traps and explosive devices.

Afrikans follow suit only to be caught and fragmented by the perverted and extreme sexual way of others. By embracing the logic that what is normal for one people is normal for all people, because they have come to accept the validity of other people's words over their own traditions, many Afrikans rush toward a European difference. They cannot see that following European culture opens them up to an alien and self-alienating way. In the European cultural context, difference in sexual practice is a fundamental measure of one''s inferiority or superiority as a human being. For the more unusual and perverted ones sexual practices are, the more progressive or advanced (i.e., superior) that individual is taken to be.

Virtually every major recognizable Afrikan scholar addressing the problem of our youth lists this progression or advancement into sexual excess as one of the most corrupting ones today. Delores P. Aldridge speaks of sexism as working with racism, capitalism and Judeo-Christianity as the "ideological institutions" serving to systematically undermine any possibility of stable, positive relationships between Afrikan men and women.[2] Na'im Akbar shares her opinion saying that sexism, materialism, Christianity, as a force insuring a perception of the inferiority and danger of women, and "an assumption of inevitable conflict between the sexes" are inextricably tied in the assault on peace and purpose for couples.[3] Maulana Karenga's four "connections" consist of the more catchy "cash," "flesh," "force" and "dependency" "connections" that undermine male/female relationships.[4] Racism is also a given in both Akbar's and Karenga's analyses.

(As a quick point of clarification, we will use the "/" instead of the "-" between male and female when speaking of intimate relationships. A number of our respected scholars have already chosen to do this because the former generally indicates complementarity and the latter contrast and/or antagonism. Unless otherwise indicated in my text, the "male/female" relationships discussed in this book are complementary, as in traditional Afrikan relationships. And the "male-female" statements indicate antagonistic or contrasting interpersonal relationships, as in historic European relationships.)

Although not the only one, sexism, or sexual exploitation, is considered a constant factor by each of these scholars. It is understood not only as a force serving to undermine the potential of women within and outside of relationships with men, but it also serves to make women the objects of men's sexual advances. Sexism makes sexual exploitation civilized. It makes it normal and, therefore, natural. Karenga's statement that (1) women have less capital in a money driven culture where everything has a price and can be bought, (2) sex is the most important cultural entertainment priority, (3) women have less muscle mass and are therefore disproportionately more susceptible to being forcibly "taken" by a man and (4) the dependency all of these create, pulls the implications of sexism together.

No matter the difference in the emphasis and terminology used by these scholars, each recognizes the extraordinary importance the exercise of power holds for the self-esteem of both males and females in intimate, interpersonal Western relationships. Each recognizes that the drive to control is so great in European culture that in intimate relationships there must be one who dominates and one who is dominated. Power gives meaning and form to virtually every relationship in the Western cultural context. These facts are even more pressing among Afrikans in a society that teaches them to view themselves as powerless power seekers.

As might be expected, each scholar is able to see the forest the trees grow in. Each recognizes that forests, like societies, are conscious, living organisms. In doing so, they have no choice but to conclude that forests, like societies, originated from a seed that grew into the tree that produced the seeds from which all the other trees in the forest grew and grow. There is a mother tree. And there is a common root system. It is instructive to further note that, in some forests, like pine forests, the trees are so thick and their droppings so acidic that no other vegetation can take root or survive there, except in a weakened, dependent state. This analogy specifically applies to European culture and its society, no matter their crocodile tears and emotional protestations to the contrary and their claims to multiculturalism.

The overriding influence of cultural context no less applies to the sexual priorities and related problems besieging the Afrikan couples who live in this New Europe. In the final analysis,

> it is of equal importance to realize that any criticism of Black male/female relationships is at the same time and in equal measure a criticism of U.S. society which has shaped us to fit and function "properly" in it. For social conditions create both social consciousness and social conduct and failure to recognize this can lead one to see racial defects where social ones are more real and relevant...It is this final contention that serves as a key point of departure for any serious analysis of Black male/female relationships. For to say we are products of our social conditions is to say the same thing about our relationships. Analysis of the major defects in Black male/female relationships clearly reveal their social rather than genetic or purely personal basis. Thus, to understand the negatives of our relationships we must understand the negative characteristics of society which have shaped them.[5]

A student once told me that sex, not money, rules the world. He argued that the power to grant or withhold sex was a more significant factor in regulating interpersonal relationships, intimate and otherwise, than control over the distribution of monetary resources. Although his argument is debatable, what is not debatable is the obsession/preoccupation with sex and money in capitalistic societies throughout the world. To fully grasp this fact, we must take a moment to explain the capitalist system through Afrikan eyes.

Sex and Capitalism

Capitalism's success is anchored in the manipulation of baser desires. It feeds on and is fueled by those thoughts and actions people are most easily tempted by and addicted to. Negative habits develop more easily and take root more quickly and firmly. It follows that they die harder and slower, therefore being the most difficult to get rid of. No thinking person who has lived long enough to have their experiences transformed into knowledge would disagree that lesser, amoral, unethical habits are easier to fall victim to and adhere with less effort than good ones. And very few thinking persons really believe that the legal profits are greater than illegal ones in capitalistic systems.

Capitalism bets on human frailty. It thrives on nurturing and exploiting people's weaknesses. Capitalism creates markets. Newborns do not just stumble into economic dependency and moral corruption. They are socialized into it. And the European economy is the most corrupt because it was created and has matured within an immoral social being. It goes without saying that, "Nothing is contradictory in a capitalistic and imperialistic economy"[6] because "in a game of power, conscience is absent from the makeup of the European."[7] Capitalism finds each individual's weakest points and strongest manipulable desires and then controls access to those desires, but not before it initially, delicately nurtures them until its victims are thoroughly hooked. Then it reveals itself for the monster it truly is by mercilessly bleeding them over and over and over again until they are no more than empty, useless hulls. Yes, individuals actively submit to this monster. But the guidelines for the interaction are systemic. The culture provides the rules of the game.

Capitalism is more than just a society's method of acquiring, distributing and consuming goods and services. It is an acquisitive way of thinking, an acquisitive drive, an "ethic" of exploitation. And, as an economic order, it is not simply the goods and services exchanged and sought or the people involved in this activity. It is the arrangement of people into mindless beings who frantically and incessantly exist in a state of preparation to hoard and consume goods and services. It is a mentality. As Amos N. Wilson taught,

An economy exists prior to money...an economic system
at its base refers to the nature of the relationship between
people. It's the systematic way people choose to relate one
to the other that makes an economic system...[8]

In a society of uncontrolled consumption and waste, the rate of
transactions, not the goods and services themselves, becomes the
greater priority.

Capitalism is a way of thinking. What makes capitalism so
damaging to the human psyche and moves it infinitely beyond the
realm of free will is what it, as an economic-philosophy, as a way of
life, does to everything. The European nature of it turns everything
into a commodity. Lest we forget, the capitalist system is an
economic form of interpersonal relationships/exchange that was form
fitted to the European mind. This acquisitive predisposition, and the
value that comes to be attributed to things once they are possessed, is
why men, and increasingly women, are never satisfied. Only when
things are not possessed, when they remain prey in the acquisition
game, when they are still coveted, do they hold authentic, useful
value. This is the driving force behind and within capitalism. Like
progress, where people seek constant change and what is captured or
mastered loses its value relative to what remains free, the same
applies to the economic side of European progress, capitalism.

If we listen closely to what entertains our children most, we
will see that music is the most involved example of this. The fact that
the music industry is most profitable among youth says a great deal
about their dedication to being fulfilled by it. Songs stay in vogue
only long enough for the next one to be produced and distributed.
They run through our memory as if chased by death. Once songs are
sampled and replayed a number of times, the unrelenting drive for
consumption automatically kicks in, resetting itself to seek out
something new and different. And the rate of turnover for the real hit
songs that children listen to increases with every year. If you notice,
the more youth oriented the radio station, the more rapidly the
"hits"rise and fall. Music, as part of the economic order, fits the
cultural imperatives.

Even though sex is a high which allows individuals to
momentarily elevate above reality, that is not its only utility. Sex is

also a commodity. Yet, it cannot be quantified materially except possibly in the form of a kept woman or man. Therefore, in order to acquire increasingly larger amounts of sex, and large amounts of accumulation is the basis of capitalism, whether hoarded or run through, it must be gotten continuously and increasingly more rapidly over time. Rational, quantitative European capitalism requires a count, and not only a count, but an ever increasing number of objects to count. The judgement of what is more requires a measurement against what is less. The capitalist system requires that you continue to increase your profits in order to just stay afloat. What you buy today cannot be bought tomorrow at the same price. Time cheapens Western valued goods but increases their costs. And, like everything else, sex is a commodity in the capitalist system. You can never be satisfied. There can never be enough sexual conquests. As with those who will quickly promise to come back and save their community after they attain some phenomenal individual success, you will never have made it, there will never be enough.

Each single transaction ends with the completion of each sexual act. The more climaxes one acquires during the game, the more capital one acquires. The measure of sexual satisfaction also becomes tied to the number of orgasms achieved in one encounter – the multiple orgasm phenomenon. The only problem is that orgasms are ephemeral. They last only until the physical sensation dies. The sexual release of tension is only temporary, so it is necessary to repeatedly perform the act over and over again in rapid succession in order to achieve some semblance of momentary peace. As the physical sensation subsides, the value of that particular sexual act loses its value. Nothing tangible remains to count. As a near immediate result, the partner's previous breathtaking attraction wanes. In the Western mind, the sensation is associated with the orgasm, not the person it was committed against. Ergo, many have the problem of not being respected the morning after.

In this game, with this commodity, the recurring, remaining choice is simple. Either push for additional sexual value through more intense sexual games with the current partner or search for "perfection" in a never ending dating game. The latter option is increasingly chosen due to the incessant drive for difference and diversity characteristic of European style progress as conquest. Like they've taken everything else to the extreme (so-called progress), they've done the same with the body and sex. The move has been from partial nudity to complete nudity, from a peck on the cheek to sadomasochistic sexual deviance. *Vive la différence* is a European cultural motto. Extreme variety becomes the spice in otherwise meaningless lives.

Morality

But because of this economic imperative and Western culture's drive to be seen as superior and universal, there is something even more important to this discussion of the abnormal prioritization of an extreme sexual orientation in European culture. The rhetoric of Western culture must make people believe that there is no such thing as a normal morality. The immoral thoughts and behaviors that Europeans and their minions engage in must be made to appear timelessly moral and normal through making morality and normalcy an individual prerogative.

Deceit is often hidden behind the promotion of confusion. When it comes to sex, in the West, morals mean prudish, frigid, old thoughts and behavior. They indicate the absence of democratic freedom. In this culture, morals, however defined, have no place where sex and difference are the priority. Licentiousness is the only universal rule. Morals are interpreted as taking the "fun" out of everything. And those who only engage in the historically morally correct behavior of the world's majority must be denounced as abnormal or somehow backward.

In such an anti-moral system where virtually everything is designed to push and pull you toward human vices, it is not enough to simply say to our youth, or adults for that matter, "Just say no." The public pronouncement, advocation, and popularization of such is irresponsible and arrogant, and speaks to such spokespeople's ignorance of the power of collective human behavior over individuals.

Sex is a baser desire as practically employed in the Western cultural context, no matter how natural or necessary it is for human survival in general. Like slaves and drugs, it is an exploitable commodity. In its use, though, it appears more as a form of interpersonal recreation than anything else. The official statistics claim that people in this society engage in sexual intercourse an average of 132 times a year, which comes to over two and a half times a week.[9] For couples, the range is from one to over thirty times per week, with age being the most important indicator of frequency. The *Kinsey Report* found that 7 percent of European males averaged one orgasm per day. It would be difficult to believe, with European's rush to progress, that the percent of European males (and females as a result of the Sex Revolution) with this daily orgasm rate has not increased dramatically in the last half-century. They have always been excessive.

This society's average annual rate of sexual intercourse per person of 132 times compares to an international average of 96 times. And, of this, Western nations disproportionately exhibit the highest rates. So let us not confuse the cultural context with the first irrelevant point naysayers will throw up in an attempt to nullify the fact of sex's exploitation in European culture. They will say that sex is universal. And, they are right. It is simply common sense that the majority of able adults in every society engage in sexual intercourse at some point in their lives. If this were not so, reproduction would not occur and human life would, long ago, have ceased to exist. But *anything* taken or done in excess is addictive. And in the West sex is not a procreative activity except by default or as a white supremacist reaction to not enough births. It is an addictive imperative. The mere fact that sexual intercourse exists among all people does not prove that the European's way is universal. If anything, the contamination of procreative sex with their perverse, recreational sex proves nothing more than insanity is contagious.

Most of us find it hard to distinguish physical from mental addictions. When we believe something has power over us, it becomes more powerful than us. This applies whether we can physically identify it or not. And so often we cannot or do not want to take the time to gain the understanding necessary to distinguish between good and bad addictions. Sex is as addictive as chemical drugs or alcohol or salt or coffee or the internet or money. And, being addictive, it becomes insatiable and exploratory. You will find a way to get it and any variation presented as humanly possible will become acceptable to you. You crave higher and higher sexual highs. That is the nature of human curiosity when manipulated by expansive, unconditioned addictions. When you combine a sick society that is progress/change oriented, with an individualistic "politics of morality" and a primary, primal sexual priority, you end up with what we see and hear all around us.

Before moving on, we must point out that "individualistic" is different from simply being an individual, which we all are no matter what culture produces us, because it speaks to a cultural personality, a selfish orientation that measures everything relative to others strictly in terms of costs and benefits to self.[10] Western social values and ideology reflect this peculiar priority that nothing is more important than the individual or that the individual's socially defined "rights" to be selfishly satisfied must be protected at all costs. Relative to others, and society in general, the single, most important drive is the satisfaction of the individual's desires. The wants and needs of the individual override all. The European mind thrives on pleasure (some argue because of an intense memory of pain and deprivation). Because of the negation of spirit, it is ultimately physically hedonist. Exploitation of other individuals, groups and organizations to gain this pleasure is seen as key and a concomitant function of being individualistic.

Although often dismissed as extreme, the Machiavellian mentality has its origin in the idea of ideal European interpersonal relationships. Within this mentality, people are naturally self-serving. They naturally exploit each other to preserve and enhance self. They use others indiscriminately and by any means necessary (usually amoral) in order to achieve a feeling of personal superiority. And personal superiority is simply measured by an individual's ability to exploit others, and do it well and without conscious. Nothing rises in value above capital (money), sex and more money and sex. It is a "take-take" relationship between individuals where the loss of one is seen as an automatic gain for another.   Each interaction is approached based on our perceived, calculated answer to the question of "What's in it for me?" Following this line of reasoning, sex is a natural commodity. And commodities are seen as forms of power. As the individual's self-esteem is intricately tied into his/her ability to exercise power over and against his/her intimate partner, in a situation where all successful interactions are judged by the loss or gain of power, sexual exploitation is an important means of gaining personal power. And even though the recording artist Tupac Shakur only became notably vocal about it late in his life, he is most remembered by many of his generation for advocating this Machiavellian mentality.[11] Throughout this discussion of the European sex imperative, the terms individualistic, individualism and, as indicated through a greater adjectival emphasis, extreme individualism are used to summarize the above mentality.

European culture is extreme individualism inducing. And, because of its culturally imperialistic orientation, it has literally turned this world upside down to make humanity fit its sexual idiosyncracies. The growing amount of neurosis and psychosis we see among individuals in this "modern" world is not a function of an advanced science's ability to detect and diagnose what has always been here. It is a creation of the spread of European culture. These things are characteristic of Europeans traditionally and continuously. They do not predate them. Others have only adopted these insane ways of interpreting reality, becoming victim to European mental disorders through forced association. Insanity runs deep in their family. It is what they have brought into the world. It is their gift.

To live and participate in a world where our guide to necessary and acceptable sexual behavior is located among those practices and mentalities of the world's greatest deviants is insanity. But to know this and still placidly watch our children be brainwashed into the degeneracies and perversions normal to abnormal others is criminal insanity. Whether intentional or not, we are preparing them, in the style of slaves seeking to increase their children's acceptability to the master, for the sexually perverted ways of Europeans. "We, as adults, have failed our children and created walking time bombs whose minds are externally controlled."[12] We are teaching them, or allowing them to be taught, that anything is a reasonable price for success, including sexual exploitation. Surely many of us have missed the sex phone line commercials that have aired on *The Cartoon Network, WB, Disney* and *Nickelodeon* cable stations. Assuredly, our children have not missed them or the Trojan condom commercials that are aired on these children's cable stations. We are allowing European culture to make its sexual perversions and extremes their second nature. This is a trained mentality and the quality of our intent does not change the fact of their systematic preparation to be used by others.

Europeans, not our children, are the voices in today's music. And they, not the performers in music videos and overly liberally rated "Black" movies and television shows, determine what will be infused into the minds of the children in our community. We must listen to what our children hear. We must study what they see. And what they see and hear is the Western mind.

The media is about the propagation of Western ideas and ideals. Western culture is commercial. Values are crafted, manipulated and carried into the individual's mind via the media. The media is the primary mechanism by which euro sexual interests are redefined as everyones.

> The corporate elite-owned and -controlled media function to create a climate of opinion, to shape social perception by framing the reality and information which basically shapes the formation and expression of opinions. They do this mainly through setting the issues agenda, that is, by controlling the "domain of discourse," e.g., determining what is worthy of public exposure and discussion. They choose what issues and information are to be emphasized, to be ignored or suppressed. Consequently, they create visibility and legitimacy for certain persons, groups and opinions and thereby impose limits on public knowledge, interest, discourse, understanding, behavioral orientation and capability.[13]

Moreover, they operate outside and above the domain of family, community or any universal morality. The media is the master of the lie. In fact, they are the crowning achievement of this "lieocracy" because they are permitted the luxury of fabrication in order to market fictional drama and comedy. The media not only makes sexual deviance normative, but it also makes it extremely appealing to the senses of individuals trained to thrive on the symbols and behaviors identified by others for them as eliciting pleasure. And TV is the main vehicle for propagating fantasy as normal and reality as abnormal and undesirable.

The contemporary society has so glorified fantasy and synthetic things that they have become more attractive than reality....The assumption that reality is not sufficient....The present society's educational and social system has a tendency of indiscriminately combining fact with fiction. Such a combination has utility when fantasy is at least a symbolic representation of fact, but more often than not, the fiction takes our attention away from the fact and/or confuses the two. The unaware child becomes contemptuous of the real because it doesn't have the predictable smoothness of the false form...the involvement of the young mind with fiction rather than fact is ultimately for the purpose of exploiting them as consumers of things and ideas, rather than as producers of both....If the child's education serves to alienate him from the natural world, he becomes disrespectful of nature and willingly abuses it...Another consequence is the pollution of self, both physically and mentally, when one becomes disrespectful of the natural processes of the body and natural powers of the mind.[14]

To make matters worse,

African-Americans watch "significantly" more, and different, TV than do other ethnic groups...In the period studied (Oct.'93-Jan,'94), blacks watched 90 percent more in late-night, 59 percent more in daytime, and 55 percent more in early morning. Overall average: 74.9 hours per week vs. 49.9 for non-blacks.[15]

This comes to over ten hours of television time per day for Afrikans.

As psychologically damaged products of white supremacist society, reality is more painful for us. We more intensely seek escape. Afrikan adults and children are more emotionally involved in the lives of the fictional characters we see on the idiot box, whether these characters are in shows or commercials. More than any other people, we act with them. We become them, emotionally tied to their pain and pleasure. We root for our enemies who play roles to win over their enemies, over us. We deeply feel their emotions. We kiss and hug and have sex right along with them. We feel their physical pleasure and pain. It has been said for good reason that television shows are things designed to entertain people in between commercials. And it seems appropriate, in this age of mass marketing and subliminal suggestion in a sex dominated commercial culture, to extend this point by saying that the storylines offered by shows and products commercials advertise are things used to superficially distract viewers while their minds are flooded with images of sex. Magic has no better slight of hand.

NBC Nightly News stated that children are spending on average only 1,500 hours in front of the idiot box each year.[16] Anthony T. Browder, however, convincingly argues that this is a very serious undercount. In his essay, "Television and Its Influence on African American Children" he says that our children "watch TV an average of 7 hours per day, as compared to 4-1/2 hours of daily television viewing for white children."[17] In his historic study, Wade W. Nobles makes the intimately related point that "the live storytelling which the parents in our study experienced as children has been almost replaced by the television for their own children.[18] More recent research indicates that the proportion of our time spent glued to the television is even greater. Jeanne A. Naujeck cites Nielsen Research findings that "Blacks spend an average of 75 hours per week watching television, with others households watching an average 52 hours per week." But her report is deeper than that because she points out that in addition to serving up mentacide, the "Black" shows that Afrikans disproportionately watch are specially designed to sell us obesity and bad diet.

> Episodes of prime time sitcoms with primarily black characters aired 60 percent more food and beverage commercials than those with primarily white characters...Black shows had an average 4.78 food commercials per show compared to 2.89 during the general prime time shows. Also, 31 percent of commercials during black shows were for candy, versus 11 percent of commercials during general prime time shows. And 13 percent of commercials during black prime were for soda, compared with two percent of commercials during white shows.[19]

Nonetheless, Browder's statistics, as well as those reported in *TV Guide*, are vastly more realistic than those given by the *NBC Nightly News*. For even when controlling for the larger percentage of children watching television who are European, this would only come to an unbelievable four hours per day.

We have missed the historical point of the intergenerational accumulation and normalization of excessive sex and violence and perversion in our minds. Though it was already quite late in the game, one need go back no further than the Blaxploitation movies of the sixties to see just how far we have regressed. *The Mack* (which has now become somewhat of a cult movie among youth who would be pimps in our community), *Superfly*, *Shaft*, *Coffee* and *Cleopatra Jones* are representative of those films which, for about two hours, gave Afrikans the illusion of power in a European world. They portrayed Afrikans as powerful determiners of their own fate as conscious imitators of European models of sexual exploitation and violence. To describe just two of the latest years in the natural progression of violence in the media

> [V]iolence on broadcast TV and cable increased by about 41 percent over the last two years...The steepest rise of all came in news programs, both network and local – a 244 percent increase...The average rate of violent incidents increased from 10 to almost 15 scenes per channel per hour.[20]

Whether on BET, NBC or HBO, Europeans control the presentation of balance. If nothing else, they regulate the distribution of these media, especially the music. With sex, as with all other cultural variables, they define how much and what kind is to be considered normal.

As we become more debased, they are made to feel more normal and validated in their belief that they are god or at least the Creator's gift to humanity. They also become more elevated and validated in their sense/proclamations of a most moral white supremacy by showcasing those among us who have chosen to take known European extremes to new extremes. Their way of elevating self is by controlling both the image of self and others. The moral degeneracy they have never stopped practicing becomes concealed in privacy, while its expression in those they infect becomes a public affair. In turn, like a bully, they point out their degeneracy as ours. Thus exonerated, they rise as the moral model.

It is in the European tradition to call other people what only they themselves are. It promotes confusion among their prey. They are the masters of projection. It is important in the game of image control to draw attention away from those behaviors and attitudes they religiously practice. If they admit to their peculiarities, they would reveal themselves for what they really are. "Superfreak," like "superpredator," is one such designation they have attributed to others. If we could see the media's influence on our minds, we would see that they have made that title stereotypically Afrikan. We have been duped into believing that wherever you looked, on the bus, in the elevator, under the desk, in the alley, just around about any corner, we could be found engaged in the lewdest sexual acts imaginable.

In our confusion over identity, we make the mistake of assuming their children are ours, too. When we note their children's love of and greater absolute purchase of rap/hip hop music and become emotionally involved in discussions about its impact on their minds, we reach to include them as ours because they buy ours. Their children readily ape our children whose performances as youth role models are regulated and selected to fit the European conception of Afrikans. Our children are not at issue because they already know our children will follow them.

However, with closer scrutiny, the attraction of European children to the lesser rap/hip hop is also quite understandable. Extreme violence and sexual exploitation nurtures their asili. Even though the art of rap/hip hop is our children's creation, the branches spawning compositions at the gutter levels of immorality form fit European children. It is natural for them to love the articulation of the world in the way they view it. European children are attracted to the lesser rap/hip hop because it speaks to things already normal in their homes. Cursing is normal in their homes. Rape and disrespect for women, children and powerless adult males is normal in their homes. Excessive drugs, illegal and legal, are normal in their homes and a central part of their lives. It is often said among the younger generation that European youth come to parties to get drunk or stoned out of their minds whereas Afrikan youth come together to mingle and dance with drinking and getting high a secondary consideration. Over half of all male and nearly 40 percent of all female college students binge drink, that is drink alcohol at a sitting until they pass out from overdosing.[21] In that the majority of college students are European, the majority of these binge drinkers are European.

We make the mistake of including European children as our own conveniently forgetting that they can and do, upon maturity, choose to remain European and become incorporated in the white supremacist power structure as did their fathers and mothers before them. The quiet yet complete assumption of power and privilege today by the "flower power" and "free love" generation of the 1960s and 1970s is an apt and ample illustration of how long a European declared humanity lasts once they have finished playing at finding themselves.

Romancing a Stone

The idea of romance is another important driving force passed down through the generations. It has been thoroughly manipulated within the mind of Europe to make excessive and unremitting sex seem human, highly desirable and sensible. As an ideal specifically created to form fit this culture's imperatives, it is a socially created instrument driving individuals to acquire more sex in search of a fairy tale reality. In Western culture, every story must be interpreted as a love story, or made into one. This fantasy world cloaks their selfish, aggressive reality under a sugary sweet emotional icing. It misdirects the actions of those who seek honest and lasting intimate partnerships with members of the other sex.

In *The Bluest Eye*, Toni Morrison articulates this truth along with other confusions we have assimilated as fragmented victims of the Western imagination. The power of a generalized lie on group beliefs about just what constitutes the basis of male/female attraction is brought to light in the narration of one of her characters.

Along with the idea of romantic love, she was introduced to another – physical beauty. Probably the most destructive ideas in the history of human thought. Both originated in envy, thrived in insecurity, and ended in disillusion. In equating physical beauty with virtue, she stripped her mind, bound it, and collected self-contempt by the heap. She forgot lust and simple caring for. She regarded love as possessive mating, and romance as the goal of the spirit. It would be for her a well-spring from which she would draw the most destructive emotions, deceiving the lover and seeking to imprison the beloved, curtailing freedom in every way.[22]

Sonbonfu Somé speaks to this confusion too when she says that romance has no place in relationships. It conceals truth until it is too late and life altering commitments have been made.

Romantic love is an attraction that cuts off spirit and community, leaving two people to invent a relationship by themselves. It is the opposite of a relationship that lets spirit be the guide. Romance ignores all the stages of a spiritual coming together, where we begin at the bottom of the mountain and gradually travel in unison to the top. It does not leave room for the true identity of the people involved to show through. It fosters anonymity and forces people to masquerade.[23]

From Molefi K. Asante we are given clarification about the global literary expression of this European particular.

...to say that romance is central to all novels is to invoke a Western literary icon for other literatures. Traditionally, African writers are not concerned with romance variety of literature...Larson is correct to see Fiedler's assertion that the "love story" is universal as another Western analysis imposed on world literature. Since there are entire cultural areas where the "love story is *non*existent, the universality of the "love story" is doubtful. There is no major African novels where the plot progresses because of a hero's attempt to attract a mate. An Afrocentric discussion of literature would guard against this ethnocentric promotion of a group universality.[24]

How quickly those of us who know traditional European cultural history forget that "romantic" love is their creation. It is barely two centuries old, even though technically, in the European language family, it goes back farther as a derivative of the word Roman. The "romance languages" are a group of languages derived from Latin which was Rome's language.   In fact, the romance languages were at one time looked down upon as an inferior breed of languages even among Europeans. It is interesting to note that on the 24 hour clock of human civilization only a little more than three seconds has passed since this word's fabrication.

But, to return to our initial point, romance fits the European mind which exists and thrives in a state of constant fantasy. For, by definition, romance is fantasy. As with most words used in European literature to describe love and sex, romance is used to make real conditions and situations which were not, are not and cannot be reality. This priority is reflected in fiction being the center of their reality. In the literature of any society, the ideas, values and concepts that are held as the most important are stated as the core/root. Dissimilar or different ideas, values and concepts are presented as having less or no value in this culture of opposites. For example, Western is contrasted with *non*Western with Western being the center or standard. In this culture, the same can be said of men being the reference point relative to *wo*men. So, it is a significant statement that the center of Western literature is fiction, while this norm is contrasted with a more peripheral *non*fiction. Lies are the reference point to which truth is a pale comparison.[25]

History tells us that the romantic part of love, i.e., the commercialization of competing for a lover by making a show of offering more and better presents than any other suitors, has its origins in traditional European society.   It reflects the natural distortion of love by a culture of things. The use of romance to court fiction has followed the familiar historical development of originating in Greece and then normally progressing through the Roman (Latin) to French to English languages.   It is a dream world in which unrealistic fantasies are made to appear desirable and possible. In the Western romantic novel and "[i]n common usage, it refers to works with extravagant characters, remote and exotic places, highly exciting and heroic events, passionate love, or mysterious or supernatural experiences."[26] It speaks to a mind that is unable to exist in the human reality.

Western patriots will contend that this interpretation and analysis of the development of romance is not true or, at least, not unique to them. They cite stories like those of Makeda, Queen of Sheba (Ethiopia), and King Solomon of Israel as well as Cleopatra, queen of Egypt, with both Julius Caesar and Mark Antony of Roman notoriety as supreme examples. But, in doing so, they take romance out of the historical context of international relations. International politics then, as now, were based on negotiation between nations, hence the term international. The offering of complimentary gifts, the exchanging of magnificent amounts of valued and valuable resources, were conscious and universally accepted forms of diplomacy between nations specifically designed to openly express a selfless desire to cease strife, create alliances, interact as equals, and, even possibly, build friendships.

These gifts served a political purpose from one people to another, not one person to another. Nations' coffers were not open to personal interests. Any Afrikan reading of this history requires an understanding of political context. We must do more than speculate about the impersonal nature of these gifts of Afrikans to Europeans. We must know that international politics since the beginnings of nations demanded the presentation of symbols expressing trust and respect from one nation to another. And what better way to express this than to sacrifice some of what you most valued.

Our intellectuals agree that romance, if that were the case, was only very peripherally related to the diplomatic agenda of these Afrikan queens. Nonetheless, if we closely study a pattern already evident throughout ancient and present history, these so-called romances have also been known to serve as a means of creating "mixed" offspring who would symbolize the union of two royal houses in an effort to increase the peace, prosperity and power of two nations. Ideally, such offspring served to unite two governments under one leadership. It is the same method by which Egyptian kings and queens gained validation through marriage to Ethiopian royalty. It is the same method by which Europeans and Asians (Arabs) came to dilute the royal lineages of Afrikans and usurped power. If anything, it is the assumption of romance in these international relationships that should cause speculation.

In the case of Makeda, Queen of Sheba, Afrikan centered scholars agree that

> Her visit may have been to negotiate a trade agreement with Solomon since he may have controlled some trade routes which were important to the Sabaeans. Thus it is interesting to speculate on reasons for the visit not usually considered in the conventional treatments of the story. One thing we can safely surmise, is that the empire that Makeda ruled was at least as important as Solomon's and if any of the traditions about the extent and scope of the empire are even partially correct, she ruled an even more substantial and more important kingdom than did Solomon...It is said that Makeda "came to test him with hard questions" which may just as easily been questions of a political, diplomatic, or commercial nature as questions to test his wisdom...There are those who might see in the 120 talents of gold given by Solomon to Makeda, a commercial or diplomatic settlement. Such a sum would be valued today at over $4 million...The level of hospitality accorded to the Queen of Sheba by Solomon was a tribute to her position and influence.[27]

As a result of these material formalities

> A trade agreement, diplomatic relations, and possibly a military alliance may have been among the things given by Solomon to Makeda.[28]

John Henrik Clarke makes the same point about Cleopatra, a Black Afrikan queen, who manipulated Roman overlords in the interests of her people.

> Egypt, now a Roman protectorate, was beset with internal strife and intrigue. Cleopatra aligned herself with Julius Caesar, who reinforced her power. Their political and sexual relationship was a maneuver to save Egypt from the worst aspects of Roman domination. After Julius Caesar

was murdered, Cleopatra, still in her early twenties, met Mark Antony and a love affair, strongly motivated by politics, began...Contrary to popular belief, Cleopatra did not commit suicide over the loss of Mark Antony. Her great love was Egypt. She was a shrewd politician and an Egyptian nationalist. She committed suicide when she lost control of Egypt.[29]

Unlike in the childish world of storybook romance, in the real world of international relations, the first and foremost priority of any leader who wishes to maintain the sovereignty of his/her people is the negotiation of power to his/her people's benefit. Bearing that in mind, these were not the gifts of one individual to another, no matter the level of royalty, but the political sacrifices of one people to another to demonstrate their desire to peacefully come to agreement. The "position and influence" of any leader is a direct function of the power of his/her people. It is not self-created.

Moreover, it is of significance to note that the extraordinary collection of gifts that these heads of state bestowed upon each other came before "romance" even entered the picture. But here as elsewhere, Europeans try to universalize their peculiarities. The fictional romance attributed to Europeans by themselves is generalized outward from their center using their misinterpretations of others' history. Ourstory shows us that romance, as eurocentrically defined, had and has no place in the Afrikan tradition of love and family.

In an indigenous context, because you don't follow romance as a guide to marriage, partners know the true identity of the other. You know the strengths and the weaknesses of the person you are going to marry. That way you won't wonder ten years down the road whether you married the right person or their ghost.[30]

Romance's origins as a fiction to promote and provide a demilitarized space for sexual intimacy is indeed quite interesting. As an honored tradition, it makes good sense in context of a materialistic society seeking to find and impersonate an emotional content. Approximately 200 years ago Europe began to take serious steps toward becoming the world's leading industrializing center. However, the problem was that their feudal system made this quite difficult because the older European men who owned and controlled the estates and everything on them, including their wives, sons and daughters, were unwilling to relinquish this power. Even so, urban factories were built. And production rapidly increased as a result of the massive influx of raw materials and other resources stolen from the colonized and enslaved[31] world beyond Europe. The need for more cheap European labor in the factories was easily resolved, but not by the forces of progress where people are thought to run to cities to modernize themselves or even because of the minimal wages offered there.

One need only look at the conditions of the factories, the urban centers they wallowed in and the loss of life and limb and mind that these conditions spawned to know that it had to be more than that. No self-interested, sane people consciously and voluntarily run to death. The source behind their rural to urban migrations was the violent and domineering nature of European patriarchy. In traditional rural European society, the father exercised absolute control over the lives of his children, grandchildren and whatever other generations that subsisted on his property. The pull of factory wages was secondary to the push to get away from a vicious agrarian patriarchy and achieve even a semblance of independence and economic solvency. In fact, for many young women at that time, marriage was for the express purpose of getting out from under their fathers' cruelty. It was a means of getting away from not only the drudgery of "slave" labor, but to find release from their grandfathers', fathers' and brothers' sexual exploitation. But, usually, their flight was to no avail. For most of them, their new mates and families practiced the same abuses as their fathers. There was no protection for females in Western patriarchy except as an excuse to exercise a selfish and pseudo-chivalrous male arrogance. And the quality of the intent of devoutly sexist men to save "their" women from others so that they can remain their sole exploiters is necessarily suspect.

The capitalists who owned and controlled the factories, of course, took advantage of every opportunity to exploit even the meager wages given to the workers. The workers' "false consciousness"[32] led them to see their spending habits not as exploitation but as acts of independence. With time they even became confused enough to believe that their spending power represented an unqualified exercise of a personal freedom of choice. So they had no reason to see the promotion of romance and romantic paraphernalia as problematic any more than the rampant prostitution or public drunkenness. Capitalists were able to successfully create a social climate fostering romance based on the needs and loneliness produced by harsh living and working conditions. Past and existing conditions fostered a need to find fantasy. Minds already socialized by glaciers, deeply engaged in a corrupt patriarchy and religiously committed to the individualistic priority of things needed little prodding toward the illusions of romantic love.

A profit motive, with no sense of the love that could exist between a man and a woman, created a market of consumer goods specifically designed to stimulate but never satisfy the romantic notions of commoners. The European haves consciously manipulated and exploited their have-not brothers and sisters without conscious. They put an enormous amount of time, energy, thought and finances into addicting the masses of Europe to sugar. In fact, during the 17th and 18th centuries, finished chocolate was the most widely accepted aphrodisiac in European society. Making rum to further numb the minds of vanquished Afrikans was not the only use that sugar cane imported to Europe from the Americas was put to. Chocolate was a major by product. And it is still one of the most widely consumed foodstuffs. Many still view it as an active aphrodisiac. Moreover, to many Westerners, chocolate is meant to be consumed in mass amounts when "falling" into, commemorating or losing "love."

Today, through the magic of credit, the socialized drive to purchase things which at least temporarily satisfy romance's sweet tooth has exploded at even the lowest class levels. Jewelry, diamonds, flowers, candy and virtually any dietary and psychological object that can be misconstrued as an aphrodisiacal gift are promoted by the media as indispensable for showing ones love. The contribution of this conspicuous consumption to the disproportionate lack of wealth and excessive debt among Afrikans in European society cannot be overlooked when addressing the romance factor. As Afrikan pawns in the white supremacist capitalist game, we should at least be curious about what happened when massive numbers of have-nots experienced levels of indebtedness they could no longer afford to pay. History runs in cycles. It was only about two centuries ago that Europe's disadvantaged found themselves in this position. Partly because of excessive and wasteful spending designed to impress their love interests with things, debtors' prisons mushroomed in traditional European society. Those who could not pay their bills went to prisons separate, at least theoretically, from those for violent and felony criminals. And the numbers of those who could not pay was enormous. So much so that debtors' prisons provided much of the riff raff who volunteered to exchange their prison sentences for a place in Europe's global colonizing forces. They were a considerable number among the pre-military invading forces of homesteaders and indentured servants in every land the Europeans stole and colonized.

We see this same pattern of imprisonment for debt unfolding in this country today. Laws that once allowed individuals to file for bankruptcy are falling one after the other. And lawyers scramble to rake in the last pieces of silver before this legal door to exploitation closes. But consumers still strive to hang on to that last limb of pretense by overextending their overextended credit to impress others with the things they have and give.

The freedom to be exploited in the factories of traditional urban Europe that came from sons and daughters escaping their fathers back then is still found in today's dating process where youth use their own and their parents' wages to buy things that symbolize a European interpretation of love. There has been an exponential increase in the things that one after the other become the most important signal of one's "love" for another and the primary means of creating romance. The "turnover" of love tokens fits a European defined progress.

Dating has increased business profits immensely. And players in this game of musical chairs are starting at earlier and earlier ages. As an example of the necessity of European progress we are now being visited by a fad called "turbo dating," also called speed dating.[33] Here an individual interviews and is interviewed by, seven or more blind dates in one night with the hopes that one or more will lead to future dates. Entire holiday seasons surrounding lovers' days such as Valentine's, Sweetest, New Year's, kwk.,[34] have become committed to the express exploitation of these commercially defined emotions.

However, we must not overlook the fact that there is an emotional component to the romance game. A broken heart goes with the territory. In Western culture, it is seen as a natural event in the life of individuals searching for love. The freedom to sift through the chaos for unrealistic, ideal partners often ends in emotional pain for the young at heart. As in all other journeys in the desperate search for completion, practicing the art of giving and taking pain becomes as common and natural as giving and taking sex. In fact, as some optimists searching for a positive meaning in all the heartbreak would argue, the broken hearts that accompany dating are practice for the more emotionally and psychologically traumatizing pain of inevitable divorce(s). As divorce has come to be considered a normal outcome of marriage, love has become increasingly understood as the expectation of being the victim of a series of painful relationships over the duration of one's life. In intimate, male-female relationships, it is expected that one become proficient at giving and receiving pain.

Speaking in the general context of European culture, pain must be normalized in all aspects of life and relationships. Romantic love is no exception. In the West, love does indeed hurt. And the pain these encounters bring has led to a parallel increase in the callousness and trepidation with which both males and females approach each other. It has helped to spread the lack of trust that has characterized the intimate, interpersonal relationships of the European for centuries among those who, up to becoming victim to Western culture and society, had proven and working means of developing strong, stable, non-romance based loving relationships that lasted for life. Fear of pain has made it easy to turn males and females into heartless predators of each other in their romanticized hunt for sex.

In intelligently discussing romance, we must continue to be clear that it is in no way an historical universal. Even the conceptualization of the idea of personal love has not been deemed necessary among most of the world's population until their invasion by European culture. The eurocentric idea, of course, based on the logic of an historical progression of human civilization to the European apex, is that it took the European to achieve and give everyone else this understanding. For too many Western disciples it took European intelligence to find true love. They claim responsibility of placing an abstraction, a spiritual context that they are still largely unaware of, into words, symbols and human hearts. In other words, love exists because they have identified and defined it.

The European lie of romantic love, and even love itself, is part and parcel of this pernicious campaign against humanity.

> We are told that 'love makes the world go round', or that 'what the world needs now is love, sweet love.' 'Love', as undefinable as it is, has been enshrined as the goal of both personal satisfaction and harmony with the eternal. 'Love' is so central to Western culture that, in spite of the fact that we cannot define it, no one doubts its existence or importance. The concept is so familiar to us, so intimately associated with our most important aspirations, that we may be excused for assuming that the concept of 'love' is universal to all Mankind....It may come as something of a shock, therefore, to discover that most of Mankind is innocent of anything like the Western notion of 'love'. Whatever it is that we mean by 'love', it is simply irrelevant to most of Mankind. The Chinese do not even have a word corresponding to 'love'. The Ancient Egyptians' two favourite words and concepts were 'ankh' (life) and 'djed' (stability). There is a good deal of uncertainty about whether the Ancient Egyptians even possessed something similar to our idea of 'love', but, if they did, the notion did not enjoy the degree of importance it boasts in our culture. It is difficult to find either words or concepts analogous to 'love' among the languages and peoples of Africa and the New World.[35]

Romance is functional for Europeans and those raised in their insanity. The elaboration on this functional cultural purpose of romance for European society is found in Bradley's *The Iceman Inheritance*.[36] It provides the distraction that allows for peace between combatants during whatever verbal and physical foreplay expedites the acquisition of willing sex partners.

In the end, Europeans are not looking for love. As it's been stylized, despiritualized and idealized in the West, it does not and cannot exist in human reality. Pure and simple, they are looking for sex. And, in the end, sex becomes just another thing to do. On this stage, women look for the candy store love fantasy through giving away their sex (using sex to get love) to men who are looking for their centerfold dream (using love to get sex). A love connection means a sex connection.

And even though this country has the highest teen age pregnancy rate in the industrialized world, this is one main reason why girls begin to engage in oral and anal sex in their early and pre-teens. It allows them to keep their sex-starved boyfriends while at the same time preventing pregnancy. So far, first year middle schoolers, or 12 year olds, are the youngest age that girls are admitting to engaging in sexually servicing males orally. However, we should know European progress and how this progress knows no lower age limit. If girls are getting pregnant at 9 years of age what would make us think that they are not performing oral sex at younger ages?

The same logic that drives teenage girls to engage in oral and anal sex applies to "celibate" priests who sodomize and nuns who fellate. Also bear in mind that this has historical precedence in traditional European male-female relationships. The forced and voluntary performance of oral sex on males by females was considered a highly effective form of control and sexual exploitation. It served the dual purpose of sexual pleasure and sexual domination. This has changed little. The need to sexually service their boyfriends in order to keep them is the main reason why we see girls with pierced tongues today. These metal "adornments," which are designed to provide greater, creative penis stimulation during fellatio, openly advertise the female's willingness to perform oral sex.

Moreover, these girls do not see oral sex as sex. It is a recreational activity just like having conversations or using drugs. In fact, in a recent poll, *Seventeen* magazine found that 55 percent of 15-19 year olds have had oral sex.[37] For some it might also be worth noting that the country with the highest percentage of teenage girls who have engaged in sexual intercourse is not this nation. Sweden is first closely followed by France in the later teens. Regardless, all of the top contenders are European.

Gangsta Boo, an Afrikan female rap/hip hop superstar, expresses the normalcy of oral and other perverted sexual behaviors among many of our youth.

> Every nigga I fuck with gots to eat my pussy. He gots to
> go down. Having oral skills is important to me. Regular
> sex is boring. It's so back in our parent's time, you know
> what I mean? And getting it from the back is my favorite
> position.[38]

This came from an interview in one of their most popular rap/hip hop magazines, *The Source*. As with so many other entertainers now who see no contradiction between their Christian beliefs and sexual perversion (as well as extreme individualistic materialism), Gangsta Boo has experienced no problem flip flopping back and forth between the two as evident in her latest move to perform gospel music.

Sadly, in too many of these cases, parents who simply do not want to know about their children's sexual behavior as long as they do not come home pregnant and/or are unable and/or unwilling to correct their permissiveness, would prefer oral sex to pregnancy as if these are the only two options. Even though well over half of the females who get married have had full sexual intercourse, the girl's virginity is often at issue. As long as the sexual behavior is unnatural (not involving the penis' entry into the vagina), she still qualifies as a virgin at the altar. This is no less insulting to our intellect than the move to politicize "born again virgins," the notion of someone who has engaged in sexual intercourse deciding that abstaining until marriage will somehow transform him/her back into a virgin. This fantasy of being born again virgins, like remaining young forever, is deeply imbedded in the ideas of ancient Europeans. Among sexually active Greek goddesses, both Artemis and "Athena were considered virgins because they had never submitted to a monogamous marriage." [39]

Oral sex is seen as a harmless and normal act to many of today's youth. It is more akin to kissing in their minds. In fact, it is rapidly becoming the equivalent of kissing in terms of how often it occurs. This causes one to wonder just how much time young girls are spending with their lips wrapped around males' penises if the average European female spends the equivalent of two weeks, or 336 hours, a year with her lips (and often tongue) connected to the lips (and often tongue) of her male lover.[40]   Again, European style progress has made yesterday's perversion today's norm. Again, what they have always done as a minority is slowly but surely being adopted by the global majority. But even as alarming as this trend in oral sex is, it is overshadowed by the fact that 40 percent of all girls are engaging in sexual intercourse before turning 15 years of age. This is up from 5 percent 10 years ago.[41]

Love is confused with sex to the point where love is sex. We find this reflected in terms like "making love" and having a "lover." We are simply confusing socially defined responses to any and every physical and emotional stimuli with the biological symptoms produced by adrenaline's rush to react to our basic, instinctual drive to sexually reproduce.   This "falling in love" or, rather, in sex, consistently occurs without us understanding the true nature of love or being able to shoulder the responsibilities that true love between two mature and responsible individuals brings.[42]   Both sexes have now been single-mindedly reduced to using whatever means at their disposal to get sex. Neither morality nor love is at the heart of the chase.   While in the heat of this confusion every encounter is translated as correct and as love, or at least having the potential for it.

Romance, as interpreted from the wisdom of Afrikan tradition, is also a substitute and indication of a misguided effort to try to locate spirit.[43]

> Separation from spirit, as we see here in the West, causes a greater emphasis on romantic love. It creates a vortex of longing for another person, for another way of connecting. Yet romantic love is only a way of finding that other connection, which is to spirit, that we are actually looking for.[44]

In this way romance is like religious fervor, drug abuse (illegal and legal) and alcohol, violence and gambling – the search for spirit in all the wrong places. The greater sales for romance novels relative to other book reading material say it all. The newest wave of romance novels, especially those which have been self-published, have seriously blurred the line between "romance" and pornography. *Soul Mates Dissipates*,[45] *The Sex Chronicles*[46] and *The Family Curse*[47] stand as compelling examples of this trend where explicit sex and sexual perversion dominate the storyline. Pornography, however "civilized," sells. It must also be noted that homosexual activities are found in a large number of such action scenes.[48] Yesterday's pornographic reading material has become today's romantic novel. The messengers of perversion have found a way into their audience's hearts and bedrooms through those books that Afrikan women, who consume the majority of book literature in our homes, buy more than any other.

2. The Safety Valve

> "[T]he animal that does not rest gets so angry and unhappy it spreads destruction wherever it goes."

> *Ayi Kwei Armah*

Tension needs outlets. This is a universal rule. "What goes around, comes around," in one way or the other. And, extreme, ceaseless tension requires elaborate outlets if it is to be kept from disrupting "normal" life. This rule applies even if, as normal in the West, life is already extreme.

Sex, like drugs, violence and religion, is a form of tension release and a guaranteed "feel good." It allows, at least for a moment, the exhaustion that follows from the expenditure of an enormous amount of energy. This exhaustion is often misinterpreted as a state of peace or tranquility. For many it gives the illusion that they are once again spiritually connected.

The less we feel good internally, the more we seek external means of gratification. In itself, this speaks to cultural differences in the need, occurrence and purpose of sex in traditional Afrikan and European societies. The more a people have nothing internally, no self love, the more "gratuitous" sex becomes the normal aspiration for its participants. And those whose minds have been wrecked by the forces of the European cultural invasion also relinquish all of their moral codes relative to baser desire in their frantic search for a return to any peaceful form of reality.

There is a reason why Europeans repeatedly bring to our attention how chimpanzees and other "related" primates use sexual aggressions to settle disputes and relieve tension. Nonetheless, we must remain keenly aware that this interpretation of the behaviors of these animals, of beings whose minds they cannot possibly have access to, like their interpretation of history, is theirs and theirs alone. Furthermore, it must be noted that animals who live in groups were neither given an instinct to abuse sex nor, as we will see, practice any form of sexual perversion. They may be what we call lower animals but in so many ways they are spiritually higher than the Europeans who study them in search of themselves. If nothing else, they do not, as our European models, kill for pleasure, practice or no reason.

It should go without saying that a tense person "needs" a lot of sex. A tense people unable to resolve their frustrations *will* evolve cultural priorities that camouflage their extremes yet enable the ongoing release of their tension or they will violently implode. That is why those few times when they are not waging war against others they are constantly agitating for it by disrespectfully encroaching on other people's spaces, cultures, minds and spirits. Europeans are not at peace unless they are at war. War is a most effective release of social and cultural tension for them. Sex, however, is more immediately effective and easier to access.

Tension releasers become cultural priorities. European culture is in a natural and constant state of the pursuit of normalcy through increasing the level of chaos. Tension is normal. It rushes to rush. Chaos camouflages their natural tension. As Westerners have become more sophisticated in the outward politicization of their mechanical, hedonistic civilization, their sexual cultural imperatives have become better camouflaged.

Sex has become their overriding priority. It is an easy release. The chronic priority of sexual excess indicates the permanence of extreme tension (like the permanence of racism) in the European culture. It does not indicate an inordinate drive to reproduce. Reproduction has nothing to do with it, except in the context of trying to stave off racial annihilation. If it did, abortion rates would not be so high and a declining population growth would not be one of their foremost fears, realities and national and international policy issues.

Excessive, gratuitous sex is correct for a society where abnormally high levels of frustration and stress are normal. Sex as an easy and extremely accessible outlet makes sense. Those things that reduce, or appear to reduce (no matter how temporarily), tension become highly marketed and practiced. They are used, and scientifically rationalized in their excesses, as normal and desirable for all progressive individuals. Moreover, because of the immorality and lies/deception that are an expected and normal part of relations between individuals, and every other form of social relationship in European culture, the level of stress normal for human society is considerably escalated before any other stress factors can be placed in the equation.

There is no mystery why these sexual extremes and perversions have reached beyond the borders of European society.

> [T]heir evil genius is their ability to drain the diseased pus of their political sores on the lands of other peoples. With consistency they have attempted to solve their problems at other people's expense.[1]

This quote speaks to the European attitude toward expansion which applies to sex as equally as internecine politics. They are inseparable because they are both tied to the same mind. European culture is a pathogen. It systematically causes or encourages social and cultural disease wherever it spreads. The need to diffuse aggression or self-destruct is all consuming. It is no less reflected at the individual than societal level. It is no less reflected in sexual encounters with each other than in the heat of military battle to destroy others.

In the capitalistic system, once you have fully exploited a market, you must find new markets to conquer and expand into. Capitalist economies must forever grow or they will die. The same culture that created and perfected this ravenous economic form also created this insatiable sex drive. When an ever expansionistic mentality defines sexual relationships, its practitioners must forever create or find new bodies to exploit because like a shark, if it stops moving, it will die. Sexual imperialism is a component of cultural imperialism.

This heightened sense of frustration must be unleashed on other individuals by individual Europeans and other groups by the European people or it returns to haunt them. Predatory sexual behaviors are in sync with the predatory European culture. They have created a world where a predator-prey mentality rules every realm of human interaction, every intimate exchange between individuals. Why would the rules of engagement for their sexual behavior be any different from those guiding every other interpersonal arrangement?

And it is at the intercultural/international level that this sexual tension has been historically vented. Long ago, the internal market was flooded. Others who are vulnerable to European aggressions become victims of the wrath of an imperialist sexual expansion based on the need to release interpersonal frustration. Those made to feel powerless against others' sexual aggressions remain easy targets for Europeans seeking release from themselves. Others become their sexual experiments, the recipients of their unwanted probing that naturally goes beyond the natural physical and mental limits of human anatomy. These victims all become new rape "survivors" in the power ridden drive to punish, abuse and control others sexually. And, no matter how these victim/survivors equal or surpass the sexual appetite of those who prey(ed) on their minds and bodies, we cannot overlook the conditions which led them to be so imitative in the first place. We must remember that extreme tension becomes part of the mood of any people under constant assault.

A Culture of Rape

Rape, however committed, is an act, as well as a weapon, of war. For Europeans, the rape of the women and girls, and even boys and men, always follows the defeat of the men in battle. It is also viewed as an effective military tactic designed to demoralize enemies into a state of vanquishment. The rape that was initiated everywhere they went in their quest to dominate the world was designed to destroy others' spirit as well as create a mulatto buffer group of surrogate pseudo-elite oppressors between them and the masses.[2]

Muslim Arabs also took full advantage of this inhumane barbarism to subdue Afrikan people after they had militarily conquered them. Wanton rape accompanied their repeated religious proselytization efforts across the Afrikan landscape[3] and the enslavement of Afrikans that is still going strong after over 1,350 years. Many hundreds of Muslim Arab slave markets provided numerous private stalls where Afrikan women were "tested out" by Arab men for sexual compatibility before they were purchased.[4] But even including Muslim Arabs, no imperialistic and colonizing nation compares to Europeans' systematic rape of other peoples.

There is ample evidence that this culture of rape did not take hold on the Afrikan continent as part of any imperialistic aggression by Afrikans until well after 2000 B.C.[5] It was a way of dehumanizing disrespect introduced by foreigners from what we now define as the North.[6] It was the beginning of our assuming a wrongful definition of manhood.

We have to stop and deeply think about the amount and duration of rape that had to have been perpetrated on Afrikan women and girls in order for us to have the range of complexion that we possess. Our rape was not committed in love. We are finding more and more Afrikans in search for peace at any cost trying to manufacture love where it could not possibly have existed. No matter how politically successful this misdirected and desperate search by the dispossessed sons and daughters of this rape for love in this rape may become, no minority of voluntary coupling cases should ever be taken as representative of the violations heaped on the majority. Europeans are not our ancestors. If anything, rape is an immediate and absolute disqualification of Europeans from Afrikan ancestralship. To be an ancestor is an honor accorded by one's descendants. It is not something to be claimed by our enemies or those among us who seek their appreciation.[7]

There is no statute of limitations on the rape of Afrikans by Europeans. It is a war crime. And war crimes have no statute of limitations. Knowing this, we must come to understand, to feel if we can, the never ending, unimaginable psychic shock over generations of our ancestors. How must it feel to be in a constant, disoriented belief; to live in a daze wondering when will you wake up from this nightmare? To have to parade around naked in front of, and be poked, prodded and violated by, ruthless, sex-crazed enslavers reduces women to what level of dehumanization?[8] Were not their women enough? To heal, we must hear our ancestors cry out for rescue from the very fiber of our soul, "This can't be happening! This can't be reality!" but to no avail.

We have experienced four thousand years of rape. And, unlike the limited research of many scholars would have us believe, this was not solely the work of the soldiers and traders scraped from the scum of Europeans who were partially paid in the currency of unlimited sex with captive Afrikans. Rape was found to be an act committed and enjoyed by Europeans at all class levels, in every occupation and religion, and by both sexes. Moreover, those who did not physically commit this crime against Afrikan humanity financed it.

> To begin with, priests were not only among the leading slave traders, but they also owned slave ships to carry the "black cargoes" to distant lands. Priests also had their harems of black girls, some having as many as twenty each. They were called "house servants" by these "holy fathers"....Sailors and unskilled Portuguese laborers had their own quotas of slaves, especially slave girls. For let this truth emerge from the many facts which are buried, and let it stand out clearly: One of the main attractions that drew thousands of white men was their unlimited sexual freedom with all the black girls and women who were enslaved and helpless in the power of their masters.[9]

And now some of us want to honor these barbaric superfreaks with ancestral honor.

Have you ever considered where the term "missionary position" comes from? It came from the sexual position preferred by European Christian missionaries who raped the women and girls on the Continent and other places they invaded to "civilize" with Western religion. It was also the only position sanctioned by these missionaries for their new converts. Terms come into use because of widespread practice or applicability. The rape of Afrikan girls and women by European Christian missionaries was normal behavior. And because of the nature of the parochial education system and the historically homosexual practices of European males, the rape of Afrikan boys could have been nothing else but commonplace also.[10]

Afrikans in denial of these facts cannot lean on the point that great variation in skin tone exists on the Continent as refuge from this truth. Their singular search for their European ancestors betrays their commitment to European cultural politics. For one thing, the variation in melanin levels among Afrikans was very limited before the arrival of the Arab and Europeans. No matter what you see on the Continent now, we were a Black people. Secondly, most of us came from the western coast of middle Afrika where the people were and still are mostly dark complexioned. When was the last time you saw an authentic drawing or painting or written description of anyone other than dark complexioned people among the Afrikans who were captured in raids and dragged along the unforgiving trails of blood to the barracoons and dungeons of no return, where they waited as death ships vied to cart them off to a deeper, more permanent dehumanization in the cultural wasteland that lay beyond the rhythm of the Ethiopian Ocean?[11]

If history reveals genetics then, apparently, for Europeans, rape is a biological drive. Although many are loath to admit it at this time because of what it would say about their motivation and scholarly lies to hide their historical behavior and intent toward others, Craig Palmer and Randy Thornhill cogently but unintentionally argue the truth of this accusation in a book titled *A Natural History of Rape: Biological Basis of Sexual Coercion.*[12] Understanding that Europeans are driven to universalize behaviors that either have not existed outside of or have been taken to their logical extreme within their society, their angry reaction to this publication is to be expected. It is not the facts that Europeans find distasteful. If European culture were to survive as the dominate means of organizing and explaining "human" behavior, this would become a useful piece of politically scientific research. So the facts themselves are not the problem. As with history, it is their interpretation that is. And, especially in this case, it is the revealing of self before it is time.

In an effort to point out this way of thinking, throughout the chapters the term "political science" will be used, but not to identify the social science discipline that studies the mobilization, distribution and exercise of group power. It will fulfill a similar but larger role of defining the conscious cultural context of Western social science itself. We will use "political science" as a literal definition to designate the *political* nature, intent and findings of Western science. Scientific proofs in all areas of study are political tools designed to validate European culture's imperatives. Science validates culture.[13] Defined this way, the term political science reflects an active, conscious, directed European science. Its "discoveries" are neither accidental nor objective. So it is this particular interpretation of rape, not what it fundamentally reveals about their peculiar cultural personality that provokes disagreement from us.

Nevertheless, rape is an act of war. When accompanying invasion and domination, it serves to project hatred onto others. In the particular case of the Europeans, it expresses their subconscious drive to make the world as they are. "It is not the unloved who initiate disaffection, but those who cannot love because they love only themselves."[14]

Like every other area of human activity, sex is a means of social conquest because it is defined by the number of others violated. It is an instrument Europeans use to force themselves into the minds and bodies of other people. In "The Psychopathic Racial Personality" Bobby E. Wright pointed out the sexual inadequacy of Europeans and the resultant psychological projection of this frustration on others through accusations of promiscuity, perversion and excess.[15] All this is done while they vent their frustration by overcompensating for their inadequacy through the continuous and extreme sexual violation of others, which gives additional evidence of their inordinate desire for ownership and control. Being rape, even if the victim is unaware due to mentacidal social conditioning, sexual violation implies the violator's unlimited power.

Perversion, as rape's complement, is a means of cultural conquest also because it destroys the victim's sense of moral decency, of what is natural to humans and of what one human could possibly do to another and walk away in peace. Being assaulted by perversions without benefit of the community's protection leaves one deeply scared and confused about truth, reality and loyalties. In the same way that the atom bombs dropped on Nagasaki and Hiroshima left those people wandering aimlessly around their devastated world in a state of disbelief, the weapon of sexual perversion leaves individuals shocked beyond knowing friend from foe or home from hell. They find that just having to mentally replay the endless debate over the sheer possibility of a human committing the act taken to destroy them continues to obstruct their sanity in this reality. Once the perversion is perpetrated it takes an enormous amount of conscious struggle to get what existed of one's sanity back. And once people are drawn into the Western sex priority, they can be taken anywhere sexually. Europeans know this. They fully recognize the importance of "subliminal seduction."

In their drive to exercise power over others, Europeans men also work their sexual frustrations out on their own women. Although relatively speaking Afrikan women by far suffer in greater numbers, European women are the majority of the ten women who are raped in this society every hour. Over 316,000 women were raped in this country in 1997 alone. According to the "The National Crime Victimization Survey," this number is included in the 430,000 women who are victims of general sexual assault.[16] It is estimated that 4.9 million women are physically assaulted and/or raped by "intimate partners" every year.[17] Moreover, European females claim their fair share of the "sixty-nine percent of all women raped [who] are between the ages of nine and sixteen years" in this great European nation.[18] And these statistics do not fully address the fact that, at most, only one-fifth of all women who are raped report it to the authorities.

Proximity, or living near each other, is one of the primary determinants of who will be victimized. And, in this hyper-segregated society, Europeans disproportionately live near Europeans. Throughout their history, European men have raped European women. No statistics, not even those fabricated during the heyday of lynching in the Deep South, have ever shown that any other group of men even came close to raping European women in the way and number that European men have.

Among other things, they use date rape drugs against each other.[19] Drugs are seen as tools in the game of capitalist acquisition of sex among a people who are the biggest drug addicts on the planet. Neither shyness nor rejection cause males or females to use date rape drugs against prospective marks. The drive to exercise absolute power over another combined with an unbridled desire to be sexually satisfied at the expense of another does. Those admitting to using these narcotics against others they want sex from are not lacking interpersonal social skills and do not find themselves ostracized or ignored by members of the other sex. It is part of the game of conquest characteristic of the European mind. Historically, for them winning has largely been a function of trickery and deceit. The victory is made more satisfying when the loser is thought to have been made a fool of. Power over another is most complete when the victim has been made immobile. Complete and absolute control is what the ultimate state of bondage that S&M (sadomasochism, i.e., deriving sexual pleasure from giving others and/or receiving pain) offers the sadist and having sex with the dead gives the necrophiliac.

A surprisingly clearheaded interview with a "professional" in the business of sexual pain is found in *FHM* (For Him Magazine).[20] In it, Isabella Sinclaire, expresses her expert opinion as a dominatrix that power, abuse, control and perversion are primary in European sexual relations. They are primary even to the point where physical contact and/or orgasm are not necessarily the desired outcome. She also makes a classically arrogant, universalizing eurocentric statement by implying that all people are into sexual pain like them. They just have to be led out of their antiquated cultural closets to enjoy it. In her words, "I believe everybody has some sort of perversion. So many people are repressing so much that it drives them crazy." But, then again, she is quite right about many non-Europeans living in Western society who hold Europeans as their reference group and attempt to become them. "If you play with a fool you become a fool."[21] However, we should know that it is not the repression of perversion that is driving those who reject the European way crazy.

At the less individual, but no less individualistic, level we also find the normalization of gang rape among our youth. Like gang activity itself, however, these practices are derived from a cultural context where they were a well practiced and normal part of life long before the Afrikans arrival. Male gangs, youth and adult, have long been part of the European social landscape. Trains, where a female is raped by a number of males, one after the other and often repeatedly, are an accepted part of their social activities.[22] And it appears that they have gradually become as normal among Afrikans as Europeans.

> Back then, when I was growing up, boys gang-banging or gang-raping a girl was a pretty common thing. They called it pulling a train. It didn't happen to any particular kind of girl. It happened to girls who were at the wrong place at

the wrong time. The boys talked about it like it was a joke or a game, like they were "only" out to have some "fun." If a girl was caught on the wrong side of a park or in the wrong territory or on the wrong street, she was a target. It was a common thing back then for boys to downgrade girls and cuss at them in the street. It was common for them to go to bed with girls and talk about them like dogs the next day. It was common for boys to deny that they were the fathers of their babies. And it was common for boys to beat girls up and knock them around. And then girls would get hard too.[23]

While this window into history comes out the memory of Assata Shakur, one of our strongest sister warrior scholars, the tradition of gang rape is a practice that is also well documented in the autobiographical confessions of Afrikan males. Two of the more popular, Nathan McCall's *Makes Me Wanna Hollar* and Claude Brown's *Manchild in the Promised Land*, are situated in the 1940's through 1970's. If it is possible, today, some fifty, sixty years later, in the European cultural tradition of confusing even chaotic and dehumanizing behaviors with progress, the practice is even more widespread, occurs more frequently and has become even more depraved, if that were possible, in its execution today.

Trains are what happens when children imitate adults, or novices copy masters. It makes no difference if the imitation is of behavior from today or yesterday. What is important is who was imitated. Trains are the child's version of the gang rapes of war and communal orgies. And they were originally initiated in the context of a particular people's military conquests among their own. Among the Afrikan community in the West today, this is most often the aggression of angry male warriors who have no sense of who their enemy is yet know that there is an important connection between the European, their rage and the probability of death if they choose to target Europeans with their rage. The same applies to similar acts on the Continent in places like Nigeria where the spoiled descendants of negroes have turned college campuses into their private amusement parks for indiscriminately practicing European-style gang rape behavior on coeds.

The sexist process of Western socialization makes any woman

or girl's voluntary participation in being gang raped highly questionable and problematic. No sane person chooses to be raped. Regardless, the sexist exploitation of women is showing itself up more and more in group sexual activities. We are slowly being exposed to the normalization of real and symbolic orgies among European youth.   Because of age constraints controlling the information available in the public record, we are only privy to the legal age side of this rapidly growing trend of children aping and bettering their elders at any and every game.[24]   But, a cursory look at what information is given in the news, tabloids and family viewing shows reveals a growing popularity in coed sleepovers.   Interest is rapidly increasing from the youngest children through college age young adults. In general, though, reasons directly related to the progressive encouragement of loose sexual relations speak to why we are seeing more and more images in the media of a number of young males and females, usually dressed in casual or sleepwear, comfortably sharing a bed together while watching television, performing some "communal" game activity or just conversing.

The rate of public awareness is, of course, related to how the behavior of these youth will be socially viewed as well as whose children are involved.   The story of European youth in during and after school sexual free-for-alls in Rockdale County, Georgia is a case in point,[25] but not an unusual one.   What is most interesting about this leaked story is that the mentacide bred in us forces us to see innocence in these younger Europeans and their deviance as aberrations. It leads us to interpret this, and the many stories like this, only as evidence of a "few bad apples" or some wayward children, when it is more common than not in European communities among parents and their offspring. The biased presentation by the media of this story itself implies that this is a group of misguided, wayward children (not teenagers responsible for their own behavior) who unavoidably got "caught up" in the peer pressure of excessive, lustful sexual deviancies. But, they are not unusual.[26]

What's even more amazing is our heartfelt belief in the idea that the parents did not know. They also supposedly do not know that their children are using their drugs or their alcohol[27] or that encouraging them to masturbate promotes sexual indulgence either. Children access their parents' R-rated and pornography collections as easily as they do their liquor cabinets and gun cases. These parents would have us believe that they have no recollection of their own childhoods. The most mind-boggling aspect of this perverted social behavior is that we somehow expect our children to not be infected with this virulent strain of insanity, when the vast majority of Afrikans would prefer to live next door to Europeans,[28] when almost one-third of Afrikan children attend secondary school where they are the distinct numerical minority, when 80% of our children go to predominantly European undergraduate institutions.[29] We have somehow fooled ourselves into believing that our children do not participate, or are only around those European offspring who would never do such things. Or, even worse, for too many of us, we assume our children should be involved if their children are. It is assumed that these learning experiences will make them less objectionable to corporate America or enable them to better get along with people other than their own. Such habits and associations will somehow change them into other people. This disguising of Afrikan mentality and behavior will somehow undermine the permanence of racism in the European mind.[30]

This illogic is their asilic defensive mechanism at work on our minds. We are so driven by their media's presentation and our own need to see them as moral human beings that we immediately and willfully search for ways to dismiss as odd and/or accept as worthy of emulation what is normal behavior for them. Some of us will even punish ourselves when our minds stumble upon the possibility that this is really them by seeking out those few Afrikans who behave the same way or worse, systematically ignoring the obvious fact that these Afrikans were raised to emulate Europeans. Even in the case of the wards of cultural stepparents, "The fruit does not fall far from the tree."

Of course, sex may not be all of their world. But it is one of the principal activities of a congenital selfishness. And if what Llaila Afrika says is true, then Europeans created and for millennia have developed a strong genetic predisposition for lust among themselves and spread this to others whom they have come into contact with and forced their culture on. I have found no reason to doubt his statement. Therefore, however insignificant as a recessive gene theirs may be, if genetics arguments are correct, we have taken on that trait.

Through the repeated and extensive historical rape of Afrikans by Europeans, we have been tainted with another's gene pool. In turn, we have attempted to rationalize what we have come to consider a biological and socialized predisposition to continuously and openly physically lust after each other sexually. Now, we have come to morally redefine what constitutes lust to fit our inability to withstand the pull of European culture's sex imperative. Lust, like distrust and self-hate, has become so normal in our community that we feel it is natural.   We blame ourselves.   But excessive sex, oral sex, masturbation and homosexuality are simply manifestations and evidence of this genetically inbred "lust degenerative behavior."[31]

House of Pain

Mental and physical abuse is unquestionably historically characteristic of European male-female relationships.   Their interpersonal histories make violence between "lovers" predictive.

> Domestic violence is the leading cause of injury to women in the nation.   Between one-third and one-half of all women are assaulted by a spouse or partner at some point during their lives. Between 30 percent and 40 percent of all women who are murdered are murdered by husband or boyfriends...Every six minutes, a woman in the United States is raped; every eighteen seconds a woman is beaten, and every day four women are killed by their batterers.[32]

> Nearly 25 percent of surveyed women and 7.5 percent of surveyed men said they were raped and/or physically assaulted by a current or former spouse, cohabiting partner, or date at some time in their lifetime; 1.5 percent of surveyed women and 0.9 percent of survey men said they were raped and/or physically assaulted by a partner in the previous 12 months.   According to these estimates, approximately 1.5 million women and 834,732 men are raped and/or physically assaulted by an intimate partner annually in the United States.   Because many victims are victimized more than once, the number of intimate partner

victimizations exceeds the number of intimate partner victims annually. Thus, approximately 4.9 million intimate partner rapes and physical assaults are perpetrated against U.S. women annually, and approximately 2.9 million intimate partner physical assaults are committed against U.S. men annually.[33]

Only a few years ago *ABC Nightly News* reported that 1,500 women are murdered every year by their husbands or boyfriends. In two-thirds of them guns were used.

Is there a consistent history of violence and abuse between "loving" couples in Western society? Of course there is. A 1956 study of homicides in Philadelphia, Pennsylvania came to the conclusion that 41 percent of the married women who had been killed met their deaths at the hands of their husbands. Eleven percent of married men's lives ended in the same way.[34] Nearly two decades later we found that 56 percent of all husbands and wives physically battered each other at least once during their relationship.[35] At the turn of the 20th century approximately 600,000 women were experiencing domestic violence yearly.[36] And, of these, 1,100 were killed. Sadly, a woman is more likely to be the victim of violence in her own home than on the street or the job. Many European social scientists agree that the family is the most dangerous and violent institution in their society.[37] This is especially the case for women and children, but in no way limited to them. The same *ABC Nightly News* report gave the related statistic that 63 percent of the children under the age of 12 who are killed are murdered by their parents. All of this violence came in the name of love and at the hands of loving mates. The relatively recent advertisement arguing that individuals would be more likely to complain about neighbors playing their music too loud than a woman being beaten in the next apartment speaks for itself.[38]

From this we can see a society where stable relationships become nonexistent for all who enter. The exercise of power over others is essential to the Western personality. And using violence and intimidating aggression against an intimate are experienced as personally empowering acts. Action produces reaction. So, especially for girls and women, rape, sexual harassment and physical, mental and emotional abuse naturally turn women away from men. The actual experience and/or mere thought of the possibility of mistreatment destroys the building of trust and, in turn, love between women and men. But we should not be confused by the image of the innocence of the "fairer" and "weaker" European sex. Violent interpersonal bouts have always been initiated by both sexes in their society.

> Both men and women assault one another in marriage, and mutual abuse is more common than either alone. Both men and women approve of slapping, shoving, and hitting one another under certain conditions. However, the consequences to women are more lethal.[39]

We have become fooled by the use of money as a subtle weapon in the battle for interpersonal control of women by men and vice versa. It is only another layer, another weapon, in their never ending battles. In a capitalist system, money forces compliance. Nevertheless, physical abuse of European men by European women is in no way new. It is well known to them. One of Mad Max's fates in *Beyond Thunderdome* is the reenactment of the punishment accorded a man who was caught being beaten by his wife in traditional European society. He was stripped, tied backward on a horse or ass, and run out of town only to return when he could loose himself and find clothes to wear.[40] This was the punishment given any man who was caught being beat by his wife. And it was common enough to be considered important enough to record in their history.

These behaviors date back to their Caucasus Mountains beginnings in factual accounts and they are clearly reflected in their myths. There was no peace among them then. There is no peace among them now. Any objective discussion of the abuse of women by men and vice versa in European society must address the logic of a longstanding, naturally excessive, interpersonal aggression driven into their genes in order to insure survival in a glacial environment. This fact, as cogently argued by Cheikh Anta Diop, Michael Bradley and others, dates the presence of their violent aggression as a vital and central part of their way of life long before they acquired the means to project it on others and rationalize it in themselves.

As all of their behaviors in extreme have been mimicked by their mentacidal imitators in an effort to be more like them, the rape of Afrikans by Afrikans continues. As stated earlier, rape and other forms of controlling violence operate hand in hand. But this behavior is not natural among Afrikans. It is ahistorical for us. Outside of fictional accounts and feminist manufactures, where is the evidence of any physical abuse of women by men or men by women in traditional Afrikan society? Where is *any* pattern? The traditional Afrikan model of male/female relationships, untainted by Europeanized universals, is what we should seek to emulate. Otherwise, some may accede that the physical abuse of women by men and men by women is a natural function, a necessary evil, of progress. Without an awareness of historical cultural context some may even become receptive to a Western debate that would make rape itself a natural, and therefore an unavoidable and acceptable, function of the human sex drive.[41] Some of us have yet to learn that

> ...dabbling in the confusion of others will only make you more confused and your divided energy will only tend to defeat the special purpose which you should have in solving the problems of your race.[42]

Yurugu

At the most fundamental level, this Western pursuit of extremes is the misguided search for spirit. It all comes back to Yurugu, the original European manifestation. As relayed to us by Marimba Ani, in the Dogon myth of the Yurugu,

> ...Amma, the Creator, ordained that all created beings should be living manifestations of the fundamental universal principle of complementarity or 'twinness'...But in one of these primordial placentas the male soul did not wait for the full gestation period to be born. This male being...arrogantly wished to compete with Amma and to create a world better than that which Amma had created...Realizing that he was flawed and therefore deficient, Yurugu returned to Amma, seeking his

complementary female self. But Amma had given his female soul away. Yurugu, forever incomplete, was doomed to perpetually search for the completeness that could never be his.[43]

It makes no difference whether you see Yurugu as real or a mythical personification. It is real in its consequences. It is the search for spirit out of being incomplete beings that drives Europeans to these extremes. They have attempted to redefine spirit as sensation and fill in their vast spiritual void with physical stimuli. Obviously, sexual extremes have become some of the most satisfying of these physical stimuli. And, in making others spiritually void like them, Europeans have opened up the path to sexual extremes for them also.

For Europeans emotions constitute the soul. When they attempt to connect with the Universe, they are trying to find emotional content. They learn about spirit under pressure. Access to it is logically defined within the context of their frantic and chaotic reality. Extremes are integral to this search to find emotional content. The adrenaline rush gives them a measurable life, a comparative base from which they can measure death. By being thrown into fear and tasting other excitements which make them believe that they are actually alive, they convince themselves that they are in touch with their spirit, or spiritually alive.

All of their cutting edge media technology naturally leads in the direction of emotional arousal because it is designed to naturally feed and nourish their asili. Horror movies and those featuring "death, destruction and domination" and sexual exploitation shock the senses. They give Westerners the illusion of a controlled spiritual experience. The masochist's desire to be blindfolded as part of his/her bondage games during sex so they will not know when "it" is coming is a most extreme example of this need to be emotionally released through surprise. And we are caught up in it with them too because we have adopted their incomplete being as our own.

Interpersonal peace has never come easily to Yurugus. Generation upon generation of survival in caves on glaciers obligated the evolution of a bio-cultural genetic structure not amenable to peaceful relations with themselves or others. Peace was only encouraged by the selfish necessity of individual or group survival.

Their sexual ambivalence and romantic love are grounded in this form of a selfish "truce," whose sole purpose is to keep intersexual peace among themselves long enough to momentarily achieve sexual gratification and/or procreate.

> The necessity of finding that small area of truce where the imperative of reproduction balances our fear and aggression is the primary task of each Western individual and the importance of that search is reflected throughout all levels of our culture.[44]

> Courtship is the subtle process whereby initial and natural aggression is 'turned aside' so that, in the end, the courting partners stand side by side to face the world with their combined and allied aggression directed outward...as courtship progresses, the aggressive movements are directed increasingly 'to the side' of the partner until, eventually, the courting pair find themselves side by side with their combined aggression directed outwards.[45]

We should analyze the extreme sexual priority coming out of a cultural personality bereft of emotional context but subliminally driven to seek any form of psychological satisfaction because it cannot recover half of its being or destroy its soul.[46] Michael Bradley may well have a point in terms of a glacially motivated sex drive. The primary cultural priorities of sex and violence indicate an incompleteness that leaves devastation in the wake of its search for fulfillment.

Inevitably, the goal must be an individual isolation attended by selective sexual relationships. They are working toward the state where individuals do not have to be with others, except when loneliness becomes so extreme that they are compelled to associate. Along with that, Europeans are seeking to conquer the orgasm. They are trying to discover, unravel and control the psycho-biological secret to its occurrence so that they can regulate the duration and intensity of their orgasms. Ultimately, they desire be able to control when and how long they can individually experience orgasm.

Masturbation, or self-administered sex, has become a readily available means to that end. Applying one's hands or tools to his/her own penis, vagina or anus in order to achieve an orgasm has long been an acceptable and promoted substitute.   Even just the acceptability and popularity of what Marilyn Manson's promoters say is a rumor that he had his spine or the lower bones of his rib cage surgically removed so that he could bend far enough forward to easily perform fellatio on himself is not an extreme example of this sexual progress in the European mind.

To this end, Bradley has taken maybe a too humanistic approach in his analysis. For in the end, he assumes that sex is not a form of aggression.

> 'Love' is that middle ground between aggression and the ability to reproduce. 'Love' is that place where we can feel unthreatened in sex, and the place where we can have sex without directing aggression toward our partner. The place were 'sex' and 'respect' can co-exist, for both ourselves and our partners.[47]

In the Western cultural context that is a highly questionable assumption. For there is no area of Western culture where aggression does not play a dominate relational role. "Love" is the lie that makes sex humane.   It may be more correct to decode the European approach to sex out of its rightful aggressive origins.   From this perspective, it would be much more accurate to say that Europeans are driven to "commit sex" against each other.

Violating "Others"

In closing, we must make sure we do not mistake the liberal politics of the few good apples as being different from the rest. No matter the image, in the end, Europeans know who constitutes their family. It has been clearly demonstrated that they will "lovingly" give to others as long as it does not interfere with their, and their descendant's, privilege.   And they are also aware that, when necessary or desirable, so-called liberal Europeans always have the option of returning to whiteness at will. In general, Europeans only publicly distance themselves from their system of white supremacy when it proves advantageous to the European cause. Sleeping with their enemies is merely another way "liberals" gain leverage for their people.

In speaking of the "other" as those who are not European, even bell hooks must admit to a viable generalization that is a constant in European power relations with Afrikans and other people of color.

> To make one's self vulnerable to the seduction of difference, to seek an encounter with the Other, does not require that one relinquish forever one's mainstream positionality. When race and ethnicity become commodified as resources for pleasure, the culture of specific groups, as well as the bodies of individuals, can be seen as constituting an alternative playground where members of dominating races, genders, sexual practices affirm their power-over in intimate relations with the Other.[48]

And, although bell hooks, the author of this and the following quote, finds the European empowering blending of race, ethnicity and gender positive, she is unavoidably led to conclude that the interactions between members of groups holding different amounts of power does not in and of itself lead to changes in relations of power.

> For white boys to openly discuss their desire for colored girls (or boys) publicly announces their break with a white supremacist past that would have such desire articulated only as taboo, as secret, as shame. They see their willingness to openly name their desire for the Other as affirmation of cultural plurality (its impact on sexual preference and choice). Unlike racist white men who historically violated the bodies of black women/women of color to assert their position as colonizer/conqueror, these young men see themselves as non-racists, who choose to transgress racial boundaries within the sexual realm not to dominate the Other, but rather so that they can be acted upon, so that they can be changed utterly. Not at all attuned to those aspects of their sexual fantasies that irrevocably link them to collective white racist domination,

they believe their desire for contact represents a progressive change in white attitudes towards non-whites. They do not see themselves as perpetuating racism. To them the most potent indication of that change is the frank expression of longing, the open declaration of desire, the need to be intimate with dark Others. The point is to be changed by this convergence of pleasure and Otherness. One dares – acts – on the assumption that the exploration into the world of difference, into the body of the Other, will provide a greater, more intense pleasure than any that exists in the ordinary world of one's familiar racial group. And even though the conviction is that the familiar world will remain intact even as one ventures outside it, the hope is that they will reenter that world no longer the same.[49]

Their "Other" still serves a psycho-sexual purpose in service to them.

Understand that slavery's seasoning was not the end of our training. The forced sexual violation of women and men and girls and boys on the Continent in the missionary schools and rectories, our villages and the more than 360 dungeons (euphemistically called castles by Europeans) that laced the seacoast where we were warehoused while awaiting the forced departure from our homeland, as well as on the treks from our villages to these castle/dungeons, and then over and over again on the ships in transport and the southern plantations and in northern urban centers where we landed was not enough. Until we were made fully compatible and user friendly, of our own free will, to Europeans in their world, our miseducation was bound to continue.

Sex education was an integral part of that process. At first, the process was limited to the few Afrikans who could be trusted enough to participate in and keep the sexual perversions of Europeans secret. Because of the legacy of enslavement and quasi-freedom, many in this chosen few were open to the opportunities to perform whatever sexual services Europeans would psychologically and financially reward them for. At that time, this training was a highly individualized process requiring one(or more)-on-one sexual conquest and behavior modification. The second stage was brought about by the media's commercial evolution that removed the moral authority from our homes, schools and churches. It made more of us question a natural moral order, especially the idea of sex as part of any moral order. The third, which is in force now, is the offspring of the second. In it we have intergenerationally internalized European sexual behaviors to the point where we willingly become them sexually of own "free will" in ignorance.

We are still being seasoned as their sport. We are still enslaved to their validation of our sexual behaviors, as all else, or we would not follow their way and rationalize our commitment to gain their love and appreciation. A people who were once enslaved as others' laborers still remain slaves to their sexual venting. We continue to be their experiment, their greatest experiment. They need to see just how far we can make their perversions go. We are their safety valve.

3. Superfreaks

> "The individualism of the West artificially detaches the
> person from the community and thereby establishes
> innumerable islands of self validation, authority,
> discretion, freedom, and power. Freedom in this context
> is tantamount to chaotic and totally impulsive behavior
> without accountability. In reality this mass of individuals
> is subject to collectively controlled centers of power,
> including the state and mega corporations...This
> disconnection from family and community leaves an
> affective and reasoning void that is filled by the
> propaganda of the state and corporate elite...This is
> modernity which mandates that every individual is
> answerable only to self, and is free of any restraint by the
> collective order or obligation to that order. The one sacred
> obligation is the maximization of pleasure (or profit) for
> self, and the avoidance and transfer of pain and discomfort
> to others."

Kwame Agyei and Akua Nson Akoto

Sex, like all else in this culture, follows a compulsory
progression. New ways of revealing more skin; new and more daring
approaches to rapping and flirting; new, riskier, still uncharted places
to perform sexual acts; newer, larger, more challenging, more
dangerous sexual paraphernalia; more innovative and intense forms
of violent sexual exploitation and control of self and others; younger
and younger as well as more divergent sexual partners; newer, more
decadent perversions, all things must be taken to their unnatural
extreme and made to go farther into the unending abyss called

progress. Europeans are in a continuous heat. They have no choice. Their culture beckons.

As participant spectators, we watch and learn what is expected of us if we are to be assimilated into their new/old world order. We operate under the assumption that their change is good for all and represents a progressive sexuality/sexual exploration. But the truth is that they are not changing at all. They are only returning to (making public) the sexual disorder natural to their ancestors. But they must present this "coming out" as a progressive change in order for others to willingly follow their lead.

Sex and Violence

In the parade of European progress, violence and sex have blended into one. In the European theater of interpersonal relationships, acts of sex are games of conquest. The past popularity of images of cavemen clubbing and dragging cavewomen back into their caves for sex, or whatever, is indicative of this underlying predisposition toward being violent during sex.

As often seen in the media, kissing and sex now come as the direct result of violent argument. With violence an accepted part of the European personality, confrontation must be normalized through its presentation into every form of interaction portrayed in the media. Sex becomes atonement. Relationships come to be seen as developing out of a series of forced confrontations where release is achieved by sexual intercourse and, this, is made to appear to gradually lead to a more intimate relationship. It appears that Michael Bradley may be more right than he thought. The level of sophistication at which violence has become normalized just in the act of kissing is phenomenal. Hate and violence promote the theme that opposites attract when they lead to the discovery of a mutual passion between a male and a female. Psychologists call these relationships "conflict-habituated." But this categorization does not define them as, or make them, abnormal. Variations on this theme are found when one person's dislike for and anger at another "turns them on." The classic silver screen portrayal of this is seen when a woman has no desire for the dashing European male but upon him locking her in his arms and forcing his kiss on her she spontaneously melts in his arms. It is the dramatic equivalent of sex's use as a release from anger and frustration.

In most other cases love scenes begin with lips slamming into each other. Kissing comes as if lips are weapons. We are entertained by images of them hitting each other with their lips and calling all of these activities "hot" and ascribing passionate love to them. Characters even jokingly complain about someone putting his/her tongue down her/his throat. The ecstacy of kissing is heightened using the cultural logic that violence improves everything. We learn from them how to do it the right way, their way. And we go home and practice. Someone who doesn't know about the durability of the human face might even wonder how many emergency rooms are visited by those needing to have their front teeth surgically reimplanted because they slammed their faces into each other in these attempts to get more feeling out of their kisses.

Yet these loving attacks are not the root of the abnormality in this physical act of European sexual politics. As they are a global cultural minority so too is their practice of kissing to show love for and/or sexually stimulate each other.

> If we look around the world we will find that kissing is not universally practiced, or at least, not as an act of expressing love (which it does not express of itself...). In most traditional African nations, kissing is called "eating dirt." You may not realize it, but you agree with them. How would you react if a stranger, or someone with whom you don't have a relationship kissed you on the mouth? How do you react to someone's spit making contact with you? Of course, if the animal brain in you caused your heart to skip a beat, withdrew blood from your gut, causing that "sweet feeling deep inside," then suddenly, as if by magic, the other person's spit will be rid of germs and viruses.[1]

Language/linguistics and common sense tells us that the form of kissing during which the most saliva is exchanged, French kissing, is purely a European creation.[2] And the European asili naturally forces this peculiarity, as it constantly does all others, to a greater extreme. French kissing has evolved to the next level called "three-way kissing", where three individuals simultaneously engage in a French kiss with each other.

The point of the above quote should be kept under serious consideration because kissing is an extremely intimate act which shows the degree to which we have become them. It is interesting to note that prostitutes do not kiss their clients because it induces a physical and then psychological attachment that they cannot afford to develop. Virtually every form of physical contact can be made to be interpreted as a form of sexual stimulation or means of increasing intimacy. All that has to be done is to have members of the reference group, or those they validate among those who aspire to be like them, practice or advocate it.

Tearing, not taking, each other's clothes off follows this prelude to a ravenous sex marathon. Violent, so-called explosive, lovemaking has become the norm as couples slam and pin each other into walls, doors, beds, the floor, the kitchen table or anything that will carry the weight. Exhausted, the couple is finally able to rest and coexist in a temporary peace. The sexual act often appears closer to two individuals attacking each other than touching each other as loving mates.

Violence stimulates sexual excitement in a violent culture. Which is to say that gentleness stimulates lovemaking in a peaceful culture. Lovemaking is a misnomer in a culture where violence and selfish individuality are normative expressions because what is occurring is not love. It is sex. We have thoroughly confused the two. Love is a purely spiritual, selfless function of which sex is an extension.[3] By itself, sex is a purely physical selfish function of which the illusion of love allows the partners to hide their selfishness. Both have their place, but they should not be confused with each other.

Spend any given hour absorbed in any form of Western media and you will see the degree to which European males, who are the target audience, derive sexual pleasure from women in pain. Websites where you can go to learn how to torture women are accessible at the touch of a button. It is the insanity endemic to Western culture that drives individuals to impose pain on each other in order to achieve life. For Europeans, violent aggression is erotic.

They are deeply into pain. And they feed their deepest desires.

Progress sees no end to this intimate connection between sex and pain as exemplified by the growing popularity of "erotic asphyxiation," the practice of choking another person into unconsciousness or death as part of the sexual gratification of the choker. Extreme sadism has deep experimental roots in their cultural personality. What have popularly become known as "snuff" films or "blue" movies, where sexual excitement ends in death for the dependent sexual partner, further dramatize this insanity.

Nothing is new here. An history of sadistic perversion tells of such honored characters as Marquis de Sade. He was so savage and cold-blooded in his infliction of pain on others that Europeans created the word sadism out of his last name. Late in the 18th century he became a cult hero to sadists for his writing on and acting out of sexual cruelties. He was the best of his ancestors and more. Besides perfecting a number of ways to asphyxiate someone for sexual pleasure, this Frenchman was known for poisoning and knifing prostitutes, sexually abusing children and holding adult orgies. He wrote several how-to books about these pastimes, of which *The 120 Days of Sodom* is the most famous. No one doubts his mastery at coupling cruelty with sex for delight. Leopold von Sacher-Masoch, an Austrian/German novelist, was a contemporary whose interests and practices ran parallel to de Sade's. The term masochism was coined after him.

As implied above, usually the victim is female and the perpetrator male. However, this violence is also a part of the sexual activities of single individuals. Adolescent European males (and sometimes females) have been known to perform autoerotic asphyxiation, or choke themselves to death while masturbating, to the tune of nearly 1,000 a year. "Erotic hanging" is another form of this sexual extreme (done in private or with others) which also often ends in death. About 50 individuals die in this fashion every year. Like their suicides are often misdiagnosed as accidental deaths, as in autocides, autoerotic asphyxiations and erotic hangings are often misdiagnosed as suicides.

The movie *Rising Sun* brought the practice of erotic asphyxiation to the attention of many in the general population as a possible erotic option during sexual intercourse. And *Kept* was one of the cinematic efforts to make the sexes equally violent in their perversions placing a woman in the role as asphyxiator. Judicial cases around the world also highlight those who have committed this insanity or other sadomasochistic style activities resulting in the death of the partner. This sadomasochistic behavior (more commonly known as "S&M" or "B&D," which means bondage and discipline) is a violent sex play found relatively common in European society. It involves everything from whips to leather and rubber outfits to binders to needles to chains to cattle prods to the mechanically unassisted side of biting, scratching, gouging, kicking, slapping, hitting, fisting (which is the act of violently ramming one's hand, fist or arm, all the way up to elbow, through another's anus opening, also referred to as "fist fucking") and "foot insertion," also called "footing," spanking, twisting, pulling teeth and even fracturing and breaking bones. This is no exaggeration. Essentially, in the European style of equating pain with pleasure, it covers most intimate sexual activities where partners derive sexual pleasure from giving and receiving pain from each other. There is no question that it is spreading very rapidly. Its popularity has even brought forth the bizarre phenomenon of S&M restaurants. And we should not overlook club scenes, like in the movie *Blade II*, which are preparing our minds to accept the next level of sadomasochism (levels which they long ago surpassed but patiently await our arrival). There is no place on the planet safe from European sadism.

Hollywood has, of course, jumped on the bandwagon. *The Cell* and *Mercy* are but a few of the films linking physical pain with sexual pleasure. It is voyeurism in its most sophisticated display. And, if it were possible, *Being John Malkovich* takes this even further by adding in a bisexual hermaphroditic unisexual identity confusion.[4] In truth, the characters in this movie are glorifying, making acceptable and normal, a psychological disorder called amphierotism. Individuals diagnosed with it are said to be able to sexually see themselves as male or female or both simultaneously. You really have to watch and comprehend that these are not movies. They are not entertainment simply for the brainless consumption of the general public. They plant ideas for practical consideration and implementation. They cannot be divorced from the cultural mind that so easily gives rise to them. They are a vision on display, a depiction of the European's present and most desirable sexual reality and truth for everyone else. Possibly more than anything else, these movies also show how comfortable Europeans are with publicly flaunting the extremes they need to experience to achieve sexual arousal.

What is sad is not what they do to each other in their bedrooms. Understanding their sexual imperative's peculiar need to combine physical power and control with emotional ecstacy, it is to be expected of them. What is sad is how more and more Afrikans who came here enslaved in chains, who grew trees on their backs as a result of whippings by their enslavers and are still the victim of a extremely disproportionate level of police brutality are now sporting handcuffs and promoting beating each other as a form of serious sexual play.

As a quick but related aside, this public renaissance in sexual depravity has sparked its own collection of superstars. Joshua Macabe Brown, Christopher Dover and Christopher Gerald McIntosh are three of the most recent celebrities in these sex games. Twenty-three year old Brown even took the time to break for a sandwich in the process of sedating, binding, gagging, repeatedly sodomizing and slowly suffocating 13 year old Jesse Dirkhising on September 26, 1999.[5] Dirkhising had previously spent time on weekends over at Brown's apartment that he shared with another adult male. Dover and McIntosh exploited and disposed of their victims in a similar fashion.[6]

But of all of the known homosexual killers, John Wayne Gacy stands as the most extreme and renowned . He earned his fame by brutally murdering 32 teenage males, all of whom he is said to have had sex with before, after and/or during their murders. Technically, his acts fall under the category of lust murders because, by definition, he raped, murdered and then mutilated those he "loved." Because his victims were of the same sex, we could correctly define his crimes as *homocide*. To our public knowledge, his record has yet to be broken, even though Joshua Macave Brown made a recent attempt at starting a similar career. Brown

> told police he sneaked up on the boy, tied him up and repeatedly sodomized him while his lover, Davis Don

Carpenter, 38, watched. The [13-year-old] boy died of asphyxiation. The men, who pleaded not guilty, are being held without bond....'Nothing was done in print, nothing was done on TV nor on radio. It's appalling that something like this was held back apparently for political reasons...'[7]

Nonetheless, like so many others, John Wayne Gacy killed the boys he slept with. Unlike so many others, he was caught for killing so many. We can only guess at how many of those missing faces on posters and the back of advertisements we receive in the mail are victims of pedophilic foul play.[8]

So, the question is not of Gacy's psychotic development or that of any other person who kills without conscience. In his exhibition of a psychotic predisposition, he is no different from others who are homosexual or heterosexual in their preferred prey. The idea of Jack the Ripper, Ted Bundy, Glen Rogers, William J. Stevens, the Son of Sam and Hannibal Lecter[9] still excites the European mind, be the thinker a participant or in the audience. Moreover, profiling killers is meaningless in a society where people from virtually every background have committed mortal violence against others. Whether dormant or not, the spirit to commit these acts is embedded in the soul of every person born and bred of the European asili. There will always be anomalies that do not fit whatever profile justice scholars concoct to give the impression that they know what they are talking about. The only questions our scholars need to be engaged in should be about a culture that continues to produce so many homosexual killers, with such consistency, and so often. Insanity is invisible among Europeans, and those seeking psychological validation by them by being them, because Western culture is insane.

To make sadists appear less insane, the scientific community has been brought in to suppress the symptoms of those "ordinary" violent sexual encounters that have the potential to take life. Since the problem of "involuntary" asphyxiation was dragged into the public domain, classes have developed in various cities to teach homosexuals and other people involved in "dangerous sex" how not to kill their sexual partner(s). European political scientists must diagnose these glitches without incriminating their culture. A correction to the problem must be thought out as if these practices are merely slight deviations from normal sex. Extreme sexual deviance is approached as if the problem is not the activity but how you do it or how far you go. Outside of "how not to" classes, the usual prescription is individual or group "therapy" on how to choke someone or give them pain without ending his/her life from eurocentric sexologists trained in the European mind's appreciation of pain and sworn to guide people into exploring the outermost limits of their sexuality.

Freudian Fixations

Culture molds the mentality of individuals in a society, and that communal mentality directs their science. It does not happen the other way around. Their greatest sex-fixated psychoanalyst Sigmund Freud did not create a mentality. He fit it.[10] The reason he was so successful in his day and continues to be the most loved, quoted and imitated student of the European mind is that he spoke to the heart, body and soullessness of the European asili. And, he was not the only one. Among so many others of psychoanalytic renown in the European camp we also have Ernest Jones, who argued that an absence of a sex priority was at the bottom of all neurosis, and Mary Steichen Calderone, who contended that children are sexually active even before birth and that masturbation was a genetic instinct. But Freud first spoke their truth, their interpretation of reality clearly and profusely through their science of individualism. In so many ways he correctly analyzed his own. Technically, the only difference between men like him and Francis Cress Welsing is that he validated and encouraged the sexually perverted European cultural personality whereas she calls it into serious question.

It is primarily from Freud's self-rationalizing psychology that we have explanations of chaos as normalcy. It is here that sex is read into every thought and action as problem and solution, as both cause and effect. Freud saw sex (and aggression) as the root cause of virtually every human thought and action, conscious and sub/unconscious. It was made into both the source and cure for the "human" dilemma.

Using his own people as the model for all humanity, he intellectualized children into conscious and dedicated sexual beings who must be left to their own devices to experiment and play with themselves sexually. Like today's commercial markets that cater to children because the permissiveness created by Western surplus combined with an extreme orientation toward individualized consumption has placed unlimited economic means in immature and highly impressionable minds (making it easy to economically manipulate them), Freud theorized that children must be allowed to engage in sex focused activities without adult interference or guidance in order to mature properly psychologically.

According to Freudian thought, the problem with adult (and some childhood) disorders, perversions, complexes and neurotic and psychotic behavior is that these individuals have been psychosexually stunted. Their natural sexual development at each psychological stage of development was arrested or took a wrong turn. As identified and defined by European psychoanalysts and sexologist, the stages, in order from earliest to latest, are oral, anal, phallic, latency and genital. In layman's terms, we are supposed to engage in sexual play (as a rehearsal for adult behavior) with those body parts identified with each stage. Individuals who grow up with "problems" did not develop properly psychosexually. They did not complete or get the most out of their stages. They did not play with themselves enough or freely. This belief system is what drives the childrearing policy and practice of Europeans. And it helps scientifically rationalize, as normal for everybody, all their extreme individualism. So, now, we have Afrikan professionals in these and related fields like Hilda Hutcherson knowingly recycling the same illogical eureason as correct for our children.[11] Accordingly, no constraints must be placed on an individual child's or adult's thought or behavior or they may be irreparably harmed and prevented from becoming fully functioning humans. Therefore, every one of their peculiar thoughts and behaviors can easily be justified as essential for positive individual development.

Without this childhood "play," Freud argued, children would develop into sexually repressed and socially confused adults. No matter how extreme or perverse the experimentation, parents are not to constrain their children with any limits prescribed by moral or social notions of what is natural versus what is aberrant. He also gave nonWesterners a European disease called the Oedipus complex by planting in our minds the idea that a son's love for his mother is really a sexual lust for her. Likewise, a daughter's love for her father is scientifically assumed to follow the same lines resulting in the Electra complex. Myth brings a people's mentality to life. And both the Oedipus and Electra complexes have their origin in Greek myth. Oedipus killed his father and married his mother and Electra had her brother murder her mother. These disorders laid the scientific foundation for the "negative" or "inverted" Oedipus complex where a son's love for his father has come to be seen as a homosexual desire for him. The same applies for a daughter's love for her mother. This is classic Freudian thinking. And his contribution to rationalizing as natural the extreme sexual appetite of his people is legend.

But Michael Bradley has opened up our eyes to a whole other side of Freud. He discusses an essay that somehow, until recently, remained hidden from the world. In it Freud connects European sexual perversions and other psychopathic thought and behavior not to incomplete or incorrect childhood sexual development but to a cultural-genetic memory of survival on a harsh and unforgiving glacier. By default, he diagnosed the people of his own genes and culture with having what in the discipline of psychology has come to be called a "control domination response" toward others and a "generalized anxiety disorder."

> Sigmund Freud...concluded that many, or even most, acute anxiety neuroses stemmed not from childhood trauma, but from racially remembered centuries-long trauma of trying to survive during the last Ice Age...survival outside the stone age caves was so brutal that the only respite from it were "perverse" sexual pleasures within the caves where Ice Age men took their frustration, aggression and fears out on their women.[12]

This is more in line with the study and conclusions of Afrikan centered scholars like Cheikh Anta Diop who have studied racial-cultural differences based on environment and climate. No wonder this 1919 document waited for discovery until Europeans assumed that their culture dominated the world and would be interpreted by all as having been "lost" as if even Freud himself did not believe it. Science is political.

But to continue with those approved theories which developed out of the school of thought that evolved from Freud's thinking, spanking has been reinterpreted as being actively sought out by children because it sexually stimulates them. This same psychoanalysis has been used to explain at least some male homosexuals as the product of a breast fixation or complex where, because of the relatively similar shape of the breast and penis, males who are stuck on nursing a breast or bottle nipple, or thumb, transfer that desire to sucking on a penis. It is only within the logic of their psychology that abnormality is proven normal and natural.

And relevant analyses do not stop there because sex and oppression/exploitation work hand in hand in this violent cultural context. To many feminists the penis is psychologically construed as a weapon, a weapon they do not have. It is seen as a battering ram. And this is rightly so in those cases where males are intentionally damaging delicate vaginal tissue by trying to drive their "manhood" into (literally through) it as rapidly and roughly as possible. We see this duplicated in our own community where there has been a gradual increase in the serious damage to Afrikan girls' vaginas due to being pummeled by the penises of Afrikan boys measuring their manhood by the pain they can give. It is as if Afrikan males are trying to use sex to kill their sisters in the way that Amos N. Wilson shows us that Afrikan-on-Afrikan killers angrily holler "die, nigga, die" as they pump bullet after bullet into those whose skin and features reflect the dehumanizing history they want to kill in themselves. Like these killers, males who take pride in having the most destructive penises even send their victims to hospital emergency rooms where surgery is required to repair damaged vaginal tissue. When coupled with a train, some of their victims do not survive the assault.

Power over others is the key to self-esteem in the Western cultural context. And sexually, power comes from control of others. In these sexual relationships, power resides in whoever, the male or female, controls the instrument of violence, the penis. Female homosexuals exercise control over penises (attached to men's bodies) through an absolute denial of its access to their bodies. Feminist heterosexuals take control by being on top and using their body to restrain its movement within them.

The idea that loving relationships between the sexes can only be fulfilling if they are accompanied by pain is not new to European culture. We are dealing with a people who historically must experience pain to experience pleasure. This is a sick society. And, as cultural historians, we know that if a similar behavior is exhibited by a significant number of people in a society over an extended period of time it is only partially a function of individual choice. So the question is not one of the insanity of individuals, but of the illness of a society which systematically produces insanity and attempts to rationalize it as normal by trying to systematically reproduce its insanities among other cultures and societies and then say that their peculiar disease is universal.

Frontiers without Boundaries

The boundaries of the sexual playground continues to expand without limits. As history clearly demonstrates, Europeans naturally have no respect for boundaries. Every nook and cranny of breathable space is deemed appropriate for sexual conquest. Opportunistic sex in places like airliners has become as normal as late departures.[13] "The Mile High Club," the name given to those who have successfully performed sexual intercourse at cruising altitude, has an unofficial membership in the thousands with thousands more waiting with applications in hand. New technology is even being designed to assist those who aspire to reach these new heights. Mile High technology seeks to satisfy culture and its customers. England is now building and fully expects to put into commercial flight in a few years "Air Buses" which ought to take some of the problem out of those seeking to have midair sexual collisions having a place to act out their encounters. Each of these superplanes will have on-board gyms and double occupancy bedrooms for nearly 600 passengers. And the same Japanese airlines who first provided telephones for its passengers are now experimenting with putting showers on board. It does not take much imagination to see what the showers will lead to in flight. If two people cannot be kept out of cramped airborne toilets, they will not be kept out of these newfangled bathing facilities. New places and spaces will continue to be found in the hunt for new sexual frontiers to conquer. Necessity is indeed the mother of invention.

And outer space is indeed the final frontier. Every other place imaginable has been conquered by the sexual invasion of Europeans. Like their ancestors scoured the planet, they now, using sex (instead of religion, economics, politics and the military) as their principal imperialistic weapon, follow suit. The search for adventure (life) is predicated on the continuous discovery of new unEuropean (i.e., wild, savage, uncivilized, dangerous, primitive) places to violate, places waiting to be made tame, modern, open and, therefore, civilized through sexual exploitation. Sex has become a primary instrument of civilizing (i.e., assimilating) others, a means of dominating them into submission and/or "enlightenment."

So it should come as no surprise that among the most odd and bizarre places these invaders can be found having sex are the tops of volcanoes and edges of cliffs, in the ocean, buried six feet underground in coffins, in mud, in nightclubs filled up to the neck with bath bubbles, while surfing and bungee jumping, in public restrooms, bathhouses, elevators and the bleachers during professional and nonprofessional sports events.[14] Risk is excitement is adventure is discovery. The list is seemingly endless. And the latest on the list is having sex in the open. Couples having their hands in each others' pants masturbating each other and girls performing oral sex on boys in public lead the list. The popularity of masturbating while driving, whether stuck in traffic of not, is also experiencing a more than general rise. Out of the house and into the street is the next logical phase in sexual exhibitionism's striving to achieve satiation through more and more extreme behaviors. The world becomes their bed and every corner and open space must be slept in. If it has not been used for sex it is still virgin territory waiting to be discovered, deflowered and violated.

But, lest we forget, these extremes have precedence. There is nothing new but the fashion of the technology and the unique positions and places it presents to the same old mentality. The only problem here is the assumption of newness because of an ignorance of history. If we cannot see the trends, we cannot prepare for the future. Chancellor Williams' instruction that if we wanted to know the historical cause and effect of a people we should "Study the migrations...Study the migrations...Again, study the migrations!"[15] is no different than us now saying that if we wish to understand where Europeans have already been and are now in the process of sexually taking us, we need to follow the trends. The only difference is that while the migrations of Afrikans relative to European invasion tend to be physical and social in form, trends tend to be psychological and cultural. Yet, trends are no less than adaptive migrations of the mind within the context of *"a certain kind of change, in a particular direction,* within a determined and well-defined form."[16] Each next generation of European youth have long been finding ways to do and outdo their parents in quantity and location of sexual behavior. Whatever direction it takes, technology is simply a tool, in this case, no more or less than one intentionally directed by Europeans to fulfill their cultural imperative of incessant, meaningless sexual progress. The car of eighty years ago is another excellent example of how the technology made for each new generation is tied to their insatiable sexual imperative.

> By the 1920s, the automobile was used extensively for dating. This removed children from the watchful eye of parents and undermined parental authority. The police began to receive complaints about "night riders" who parked their cars along country lanes, "doused their lights, and indulged in orgies"...In 1929 Jewett introduced cars with a foldout bed, as did Nash in 1937.[17]

This drive for privacy among children raised to be highly individualistic continues along a straight and progressive line where sex becomes the end in and of itself. Still, little has truly changed. Remember that "premarital intercourse was an accepted practice in preindustrial villages"[18] throughout Europe.

Extreme individualism has also broken the bounds of age with respect to sexual relationships. The anybody with everybody sexual free-for-all is assisted by the popularization of spring-winter liaisons. The seemingly arbitrary confusion as to age-mates is intentional and in line with anti-group identification. It is in line with the extreme individualism continuously seeking a way to be fulfilled in every possible, sexually capable person. The return to the silver screen of the classics in sexual confusion, like Vladimir Nabokov's *Lolita* where a 40+ year old man has an affair with a 12 year old girl and *Jerry Lee Lewis: The Story of Rock & Roll* where he marries his 13 year old cousin,[19] plants the idea of child sex and incest in impressionable minds and helps undermine any traditional foundations explaining the connection between age and intimate relationships. Stories of both male and female school teachers who were caught and/or are serving time for "falling" for one of their students are public examples of just how far this extreme has gone. The love-hate attraction of European female teachers to young Afrikan male students is a story to which most of us have not even thought to visit.[20] The public has only been exposed to a very small number of the adults who sit at the tip of an iceberg of sexually immature and unrestrained educators. They remain hidden behind the image conscious administrative bureaucracies of the public and private schools at the secondary and collegiate levels.

　　This lack of boundaries when it comes to age has had untold effects on the minds and bodies of young and old alike. The problem is most evident when tracing the trends for the diseases that are passed between individuals through sexual intercourse.

> AIDS has consumed the elderly population as well. Between 1992 and 1994 adults aged 60 and over represented the fastest-growing segment for AIDS infection with an astounding 71 percent increase...Today, persons over 50 account for 10 percent of all reported AIDS cases nationally.[21]

Like other more mature individuals in this society, age has not made our elders immune to the adverse effects of the AIDS passed on through excessive and unprotected sex. The disproportionate presence, and greater rate of increase, of AIDS (and STDs) is not limited to Afrikan youth and adults. It is more destructive in our community for all age groups. And the natural health issues of aging, combined with the unnatural way that people age in Western society, make our elders more vulnerable to it. Because too many of us have bought into the European model that blurs meaningful boundaries based on age, our elders are also feeling the effects of this manmade and planned attempt to increase the rate of our genocide. Knowing the prognosis of AIDS is just as ineffective in stopping many people from engaging in excessive and unprotected sex as an awareness of the dangers of drugs, alcohol and cigarettes is. Once you are addicted to sex, even if you know it can kill you, it doesn't make a difference, whether you are "young and dumb" or "old enough to know." You can't stop. As we already pointed out in discussing the driving force of capitalism as the exploitable baser desires of humans, this is a culture of extreme addictions without caution. Sex is no exception.

Through undermining age boundaries, sex is being used as a tool to destroy tradition. Everywhere, in every aspect of life among those under the influence of European culture, the drive for progressive individualism must destroy all established boundaries, no matter their purpose or origin, in order to issue in the new/old European world order. As choice as to thought and behavior comes to be seen more and more an individual function, socialization and sanctions come to fall more and more in the domain of a self-directed European culture. Every tradition, except the European, comes to be seen as negative and dehumanizing. As in the remaking of the Creator as European science, all the old must be destroyed or made to seem as only antiquated and meaningless but fondly cherished symbolism in order for European culture to dominate the world. Within this confusion, Afrikan women who want to remain Afrikan are being forced to sift through a younger and younger pool of Afrikan males in search for men as mates. Again, as with feminism, it has taken the intelligence of Europeans to undermine the millennia old meaning behind relative chronological and mental maturity of males and females in mate selection. Of course, if the pairing is of two males or two females relative age is irrelevant.

Outer Space

Science fiction is the most revealing vision of their future, present and past. It tells you more about who they are and what they know about themselves that they consciously work to conceal from others than even their contemporary rhetoric. It is the imagination that is the window to the European mind. And it is the fictional futuristic scientific mind that is most revealing of that thought.

Their science fiction also shows where Europeans see sex as going. Their sexual vision of progress is in their science fiction. The future images of humans and mega-advanced beings is very telling of their vision of being masters of the universe and the evolutionary theory that undergirds it. Unless out to destroy humanity, these beings are portrayed as sexless, genderless, soft-spoken, effeminate, monk-like, compassionate aliens. They are presented as the next level or a utopian stage in the evolutionary progression of the currently civilized humans. The images of advanced beings are pale and colorless (absolute albinism), without muscle tone and with enlarged, elongated heads. Unlike most Europeans, as compared to the rest of humanity, though, these beings are supposed to be hairless. Some even exhibit no "baser desires." Therefore they do not engage in sex as we know it. They fall into the loose category of hermaphrodites who have the ability to perform self-sex at will, and without outer signs that it is occurring. In fact, whether they are identifiable heterosexually as male or female or not, a common theme in science fiction movies is where these "advanced" aliens have to be reintroduced to interpersonal sex by relatively primitive Europeans. This theme is found in *Demolition Man*, where humans have to be reintroduced to the physical act of sexual intercourse, and Woody Allen's *Sleeper*, where you get sex via a pill or by going inside a sex machine. Otherwise, European science fiction is laced with homosexuality, bisexuality, unisexuality, interspecies interbreeding (i.e., bestiality) and other forms of sex and gender confusion that takes us beyond where even they have gone before. The movies *Dune, Star Wars* and *The 5th Element* are clear examples of this.

But a hermaphroditic unisexuality remains the dominant theme. The mascots for alien cults celebrated all across European society fit this description. They see this super white creature without sexual identification who possesses an extraordinary brain-thinking capacity as the next stage in their genetic evolution. If one believes in the European theory of evolution, then one must believe in their superiority, no matter how much one accepts the postulate, outside of historical and political context, that we are all human. Their evolutionary theory proposes a survival of the fittest framework wherein the last to evolve (come on the civilization scene) are the most advanced. They being the last, can believe in their genetic superiority as the most advanced human "species" as evidenced by their global conquest and control. It is only in this evolutionary context that they can willingly admit that Afrikans were the first and that it was out of Afrikans that they evolved. And it is with these assumptions that we inferior types must accept their advanced interpretations and redefinitions of sex and sexuality.

The latest trends, although found from the beginnings of European science fiction literature and cinema, is the mating of human and alien life forms. In oppositional European thought, aliens must either be destroyed or mated with. It appears as if this is the last hope for expanding the limits of sexual activities. If only life can be found out there, and they can find a way to have sex with it, they could open up a whole new frontier of excitement. The search is for the ultimate sex machine. This characteristic scientific imagination is reflected in Gene Roddenberry's fiction of Captain Kirk's sexcapades across the universe in the original *Star Trek*, Data's revelation that he was programmed to expertly provide sexual pleasure in every way known in the universe in *Star Trek: The Next Generation*, Jadzia's reminiscing about her life as both male and female on *Deep Space Nine*, the general interspecies interbreeding on *Star Trek: Voyager*, the effeminate genderlessness of the aliens on *Earth: Final Conflict* and, now, the normalized interspecies sexual activities on *Enterprise*. (One only need glance back at *My Favorite Martian* and *Mork and Mindy* to see the evolution of this character on television. It is not new.)

But until that futuristic time where sex is purely a willed mental function or humans evolve to the point of having male and female organs so that masturbation becomes sexual intercourse, they search the skies for voluntary extraterrestrial male or female sex slaves or, preferably, both in one. Essentially, the search is for an intelligent dildo, or a sophisticated, but obedient vagina/anus. When not focused on this possibility, they then direct their efforts toward cloning the perfect sex toy. The *Stepford Wives* was a weak, but evident example publicizing this imagination. The evidence of their dedication to this eventuality, however, brings up one important question. Regardless of whether earthlings are the only beings in the universe or not, why is it that extraterrestrials only single out Europeans for sexual exploitation, experimentation and fantasy when they are by far the minority on this planet? Why is it that these explorers singularly and consistently limit themselves to European bodies? Why is it that aliens only select Europeans to sexually violate, experiment and play with? One is left to assume that the propagated beauty of whiteness is truly an intergalactical phenomenon.

Revealing Flesh

Naked intersexual public, semi-public and private club activities in a society that uses clothing as a means of inciting sexual attraction is not an indicator of the liberal enlightenment of the participants. In this cultural context the absence of clothing that is supposed to signify an open appreciation of the human body is as perverted as garments covering one from head to toe. The idea of free love through sexual satiation (if sexual satiation were a possibility in Western culture) draws many more individuals to the idea of nudity than does the need to remove any of their newfound notions about the constraints of clothing.

One cannot disconnect nudist camps, nude or topless beaches from orgies, wife-husband swapping or male and female strip clubs. The nudist camps found throughout Germany, France, Azania (misnamed South Africa by European invaders), this country and everywhere European culture dominates are culturally no different than Las Vegas' or New Orleans' best showplaces.[22] Moreover, they are not new. The Adamites of Germany and Holland and the Wandervogel movement early last century among German youth are but a few examples of nudist sects and popular efforts in a culture that periodically attached shame to the human body to conceal their inordinate interest in it. What some consider a private and tasteful nudity shares an intimate historical origin with the debased erotic display of flesh for profit. They are inseparable in their origins because they came into being for the same reasons, reasons found deep in the mind of traditional European society. The insecure express themselves in extremes. Their fixation on the naked human body is not out of artistic appreciation. For the European, nudity is in and of itself erotic. This connection is reflected in their cultural history.

> In Europe, on the other hand, there are numerous illustrations from the medieval period showing men and women sharing a tub, or bathers being attended by servants of the opposite sex...this was a practice that led to abuses. Stews, bagnio, and bordello, which had signified only bathing places...began to take their modern meanings...By the reign of Richard II the baths had become almost entirely brothels.[23]

> Where they did manage to wash, the women were unlikely to have any privacy in the crowded houses, and mostly adopted an attitude of indifference to modesty...'I have seen them washing themselves naked much below the waist as I passed their doors, and whilst they are doing this, they will be talking and chatting with any man who happen to be there with the utmost unconcern, and men young and old would be washing in the same place, at the same time...'[24]

What we must be careful not to overlook is nudity's relationship to the natural progression of several perversions at the group level as an industry. Even though their fantasies are often fulfilled elsewhere for a price, strip clubs are places where groups of males come to fantasize about the females paid well to tease them with visions of exotic and multiple partner sexual conquests. The mind is turned into a sexual playground until the playground has become normal enough to force its way into reality. Strip clubs (like swinger and spouse swapping clubs) are way stations between the original Greek and Roman orgies (such as the *Thesmophoria* and *Fasti Praenestini*) and a return to that fully orgiastic society. In viewing the continuum in the European sexual tradition, they are the enterprise that makes the transition from brothels, which date back to the 6th century B.C.E. Greece to the orgies clubs coming into vogue today. Strip clubs recreate the vision that, progressively, only orgies can fulfill.

Child's Play

The fallacy that individuality is not guided by cultural imperatives allows us to believe that the exploitation of children in the media and these mean streets is the work of only a few bad apples. However, history tells us differently.[25] Children have historically been the victims of Europeans, both adults and other children, and those around the world who mimic their way. Relatively recent stories, like Mark Pazniokas' "Yale University professor...pleading guilty to child porno charges,"[26] are bringing the depth of the contemporary expression of this European hobby to public attention. And movies like *3M* and *Kinjite*, a movie about Asian child prostitution in this country, capture some of this highly organized trafficking in children. The exploding market in child (or "kiddie") porn/sex is the most glaring example of this complete disregard for innocent, defenseless children.[27] On the web, naked children are some of the most sought after attractions. While they reap none of the profits, they are big business for sex peddlers who provide thrills for sex maniacs who seek sexual excitement through manipulating the least powerful humans.

Most shocking are parents who use their own children in this way. On the 9th of August 2002, *NBC Nightly News* broadcast a story about a worldwide child pornography ring that was the brainchild of the parents of sexually abused children. Explicit pictures of parents sexually abusing their own children were delivered upon demand to an apparently large collection of eager customers. The internet, of course, was the medium these parents used to transmit these sordid images. According to that report, ten adults and thirty-five children in this society were involved. As always, Western media gives only the tip of the iceberg when it comes to sexual perversions they have not yet been able to force as acceptable/normal on the rest of the world. It never fails to paint normal European behavior as abnormal, as a function of a few bad apples and not a nation. On the same night *ABC World News Tonight* presented the additional information that ten European parents in Old Europe were discovered to have also been involved in selling their pornographic behavior with their own children between the ages of two and fourteen. Here children were also "swapped" by parents and requests fulfilled for internet clients for particular forms of pornographic activities such as hearing the child crying while being spanked and/or sexually abused. Only the European mind naturally sees innocence as something that *must* be exploited.

Physical abuse in child sexual exploitation manifests itself in numerous ways but what must be the most terrifying for these children is the practice of choking them to, or near to, death while they are being sexually assaulted.[28] It, too, is becoming progressively more popular. Yet, this extreme is only one form of the exploitation they receive at the hands of adults who have no sexual morals where age, or anything else, is concerned. No matter how one might wish to measure the degree of any of these extremes, though, using children for sex is an inexcusable violation of their human rights. It is even more alarming and shameful that many of these adults are supposed to be directly responsible for their care and welfare because they physically brought them onto this planet.

The global sex slave trade and prostitutionalization of children is a real and massive phenomenon. It is fed almost exclusively by the ungoverned cravings of the European homosexual pedophile. In many places, tourism and child prostitutes are synonymous.[29] And many European males seek out international travel packages that specifically include this activity.

Pacific Rim countries rank high on the list of best tourist sites for European males. Even though other countries around the world jockey for larger shares of this perverted pie, Bangkok, Thailand continues to dominate the field as the world's number one tourist attraction for European males in their global search to discover and rediscover child sex.

> Thailand alone now has 1 to 2 million prostitutes (perhaps 8 percent of the country's female population); about half of these are children.[30]

That AIDS kills more people in Thailand than anything else and that many of its victims are children is clear evidence of their exploitation by European male homosexual tourism.[31]

If the estimates that 40 percent of all prostitutes in this country and 50 percent in Bangkok are children is correct, one has to wonder just what percent of all children on this planet are prostituting themselves in service to European males and their imitators. Globally, outside of Western countries, child prostitution only occurs among dependent people who are under the thumb of an imperialistic culture that is immoral enough to cultivate sexual exploitation among its subjects. Child and adult prostitution become cash crops that dependent nations produce for consumption by their political and economic neocolonizers. Also in Bangkok, as in other nations that serve as tourist traps for Europeans, the level of sexually transmitted disease among children ranges from 30 to 50 percent. And here, as in other nations, history is ignored. The source of the introduction and spread of venereal disease is ignored and the indigenous population is now blamed for their imported moralless promiscuity.

This exploitation is just as easily seen in this country, the place from which reservations for most of these international jaunts are made. Just barely on the other side of the Rio Grande, the insanity of the Western sexual reality is recognizable in one pedophile's self-serving rationale. His responses when confronted with his blatant disregard for the human right of children not to be sexually exploited epitomizes the classic victim blaming mentality of the psychopathic racial personality who cannot accept blame for his individual or group immorality. When confronted by a *60 Minutes* correspondent about using impoverished Mexican boys just this side of the Rio Grande to satisfy his sexual perversions for virtually pennies, he responded that it was their doing, not his. If anything, he surmised, he was the victim because *they* were the ones who were exploiting him for financial gain. He neither understood why there was a problem nor why he was being questioned.

His confusion is not abnormal. It is a natural function of the sexually exploitative nature of the European mind. The heterosexual politics of foreign "aid" follow these same guidelines. Using those being assisted for sex is an area requiring major research. One would have to be blind to European history not to expect the findings to reflect the same pervasiveness of exploitation that is now being uncovered about Western clerics. In the meantime, it comes as no surprise that

> In February the UNHCR [(United Nations High
> Commissioner for Refugees)] and the UK-based charity
> Save the Children published a report revealing details of
> the sexual exploitation of refugee children in West Africa
> by staff of both local and international aid agencies. West
> African refugee children described being sexually exploited
> by aid workers who offered as little as a few cents or a
> biscuit for sexual favours...It is said about 70 people –
> workers for more than 40 non-governmental organisations
> and UN agencies – were suspected of sexually abusing
> teenage children in the region. Teenage mothers said they
> had to sell their bodies to feed their children.[32]

And their real lack of concern over this matter of their employees
sexually exploiting powerless children of color is reflected in their
proposed solutions. Ruud Lubbers, the high commissioner, is giving
refugee women who have been left with no option to feed their
children but prostitution the "task of distributing food in refugee
camps" as if destitute people cannot still be bribed for pennies.
Beyond the virtually unenforceable "ban on sex between employees
and young refugees" (given that there is no one to enforce the ban and
those who would be placed in the position to enforce it are most likely
the worst perpetrators) and the real probability that the number of
exploiters given is a serious undercount, they are also attempting to
increase the number of female workers in the camps. Two quick
problems crop up here. First, this does not reduce the number of male
workers, as if even a reduction of male workers necessarily means a
reduction in the abuses. And, secondly, homosexual female aid
workers are as prone to exploit this sexual gold mine for unethical and
moralless predators as heterosexual and homosexual male aid
workers. So, increasing their presence will probably only worsen the
situation. In the end, the question comes down to just what is the
nature of the aid offered by the West?

Eye Candy

D.H. Lawrence, an early 20th century English novelist, defined pornography as something intended to arouse the viewers or readers or listeners sexual desires.[33] As someone Europeans consider one of their best writers and whose literature faithfully mirrored their extraordinary obsession with sex, we have a valid tool for defining the Western preoccupation with sex as pornographic. However, while doing so we must remember that he blamed the "underworld" people who manufactured and promoted pornography for devaluing, insulting and dirtying the pristine act of sex by showing it as a sordid, lustful, cheap bazaar. And while he described pornography's male following as "vulgar" and without moral principles, he was insightful enough to recognize that this clientele was present among all social classes.

Obviously, since his thoughts on this phenomenon were published some seventy years ago, updating is required. But the core definition stands as is. His definition was prophetic in outlook as to who today is involved in pornographic behavior. Lawrence had the insight to see the youth of his day as "open" enough to usher in a new world where sex was no longer something that could be exploited by pornography because they were geared to make private pornographic sexual behavior public and practical. He understood the European model of progression to the degree that he was able to see that yesterday's pornography is today's family programming. But he could not see where "modern" pornography must go in its return to its ancient extremes because he probably had no real knowledge of the pornography of his ancestors. Back in the day of his remote ancestors, "Actresses sometimes appeared nude and performed sexual acts on stage."[34] And written, staged and spoken pornography has not declined since ancient Greece. The work of Pietro Aretino, an Italian producer and collector of pornography at the beginning of the 16th century, is a case in point halfway between then and now. Understood in historical context, today's brave new world sexual order is no more than a return to their roots and normalization among others of perverse and pornographic sexual thought and behavior practiced by Europeans but hidden from others for centuries. This interpretation of their collective deceit, however, was not part of his thinking because of the defensive need of European intellectuals to help project their people's behavior as universal. So, in typical European arrogance, he elevated this adventure of progress into an honorable challenge worthy only of those with the courage, strength and vision to take the road untraveled.

Looking back, one can see that the so-called sexual renaissances in Western society have only been part of natural European cyclical shifts from denial to active admittance in response to increases in their imperialistic cultural power relative to others. There was never an absence of these behaviors among Europeans. But there was an understanding that they needed to gradually introduce their peculiarities to others. True to Lawrence's vision, European youth, their children and children's children have made a priority of laundering their forefathers' and foremothers' sexual perversions. Like Sigmund Freud, D.H. Lawrence knew his own. Today, the question is not of the pornographic nature of certain sexual behaviors or their public presentation, but of how to pressure more and more people into it so as to make it appear as normal, legitimate behavior. Indeed, using Lawrence's definition of pornography as simply "something intended to arouse the viewers' or readers' or listeners' sexual desires," this society becomes increasingly more pornographic with every passing day. But also in using his definition, the word itself becomes harmless and meaningless.

Nevertheless, the question as to whether Western culture/society is pornographic is quickly answered by looking at the value placed on pornographic material, in terms of what people will do to get it, the extremes that people naturally take the behaviors portrayed in pornographic material to, the value placed upon those individuals, particularly women, girls and boys, who are exploited for their pornographic favors and performances, and the dominance of sexual innuendo in all forms of media. Obviously, there is very little that Westerners will not do or sacrifice to engage in sexual activities. Obviously, there has been a progressive increase in the range and complexity of what is considered normal sexual activity. Obviously, and in spite of feminist and children's rights initiatives, women and children have remained, and even become more, devalued as to their humanity in sexual activity. To speak in European sexual lingo, they remain objects whose pleasure and pain are secondary and peripheral to the satisfaction of the dominant male.

Based on this, an assessment of what is officially defined as pornography today is in order. We should first know that the pornography industry is "larger than the record and film industries combined."[35] Of course, we are talking about a difference between that which is and that which is not officially defined as pornography as only a matter of degree. The recording and movie industries are only a shade away from the pornographic if, in many cases, at all. There is so much grey area that they are often indistinguishable. Moreover, official numbers rarely and barely touch the illegal pornography market.[36]

Nonetheless, in 1986, the pornography industry, including movies, video tapes, phone services (although not including other services which are also growing at a phenomenal rate such as prostitution or escort services that tend to be indistinguishable as well as inseparable from these activities[37]), computer sites and magazines, was estimated to be worth $2 to $10 billion by the U.S. Attorney General's Commission on Pornography. That same report estimated that the number of theaters exclusively catering to adult audiences to be somewhere around 700, with a whopping 1,600 adult videos produced in 1986 alone.[38] Nearly a quarter of all video sales in the 1980s went to pornography. This does not speak to the million hotel rooms that provide pay-per-view sex videos. Today, $7 billion is the most common estimate given the pornography industry. In 1980 the circulation of "skin" magazines such as *Playboy, Penthouse, Oui, Gallery, Hustler* and *Player* stood at well over 10 million. However, their sales have dropped off considerably since then. The yearly profits of many of the smaller magazines have even become eclipsed by the sales of *Sports Illustrated*'s single annual "swimsuit issue" alone. It is also worth noting that "of the 852 new consumer magazines launched in 1997, the top interest category was "sex."[39] But before we take the decline of "skin" magazines as an indicator of disinterest or moral elevation among readers, we need to focus our attention on the changes in Western media technology that have allowed these sexually explicit publications' loss of sales in stores and at newsstands to be recouped and increased.

In doing so, we first need to briefly look back in their time. Because we often make the mistake of thinking that pornographic reading material as a relatively new phenomenon in European society. Not so. As early as the 4th century we find "pillow books" instructing men and women in the "art" of sexual intercourse.

Literally hundreds of these manuals have been published since. The most popular modern book teaching sexual intimacy to European couples has been Alex Comfort's *The Joy of Sex.* Of course, it requires a highly individualized society, where information of a personal nature is not passed down or respected over ones own ignorance, to historically and consistently produce sex manuals.

VCRs, DVDs, camcorders and digital cameras revolutionized the pornography industry. They almost singlehandedly brought about this transformation in the sales and availability of pornographic motion pictures. Unquestionably, the decline in magazine sales, XXX theaters and peep shows was matched by a corresponding jump in video sales and X-rated cable stations. The *Playboy Channel, DirecTV, EchoStar* and the *Hot Network* are some of the biggest cable (and pay-per-view) channels airing hard core sex films. The *Spice* cable network (an adult movies channel) ranked only below *HBO* and *The Disney Channel* in subscribers in 1998. This video explosion has also produced a significant decline in the number of adult movie theaters. Personal video cameras and players allow for the privacy that pornographic viewing still demands. The use of personal computers equipped with webcams to film and send out amateur pornographic imagery from private residences to paying customers in cyberspace dramatically increased the viewing audience of skin flicks.[40] And with this privacy and advanced technology has come a cleaner image for pornography. Also, since the early-1980s deregulation of the types of services that could be accessed through the telephone, the phone sex industry has become a dominant pornography market. Its profits have increased at a faster pace than any other business in the sextainment industry.

As reflected in commercial television, regular prime-time, family shows like *Friends, Mad About You* and *Girlfriends* have made pornography normative viewing in homes all across society. Some form of pornographic imagery is a regular pastime of the actors on these prime time, family shows. It has become something everybody, who is anybody, watches as readily as the news, talk shows or cable movies. The intent is important here because the actors in these shows offhandedly but specifically state from their scripts and cue cards that this is what they are watching. The viewing of pornographic erotica by these actors is stated almost as an aside, as if it is a normal and natural part of every family's entertainment. Such cunning indicates European culture's propagandistic intent. Indicative of this, *Playboy TV* has taken this implied pastime to the next natural level by having the day-to-day sex lives of several couples, who live in a loft with a female porno star housemother, aired live on a program called "7 Lives Exposed."

At the theater and video rental stores, R-rated movies primarily designed for European family audiences like *The Devil's Advocate*, *American Psycho* (a movie really emphasizing "spectatoring" or the act of gaining sexual stimulation and satisfaction by watching oneself perform sexually) line the shelves. This self-indulging fascination with self is not new, as evident by the popularity of ceiling mirrors and camcording equipment in bedrooms. *The Amazing Mr. Ripley* (which is really no different from *Eye of the Beholder*, except that one dealt with a heterosexual fantasy and the other a homosexual one) give one some insight into the tip of the iceberg of the progressive glorification and marketing of sexual perversion in Western culture. Art reflects culture.[41] And, here, "reality is stranger than fiction."

Cybersex

The National Council on Sexual Addiction and Compulsivity estimates that there are 2 million addicts hooked into sex on the internet. With around three hundred thousand sex/pornography websites, there seems to be no end to the number of places where one who is addicted to sex or not can go to explore his/her sexuality. In March 26, 2001, the *ABC Nightly News* reported the number of pornographic websites to be approximately 100,000. So this tripling of pornographic sites in less than three months indicates the extremely rapid growth in this sexual marketplace. It should be noted that cyberspace entrepreneurs who have failed in trying to profitably market other commercial products are increasingly turning to pornography for income. Morality is not an issue in the capitalist system. Only profit is. And immoral people use the excuse of simply exploiting the natural vices in other people to excuse their own greed and feeding of those vices. And while some of these sites disappear because the nature of their perversions require them to rapidly relocate on the web to avoid prosecution, new sex/pornography sites appear every day. There is a very strong and growing perverted pornography internet underground. Like drugs, it is the curious and hard core addicts that give life to this industry.

> According to Yahoo!..."sex" is the most commonly requested search term, with more than 1.5 million search requests a month. In fact, one of every four searches requests a sexually related topic.[42]

Interestingly, the most sought after sites feature bestiality and sexually violated children.

Fifteen percent of all cyberspace explorers have logged onto sites featuring images, voices and/or written sex. Of that group, nine percent consistently seek sexual stimulation at least one and a half hours every day of the week. It seems that sex equality in excess, perversion and addiction has occurred because, although women seem to prefer verbal stimulation while males opt for visual imagery, apparently, comparable proportions of men and women spend similar amounts of time playing cybersex games.[43] At minimum, what these reports miss is that, for children (being the least likely to be willing to be surveyed and who we perilously make the mistake of assuming that our permissiveness will stop their curiosity here), cybersex, like masturbation, is training for participation in and defense of a socialized sex priority. Their curiosity leads the over 15 million of them who are online to more thoroughly and consistently explore the internet. In knowing this, there are two things about which we should not be naive. First, many do have access to credit cards, as if credit cards are necessary to access X-rated photos (sexual penetration) on web sites, a mistaken assumption many parents make because in more and more cases they are not. Payment is only required to go further, usually from still to moving action. Moreover, children (and adults) save pornographic pictures and videos on disks and forward or hand copies of them to other children. And, secondly, those adults desiring to sexually violate children know that lonely, bored and curious children freely navigate the web seeking conversation and companionship in private. Those Afrikan parents seeking to bridge the "digital divide" by bringing their children into contact with computer/internet technology must remain conscious of this powerful corruptive undercurrent. There must be a continuous monitoring of our childrens' interfacing with all forms of Western media information to prevent even more advanced levels of sexual seduction.[44]

The same critical eye must be kept on video games whose over-the-counter sales and rentals remain essentially unregulated (further exacerbated by sharing and exchanges among friends). As with much rap/hip hop, most parents have little to no idea of what their children are playing with. For example, "Grand Theft Auto III" is a very graphic video game featuring a car stealing ex-con who has sex with prostitutes (killing them for extra points). Eurocentric media defenders argue, however, as they continue to do with all profitable "toys" that increase profits through escalating the violence and sex imperatives in impressionable minds, that these games are good because "they allow children to vent without hurting anyone." Apparently, these experts spend very little time observing the venting process among children, and between children and the adults who are spoiling them or must deal with them as a result of other adults having spoiled or abused them. These games allow them to fine tune venting tactics (now and as they mature into a world that promotes the exercise of aggressive power/violence in response to intimidation and obstructions to their "personal freedom" to exploit), not dissipate their frustrations and anger. "Duke Neukum," a slightly older video game, features prostitutes, strippers and sex at the push of a button (which the students I have interviewed say you cannot see but are *clearly* aware of it happening). The more current "James Bond 007: Agent Under Fire" follows in this tradition.

This assault is even more intense and destructive on the internet where, in predator-prey, cat and mouse fashion, our children are being systematically and continuously hunted down by pedophiles/homosexuals. Afrikans who have allowed their children to be raised in the unmonitored, permissive style for fear of suppressing their natural talents, cannot interfere with their children's "personal freedom." Very recently, this corruption attempted to find its way into our home. Even though my daughter's e-mail was set at young teen (which limits what websites she can access), I was shocked to find she had received an e-mail from an unidentifiable source with websites embedded in it directing her how to go and "See Tommy fuck Pamela for FREE!!!" Even without the visual connection the language adheres to their memory. Thankfully, because I regularly monitor her e-mail, I was able to delete this example of Western perversion.

Because many of us cannot think outside of the European cultural framework, outside of their box/matrix, we are unable to see that, while we leave our children alone with their personal freedom, their privacy is being relentlessly infringed upon by a corruptive European media. Their privacy is dominated by European cultural imperatives. They only think they are free because they believe they personally originate the insanity that orders their minds. Personal freedom is only an illusion in any society governed by an ideology that systematically exploits impressionable, vanquished minds. And the Western ideology of exploitation that purports to advocate personal freedom knows no ethical boundaries with regard to age or innocence. Immorality allows the immoral to seek out new markets anywhere and everywhere. Everyone must be drawn into their corruption.

If their children are not limited to a home computer they might supervise, Afrikan parents who want their children to fit in and become successful by exposing them to all of the European's interests and habits must play ignorant to their general access to the internet because their tattered sanity requires them to believe that the "few bad apples" theory applies to pedophiles and homosexuals. Pedophilic homosexuals are experienced and desperate hunters. They make use of every tool at their disposal. It only makes sense that the predator places him/herself where the prey is.[45] It only makes sense for them to find their way into the places where our children frequent, in real or cyber space. Predators go where there is prey.

Virtually every child is vulnerable in the hands of a manipulative, experienced, determined adult. No child is trained well enough to compete with a determined adult mind. And these sexually perverted child molesters have been about the business of working within those Western institutions where children are voluntarily and involuntarily isolated from their parents and family.

They blend in with "normal" heterosexuals where they can launch attacks on the minds and bodies of children. They have thousands of years of practice. It is far from a local European phenomenon. Where the West goes, they go. They represent the church, the state, the private sector and private citizens. Europeans have always been aware of their significant presence as a defining characteristic of who they as a people are.

Yet, due to their greater access to resources at this time, adults play this game much more than the children. Beyond the sites, the web has become a highway where digital cameras, whose "film" development does not have the limitations on nudity of the local drug store processor, are used to take and share nude and sexually explicit pictures with the curious and the adventurous. It is the virtual and real dating game taken to its progressive, hypersexual level. But there are consequences to this madness. As if they were needed, studies are showing that sex/pornography sites, as well as the personal show and tell pictorials, are addictive. In being so, they are unquestionably damaging to serious intimate relationships, especially marriage, as if the divorce rates are not already high enough.

For the more discreet voyeurs of sex/pornography material on the web, the result is no less damaging. It is assumed that viewing without participation is harmless. The propaganda surrounding this promotion of cybersex has put forth the myth that a vicarious involvement is safe sex. But sexual diseases are of the mind as well as the body.

Prepubescent Obsession

European males have a prepubescent obsession. Their goal is to have someone so young as to be physically immature (undeveloped), unblemished and so naive as to fully trust them. This applies whether they are dealing with young or adult females. Many "working girls," wives and girlfriends use vinegar or astringent lotions or gels to "shrink" their vaginas so they will feel like they are still virgins upon entry. The European male, and others raised as such, not only desire virgins because it indicates the females sexual innocence at marriage, gives him a greater sense of power over her because of the assumed lack of experience and insures the ever important cultural priority of conquering a new/fresh body, but because of the excitement given by the pain that the first penetration is almost nostalgically said to bring to the female. For these and other related reasons "deflowered" females dress up in schoolgirl uniforms in an effort to appear immaculate, innocent and prepubescent. Either way, whether the female actually is without visible breasts or buttocks or is just giving the appearance of being so, at the subconscious level, it's a case of men desiring females who look like boys. By default, this classifies most adult European males as homosexual pedophiles in that their conception of beauty is of the shapeless, prepubescent, virgin boy. And, having an even lower self-esteem than most others, European girls try even harder to make themselves into what European men want. Unlike the plausible but neutral rationalizations offered by European sexologists that anorexia nervosa is a condition characteristic of girls who attempt to look as thin and shapeless as European boys so they will not have to grow up and face the responsibilities of womanhood, in reality they starve themselves and/or regurgitate digested food in order to attract the males who do not want them to look physically grown up.[46] European women know their men. They know how to attract European males by using their domination-oriented egos against them. They know that to be thin presents a certain image in the European mind. It is to be fragile and vulnerable, to need protection and discipline.

Moreover, the usual Western, immature, selfish individualism is evident in this effort to stay forever young. The anorexic physique is incongruous/incompatible with motherhood. It is anti-maternal. It devalues breasts and buttocks. It reflects a highly individualized social application of their anti-family mentality.

Their Oldest Profession

It is said that prostitution is the oldest profession in the world. But I beg to differ because as we know, in Western culture, historical facts and truth are political. And through the use and lies of political science, we also know that Europeans are about the business of attempting to make what is and has been originally peculiar to them universal for everyone. Prostitution is normal for them because even the "family" can be reduced to an individual operating alone and against all others. Each family unit is individual and operates in an antagonistic posture toward other families and individuals. Extended family situations exist only when they prove economically and/or politically expedient for the nuclear families involved.

Originally, extended families lowered the probability of prostitution in European society, of a woman selling her body to provide for her children's and her needs. The extended family provided the strongest safety net of social welfare ever for women whose husbands had died or divorced them or whom they had divorced. But this did not last long, not even in Greek culture. The national and global sex trade in free and slave European women commanded a large market then as now.[47] Without extended family, women in traditional and present European society who are caught without a job or support, especially if children are involved, find themselves between an economic rock and hard place. It is for this reason that prostitution arose as a common social practice in the streets, home and workplace. And history shows that this reason made prostitution an original European creation and tradition. It has an extensive history in traditional and ancient European society.[48]

It is interesting to note a related European cultural continuum in passing: the use of graffiti to convey sexually perverse thoughts and sexually slander others.

> The names of waitresses and prostitutes are found scribbled on walls at Pompeii. The graffiti refer to the women's vices and attractions, and announce that some women can be had for two asses – the price of a loaf of bread.[49]

We would be remiss if we did not note graffiti's historical continuity in European culture. Its use as a means of using foul and degrading language to describe sexual acts and the character of individuals, as well as giving out phone numbers, addresses and places where sexual favors can be easily attained, litters the walls of virtually every public men's and women's restroom. It has always been a corrupting agent for the minds of innocent children who frequent public restrooms. Obviously, graffiti's popularity as an obscene literature has not declined since Rome. Pornographic graffiti is so ordinary that psychologists have even come up with a term for the obsession to write obscenities on public surfaces, especially as it applies to statements about sodomy and feces – *coprography*. Again, a people's language identifies and defines them.

Nonetheless, prostitution does not predate them in human history.

> The word prostitute is especially politically significant because of the way it is manipulated by members of the religious community. The assumption is that it is a practice natural to human civilization. If everything in your society has a name, which it does, then prostitute is not a quality of traditional Afrikan society because it has no name there. And this has a lot to do with the nature of the community and perceptions of family structure. A woman would never have to sell herself to feed her children.[50]

Claims about prostitution being the "oldest profession in the world" do not refer to the Afrikan world.

As since their classical societies, many women without husbands and not connected to family must continue to fend for themselves using the only asset they believe they were born with. With men the major consumers in this morally corrupt society, the quickest way women are allowed to make money is to sell the only asset these potential customers are interested in – their bodies. Because of the sexist nature of Western culture, women's minds, for the most part, are not respected. Look around at the number of prostitutes, strip clubs, full massage parlors, escort services, phone sex lines, datelines, partylines, personals, kwk., and then tell us that women are respected in Western culture. The only human capital many believe females possess that is worth paying for is their sexual services. Earlier evidence to this effect comes from the *Kinsey Report* which found, in the middle of their 20th century, that nearly three-quarters of all men in this society had paid for a prostitute's service at least once in their lives.

However, as previously stated, prostitution is the direct result of an overemphasis on the nuclear family structure in European society. The frigid, harsh environmental conditions that produced an extreme individualism naturally led to a selfishness among family members. This neurotic preoccupation with the nuclear family structure of an detached and wholly independent father, mother and child[ren] unit is not a universal ideal among humans. The extended family is the natural state of the vast majority of the human community. And, as Afrika is the cradle of civilization, and therefore family, it is where we find the tradition of the extended family most pronounced. Proportionately, more extended families are found on the Afrikan continent than anywhere else on this planet. As further evidence of our genetic, cultural connection to the way of our ancestors, Afrikans also have more, and more extensive, extended families than any other group in this country.[51]

The prostitution that is rampant on the Continent today is a function of its introduction from outside, a massive impoverishment of the majority of the indigenous population and European tourism. Our scholars have no doubt that "both homosexual and heterosexual prostitution were introduced by Europeans into Africa."[52] There is no evidence of it before the arrival of people from the north. And it is quite obvious that, in the midst of enormous wealth, Afrikans have been reduced to a state of poverty. That the average lifespan on the Continent is 52 years, as compared to 73 and 76 on the European and North American continents, respectively, is primarily due to this fact and the disease and wars that poverty, the perennial divisiveness of neocolonialism, and the perception of scarcity bring. But the most important factor in this modern equation explaining Afrikan prostitution, is that Afrika, as a continent, is no different than many other countries that serve as economic and tourist satellites for the European nation. Today, prostitution is everywhere in service to Europeans and national elites. Prostitution of the natives for European tourists is most rampant throughout Central and South America (except the southernmost portion of South America), the Pacific Rim (disproportionately in Bangladesh, Thailand, Korea, Taiwan and the Philippines) and Afrika (disproportionately in Senegal, Gambia, the Ivory Coast and Kenya).

And we should not overlook the fact that heterosexual prostitutes on the Continent, as well as in other places the people have color, are not limited to females. Most notably, European females from the North American continent vacation in the Caribbean Islands for this express purpose. A glaring piece of evidence to this effect is the dramatic increase in the number of young Afrikan males, especially between the ages of 14 and 15, who are dropping out of school to secure the relatively lucrative employment provided "beach bums" in the sexual service of European women. As reported in a study conducted by Dr. Joan Phillips, the sex tourism trade is openly exploding as European females with means arrive on vacations with dreams of fantasy islands inhabited by willing, mesmerized "post-colonial Mandingoes."[53] In the eastern hemisphere, women from old Europe, especially the Nordic/Scandinavian countries, visit or retire in Afrikan countries like the Gambia so that they can be more cheaply sexually serviced by the melanin rich "natives." *Waiting to Exhale* was a white girl's story.

The same historical understanding about the birthplace and natural home of prostitution applies to sexually transmitted diseases. Where is the evidence that they existed in Afrikan society before the European?[54] They, like so many other diseases now found among humans, were carried out into the world by Europeans from Europe. No where else were the conditions of filth ripe for the development of plagues and disease for so long that human physical tolerance reached the point where they could carry them around, literally as walking, talking pathogens, and expose/infect other people with fatal results for tens of millions without themselves being infected by the lesser illnesses of others.[55]

Terms of Endearment

European languages are harsh and vulgar. Being their neighbors, the ancients were the first to see that "the Greek tongue is a noise of words, a language of argument and confusion."[56] The terms most used for sexual intercourse throughout their history favor the derogatory especially with respect to the female participant. In this collection of terms of endearment we find nailing, fucking, screwing, pegging, pinning, humping, balling, banging, bopping, jumping someone's bones, action, scoring, hitting, hit and run, gettin' nookie, grinding, icing, occupying, drilling (extramarital sex was coined "offshore" drilling), playing "poor man's polo," wearing it out, tearing it up, gangbanging, wenching, boning, driving, impaling, shooting, stabbing, slamming, ramming, busting, jamming, "tapping that ass," "hitting it from the back" (for sodomy), killing it and, one females who see themselves as something to be conquered tend to say, "take me." And, most often, those that could be considered positive, like "making love" introduce romantic notions by confusing sex with love. Euphemisms like "making love," "sleeping together" and "going to bed" give the illusion that these all too often violent acts of control and domination are as harmless as taking a nap. The number of terms for hate as compared to those for love in the English language reflect this negative tendency in their thinking.

Mental Rape

There is no need to mince words or use polite euphemisms. Masturbation, or what is commonly referred to as "jacking/wacking off," is a principal avenue for the private expression of mental rape, of visually fantasizing the act of having sex with another person in your mind, by European males.

> A critical distinction between Black and White males is the tendency of White males to use substitutes of masturbation, fellatio, and fantasy for direct sexual intercourse. Masturbation, for instance, is more likely to be the source of the first ejaculation for the White male, while intercourse is for the Black male...A larger percentage of White males reported being sexually aroused by being bitten during sexual activity, seeing a member of the opposite sex in a social situation, seeing themselves nude in the mirror or looking at another man's erect penis, hearing dirty jokes, reading sadomasochistic literature, and viewing sexy pictures.[57]

European females are not exempt from these peculiar cultural propensities. Masturbation has a rich tradition among ancient Greek women. They were not above or below the cultural need to continually heighten their sex drive through constantly stimulating their own sex organs.

> [T]he Athenian atmosphere was not conducive to homoerotic relationships between women. Therefore, masturbation seems to have been viewed as an acceptable outlet for women's sexual appetites...Some vase paintings depict phallic instruments being used by women for self-stimulation...In this sex-starved climate, resort to onanism among women would be most expected.[58]

> Greek women made penis shaped objects made of leather called *olisbois*, a word derived from a verb meaning "to glide" or "slip." Today, such devices are called dildos and are widely used in western cultures.[59]

The *Kinsey Report* found that 96 percent of men and 85 percent of women masturbated. And both the *Hite Report* and *Redbook* surveys of the mid-1970s showed that the majority of European females, both single and married, masturbated regularly. The findings showed that 82 percent and 70 percent, respectively, admitted to self-sexing themselves. *The Sorenson Report* revealed that three-quarters of all 13-15 year old boys and nearly the same percent of girls masturbated.[60] Of course, his report had the same flaw as the others in that the respondents and the findings applied only to Europeans.

The specialty market that has developed around masturbating reflects this preoccupation. Masturbative devices control a significant amount of the profit from the sales of sex related and enhancing products with products ranging from leather dildos to chromed to rubber to butterfly vibrators that strap on to anal violins to vaginal balls to inflatable dolls with "functioning" vaginas and penises to dydos, which are surgically implanted sex aids, to a family of *Accu-Jac* contraptions with attachments which simultaneously fit over a combination of penises and into vaginas and anuses allowing for group masturbation. Easily overlooked in this specialized list is the wide variety of fruit and vegetables like bananas, cucumbers, squash, zucchini, gourds and potatoes, other foodstuffs like sausage and drumsticks, and nonedibles such as candles, tennis racket handles, baseball bats, vacuum attachments, telephones, bottles and a host of other unrelated, but common, accommodating items bought and used specifically for masturbation. One thing we must remember about these devices, which are already indicators that basic, natural sexual intercourse has been abused to the point where it has lost its excitement in a mind that craves it, is that artificial stimulation to achieve an excitement that natural stimulation no longer does, translates into extreme excess. Extreme excess develops when something is done so much and so often that what is natural and normal no longer works. In this light, we must also be aware that mechanical sexual stimulators are becoming increasingly more popular among teenagers.

Afrikan males and females, in becoming more efficient at aping European male behavior, are also on the road to perfecting this disturbing art of fantasy. This mimicking is not new because our general imitation of them is not. Imitative masturbation came about because we were forced into their presence early in this society.[61]

Imagery and fantasy are very intricate parts of masturbation. Successful manually performed orgasms usually require the male to imagine himself having sexual intercourse with a real person (and in addition to females fantasizing more and more about males, in this modern sexual free-for-all we find females mentally raping other females, males doing the same to other males and various combinations thereof which may or may not include animals, plants and things). Through this fantasy that accompanies the vast majority of successful masturbations, the individual in mind is sexually manipulated/exploited in whatever way the mind needs to see in order for the body to achieve orgasm. Most European males have had sexual intercourse with every desirable female they encountered, in their minds and the privacy of masturbating. This, like real sex without the permission of the other involved, is here being defined as mental rape. Although this term may seem a mite harsh or a slight exaggeration, in the Western cultural context it is a most appropriate concept for this overemphasis and preoccupation with sex that uses other individuals to achieve an orgasm without their permission. In this respect, masturbation is a form, a tool, of conquest. It follows the historical pattern of European imperialism in all aspects of their being. In this case, that which you cannot have you "take"/conquer in another way. In the predator's mind, regardless of how it is done, if the sensation gained through exercising power over another is the same, then that act of conquest is psychologically the same.

Mental rape is not a victimless crime. Regardless of how one plays this out in his or her own mind, as well as the potential for those thoughts to modify actual behavior, there is nothing natural or harmless about rape. Someone is being sexually used without their consent. They are being violated without their knowledge. Mental rapists are getting around the natural avenue to sexual intercourse with members of the complementary sex.

Not surprising, many "sex symbols" take great pride in knowing that they are being sexually violated by many others who they do not know and would never touch. It is all part of the stardom game. Such attention becomes their financial and emotional livelihood. For them, it is profitable to be used. And, although pornographic videos are making still life less attractive, pinup models are a classic case in point. Currently, posters and calendars of pinup women (and currently to a much less degree men) are experiencing record sales. Interestingly a number of women are now buying them as gifts for their men (but not vice versa). It seems that females are buying them as an incentive for their male lovers to masturbate more so as to practice and increase their sexual staying power and, presumably, to distract them from having affairs.

However, the average female (at least in the Afrikan community) is not so impressed with these unsolicited physical examinations. Most consider it an insult to be "undressed" by another's eyes. They take no great comfort in being unable to control being violated against their will or knowledge. Mental rape, like the use of date rape drugs to rape, is a cowardly act, driven by the need to have what is not yours. Stalker/rapists who fulfill their masturbative mind,[62] are no different than the common serial mental rapists except that they are brazen enough to act out their psychotic and sadistic perversions on real people. In this masturbatory culture, everyone, voluntarily or not, becomes an active participant in a massive, never-ending orgy. The difference between ones sexual imagination and actual practice is nonexistent because fantasy and reality blend into one.

Historically, in the European community, this "sexual imagination" indulges itself through voyeurism. Voyeurism is a common but special sickness of the European mind, and is inextricably tied to masturbation. European males are known to derive great sexual pleasure from watching two females engaged in homosexual acts. And European females' appreciation of this voyeuristic attention continues as evident in the number of them who elect to adopt the homosexual sexstyle because males think that it's "cool." Seemingly everybody wants to see and hear others engaged in sexual acts. Although the range of activities falling under the voyeurism heading that have taken form in the European community are too many to list here, it is important to critique at least one of the rationalizing theoretical foundations they give for why it exists and should be considered "normal" individual behavior.

A number of their psychoanalysts and sexologists argue that a predisposition to peep results from children seeing their parents and/or other adults engaged in sexual activities. According to this logic, children's curiosity is intensified when they first observe such a "primal scene" and then seek to repeatedly watch adult sexual activities in secret. The Western adult's voyeuristic tendencies is said to result from this early introduction and attraction which left the child's visual sexual appetite permanently altered toward an increased viewing of other's bodies and sexual activities. If that is so then an historical overview of children's freedom to view their parent's sex bedroom activities in European society is in order.

Although European children's access to their parent's private sexual relations began long before their traditional society, that is where it exploded. As Europe came out of its second dark age, the vast majority of their nuclear and extended families lived in one room cottages. The extended families consisted of parents, their children and usually other unrelated, but sexually active, adults. There were no barriers in these cottages during daylight or at night dividing adult from children's sleeping places. There were neither walls nor hanging sheets creating private spaces. Therefore, adult sexual activities were readily visible to children. There are only two general qualifiers to this fact. First, most sexual activity occurred at night when it was dark. But it is no secret that our eyes very quickly adjust to darkness.

Moreover, for most of the year the European climate was frigid, another reason for close, adult, homosexual or heterosexual, sleeping arrangements which promoted sexual relations. These sleeping arrangements continued into this country's colonial period for men and women, as well as boys and girls during the cold seasons. They called it "bundling." And although historical documents indicate that both parties were clothed, in the case of boys and girls, pregnancies were not uncommon. For adult male and females, the outcome was, of course, irrelevant. Moreover, a fireplace, or at least open fire, was needed to help give the cottage a semblance of warmth through the long, cold nights. Fire gives off light. Second, the cold or coolness of night would have forced most sexual activities under the covers. However, the heat generated by sexual activity has been shown to lead many couples to shed their coverings. This second qualifier, though, explains nothing of summertime. The heat of summer would have made covers unbearable. We must also remember that the names Lady Godiva and Peeping Tom became famous during the 11th century in traditional European society.

Of course, in contemporary Western society where privacy is afforded by homes with multiple rooms and locking doors, the variable of quantity has to be worked into this theoretical formula to truly understand the relationship between the opportunity and probability of children seeing their parents and/or other adults having sexual intercourse. The more parents and/or other adults engage in sexual intercourse, the greater the opportunity and probability that their children will stumble upon (and repeatedly see and/or hear) them engaged in sexual intercourse. And, we cannot overlook those "passive scopophiliac"[63] parents who strive to be caught in the act by their children. Moreover, today, due to easy access to adult media (and adult themes and language being constantly downgraded so that what was adult thought and behavior becomes viewable to children), they do not have to steal peeps through their parent's bedroom keyholes to see people engaged in sexual intercourse. Cable, video rentals, theaters and music videos suffice to fill this void.

It could also be effectively argued that the practice of masturbation was also initially and specifically designed to serve the selfish power interests of European males. In a patriarchy that required complete and total submission of women to men and where women primarily served the function of men's sexual servants, distantly followed by reproducing and performing "women's work," the use of sex by European women as a tool to gain political leverage and gain justice from men as their counterparts on the Afrikan continent had done for many millennia was unacceptable. European men were warned about this vulnerability early, as evidenced by the ancient Greek play "Lysistrata," in which sex is withheld by women on both sides from male warriors who refused to stop European infighting between Athens and Sparta.[64] Such an idea is historically ludicrous in European culture. That, if for no other reason, is why "Lysistrata" is a comedy. The idea of women withholding sex from and/or exercising power over men was, and still pretty much remains, laughable in the European mind.

There is no doubt that dependency on another for a needed and/or highly desirable service can lead to the successful negotiation of power by the holder/controller of the service. Afrikan women have long recognized that withholding sex from their men is a useful tool, as a threat judiciously used, that will keep their autonomous power safe and bring peace when men refuse to cease disagreements that disrupt communal life. European women, however, have always been thwarted in the possibility of commanding such power by the common desire/ability and pride with which European men take in servicing themselves sexually and/or having women other than their wives doing so. This self-service comes in the basic forms of homosexuality (sodomy and fellatio), masturbation and prostitution (from women dependent on men's patronage who work on the streets to those who are set up by these men in luxury homes in another part of town).

Llaila Afrika reminds us that

> Ancient European females/males had four simultaneous mates which were (and are) the (1) breeder - so-called spouse (2) prostitute (3) lover-homosexual mate (4) and concubine (girlfriend or boyfriend sex acquaintance).[65]

And, in so many cases, this was not done in secrecy from, or without the approval of, their wives.[66] It is difficult to imagine, except in those cases where the male wishes to be dominated or the female has greater income and/or wealth, that the wife would be able to control her husband by regulating his supply of sex. And, while I concur with the above quote in its entirety, we need to be sure that we consider the relative differences in male-female privilege in European society. In a capitalistic society, each additional mate requires additional income and/or wealth. And, because men disproportionately controlled the sources of income and wealth they *tended* to disproportionately have more extramarital mates than females. Prostitutes financed by European men have no more of a reason to be loyal to European women than Afrikans paid by Europeans have to be loyal to the Afrikan community. Relating directly back to the subject at hand, if masturbation were not designed to decrease the probability of women's "abuse" of their sexual advantage, if European males did not begin the practice of self-sex and homosexual sex to subvert European women's efforts to secure political leverage, it served to prevent the need to invent it for protection from the sexual manipulation of European women.

Masturbation is not a practice found among ancient/traditional Afrikan society. To say this is not to say that the Afrikan way was perfect, only that the European was and is different. There is no scientific evidence that identifies this practice in the traditions of any Afrikan people prior to our physical invasion and cultural violation by Europeans. In *Love and Marriage in Africa*,[67] John S. Mbiti speaks of it as natural to us, but does so without grounding his argument historically relative to a European presence. He does not go back far enough. Moreover, Mbiti's statement is made in service to Europeans as they are his primary teachers and validators. The following statement by Jomo Kenyatta's falls into the same category of compromise.

> Before initiation it is considered right and proper for boys to practise masturbation as a preparation for their future sexual activities. Sometimes two or more boys compete in this, to see which can show himself more active than the rest....Masturbation among girls is considered wrong...[68]

Afrikan truth must be sought in uncontaminated Afrikan cultural history. In order to get at Afrikan truths, we must [segregate] traditional African institutions from those later influenced by Islamic Asia and Christian Europe. In this way, and in no other, we can determine what our heritage really was and, instead of just talking about "identity," we shall know at last precisely what purely African body of principles, value systems or philosophy of life gradually evolved from our own forefathers over countless ages, and we will be able to develop an African ideology to guide us onward. In other words, there can be no real identity with our heritage until we know what our heritage really is.[69]

Not surprisingly, my conversations with Afrikans born and raised on the Continent show that the masturbative practices Kenyatta describes, even if accurate for his people the Gikuyu, are not normal for Afrikans. Even so far as Afrikan culture and society have been systematically assaulted in wars with European sexual imperialism, his description still does not apply for the Akan, Ibo or any other Afrikan tribe practicing their traditions today. Most are appalled at the idea of what he describes as normative. As in the cases of homosexuality, the confusion about tradition has probably arisen out of not taking enough time to distinguish between the traditional behavior of Afrikans before Europeans invaded and that which was unnaturally adopted after their arrival and has since, through historical forgetfulness, moved in the direction of becoming tradition. This is discussed in detail in my forthcoming book *Homosexuality and the Effeminization of the Afrikan Male*. Of course, the thought, the possibility of cultural imperialism at the level of sexual behavior has to occur in one's thinking in order to take the time to consider this extremely relevant factor.

Additionally, in Kenyatta's case, as in many others, there is also the question of the confusion infused through the European influence. Regardless of the nickname "Burning Spear" given him due to his notable efforts as a leader of the Land and Freedom Army (named the Mau Mau by European colonizers) in their efforts to oust Europeans from their land, Kenyatta was educated by and slept with the European. How can you lead a movement to expel Europeans from your country but at the same time fight to keep one of their daughters in your bedroom? As Amilcar Cabral pointed out, "political leaders – even the most famous – may be culturally alienated people."[70] Still unknown by most of us, he also denounced the Land and Freedom Army's revolution against their European colonizers after his release from prison, as well as defended the right of Europeans to recolonize his land and people, expressing a love for his people's enemies to the end.[71]

We find a similar pattern with Nelson Mandela since his release, even though a reading of Winnie Mandela's thoughts reveal that little has really changed. We need to consider these factors when we look at what of ours is consistently being used in others' classrooms and on their reading lists and bookshelves that validates any universality in their way. The question of validity always arises from the difficulty of disentangling our truth from theirs because of the mentacidal contradiction all Afrikans have inherited to some degree. How can you see Europeans as normal and natural without believing that what you mimic of them is not originally of you? It is easy to ahistorically see them in you when you see them as you.

Kenyatta's historical or absolute confusion is no different than that of his literary European counterparts. One of the most repulsive examples of the attempt of the mind of the European to normalize this sexual perversion combined with racist fantasies of Afrikan submission to these perversions is found in Steven King's "Dedication."[72] From the mind of one of their most celebrated fiction writers comes the idea of an Afrikan woman lapping up a European male's semen hours after his masturbation. The implication being that his sperm somehow genetically influenced the superior intelligence of the son she afterward gave birth to. This is an unforgivable insult to our character and intelligence yet quite characteristic of the European arrogance of assuming that literary license in fiction gives them the right to play with their insanity at others' expense.

Our confusion, or refusal to be Afrikan, has even led a number of desperate Afrikan male rites of passage program leaders to go so far as to resort to moral compromise because they have surrendered to the notion that these males cannot exercise self-control. They are instructing their wards that masturbation is acceptable because it is, next to abstinence, the only form of safe sex. "The bandages themselves are infected with the very disease that attacks the host from within."[73] We must remember that if people, in a moral society based on honesty and internally driven self-control, do not tolerate a behavior people will not do it. If anything, these young Afrikans should be brought up not down.

Along with the explosion of prostitution and places of ill repute over the last few hundred years, masturbation has become a socially acceptable and socialized method of maintaining a high level of sexual arousal through the constant and uninhibited repetition of attaining an orgasm.[74] Just as the blood cells of a chronic alcoholic become biologically altered to ingest, and therefore crave, alcohol, the mind of the chronic masturbator is conditioned to seek out a perpetual feeling of completion through repetitious orgasm. Masturbation may not lead to blindness, acne or insanity, but it does, as every other habit in the West, lead to seeking more and more extreme forms of risk to achieve sexual gratification. It reinforces the need to constantly be on the prowl for sex and new ways to engage in it.

The lie that masturbation leads to physical and/or mental disorders is an old tactic used by Europeans to control the natural propensity toward excess among their own when they really do not want it controlled. This pattern of lying that eventually leads to a breakout in the behavior, followed by a normalization of its excess, is found so much in their history that they must, even if only subconsciously, know what they are doing. One of the better examples can be taken from the 1970s when government media promoted the lie that using marijuana naturally led to using and becoming addicted to heroin. When this scare tactic was discovered by the youth for the lie that it was, their use of marijuana and other drugs exploded in defiant response to their parents. Denial in an overly permissive society is contradictory. It naturally breeds a craving for that which is denied.

Things done repeatedly, especially when done out of emotional desire, develop into strong, often unbreakable, habits. The goal is to standardize, socialize their children into their sex imperative, to recreate their children in their own image, to make their children habitually, subconsciously driven to seek sex for the sake of seeking sex. It is in line with the singular pursuit of individualistic self-satisfaction. "Sexual lust (sex without the intent or purpose of procreation) between men and women is a high form of masturbation."[75] And masturbation is a high form of homosexuality.

> Homosexuality is also another form of masturbation. This form of masturbation uses another person (of the same sex) as the masturbating device...Consequently, void of gender and sexuality the homosexuals become two parties of the same sex that masturbate each other.[76]

Obviously, masturbation is a cultural specific and not human genetic function because it is not a generalizable universal. Its prevalence around the globe is marked by the spread of Western culture. That does not mean that it is not genetic among Europeans. But, it is not found among Afrikans until after the invasion of Europeans and, even then, not until Afrikans unwittingly or voluntarily imitated European lifestyles because of a burning desire to be integrated as the result of abandoning their own moral imperatives. Historically speaking, it is a very recent sexual perversion in the Afrikan community.

As an aside worthy of serious consideration, the psychologically deforming mentality white supremacy brings to European males also deserves a moment's consideration. The logic Francis Cress Welsing uses to explain the ingesting of Afrikan male semen by European males as a means of attaining color would suggest some added serious psycho-sexual problems for European males. It causes us to ask if European male anxiety is related to the current staggering escalation of real and imagined sexual impotency among European males? Or, is it simply a massive confession of sexual inadequacy analyzed in the Freudian subconscious fashion of not being able to get an erection when it is time to have sex with a female? Or is it both? As the overuse of land causes a barren field, "excessive ejaculation of sperm causes impotency."[77] Sperm, like money and other things, is seen by European males as a limited resource that must be spent as quickly as possible before it becomes exhausted. Here also, we see evidence of the excessive and wasteful nature of European progress.

Findings taken from a survey of mostly European respondents have indicated that impotency has come to disproportionately affect males at younger and younger adult ages (30 and under). While evidence also indicates that impotency among European males in general has remained relatively constant, and that the seeming rise in cases is nothing more than a greater willingness on their part to admit it, there is no doubt that women's sexual aggressions have further contributed, at least psychologically, to an already damaged self-esteem when it comes to European males being able to adequately perform sexually. This phenomenon has been mislabeled the "new impotence". And there is no question that a male's mental state significantly impacts on the quality of his biological functions. Even so, the lowering of the age at which impotency is occurring would suggest an intergenerational increase in individual masturbation, especially among Europeans.[78] We should also note that an overuse of the male sex organ to induce orgasms is also associated with premature ejaculation.

The purpose of the commercial entertainment media (be it in the form of the internet, movies, TV shows and advertisements, videos, CDs, DVDs, clubs, radio, billboards, posters, books, magazines, art, kwk.) is to keep the individual in a constant state of sexual arousal. Like with any form of corruption, European media knows it need only expose the viewer to one small piece of lust, and it will take on a life of its own in his or her head. If you plant a defective seed in a fertile, idle, curious mind, separated from its spirit, it grows and grows into a defective vine that overtakes and chokes the life out of whatever healthy plants are growing there by arresting their development.

Entertainment icons are used to promote this nonstop masturbation. Afrikan males who have no inhibition about grabbing their crotches in a symbolic public masturbation, like the proudest of their "breeder" forefathers during our enslavement, are constantly displayed on stages around the world. However, their attempts to hold onto a fleeing manhood must be understood in cultural context. It should be seen as the present counterpart of an old European tradition. King James, of the King James version of the Bible fame, was known for playing with himself. "[H]is fingers ever in that walke fidling about his cod-piece...."[79] The codpiece became popular during Europe's 15th and 16th centuries. As the women's bustle and corset of that time was designed to give the illusion of an expansive posterior,[80] codpieces were invented to attract attention by making male organs appear larger than normal for Europeans. Obviously, females were not the only ones who neurotically acted out a form of penis envy in European society. Males used padding to give the illusion of being as large as the Afrikan men they psychopathically considered their sexual competition. Rolled up socks are the stuffing of choice for European males today.

Decorated codpieces and "fidling" were common in that time. And this masturbative practice has been passed down through the European ages. Then and now, the most important point is that this constant playing with oneself's significantly contributes to their sex imperative. For it does little more than serve to help keep the practitioner in a constant state of sexual stimulation. We still find codpieces used as sexual signals in modern entertainment media as shows depict males placing rolled up socks or other items in their pants to give their penises a larger appearance. Not too long ago one could clearly see this boldly displayed in the musical group Cameo's dress.

Yet, this is but one manifestation of an overemphasis of the size and importance of the penis in the European sexual cultural continuum. Males being "encouraged" to grab their crotches and plant their hands halfway into their pants are bits and pieces of evidence showing the media's search to find more and better ways to stimulate its audience into a constant state of sexual readiness. On the other hand, Western psychology itself would point to this habit as problematic and indicative of mental imbalance. A constant obsession about one aspect of one's anatomy not only indicates a neurotic fixation, at the least, but it also implies that the overemphasis is designed to cover up a deficit. As with Michael Jackson or the character Al Bundy in *Married With Children*, it may demonstrate an absence of or immaturity in sexual activity.

Of course, European females have not been remiss in this practice. As the other in a sexually oppositional, competitive culture, they have also spent a good deal of time mentally undressing males and playing with themselves. It is also not new among them. Only the feminist movements have made it more visible and of public knowledge.

Orgiastic Society

Sexually speaking, European society is an orgiastic society. It is driven by the ideal desire to attain of multiple orgasms with multiple partners in a limited time frame. It is driven to make sex play in the group context. Collective sexual deviance is facilitated by the need to celebrate their sexual priority through the immediate access of as many different sexual partners and positions and acts as possible in one time and place. Group sex allows one to wallow in sex. Orgies, historically in "civilized" European culture, were typically reserved for the elite as a fashion statement of privilege. This made it easy to publicly hide this perversion from nonEuropeans.

This secret nature speaks to the origin of the word "orgy" itself. The ancient Greeks and Romans used this word to describe these types of exclusive rituals of religious worship practiced in honor of certain gods such as Dionysus, who was also called Bacchus, and Saturn. Regardless of name, these mythical characters were the epitome of sex in extreme. In Dionysus' case, he went about the countryside planting grapes (the fruit symbolizing sex for the Greeks). He was followed everywhere by groupies who had sexual intercourse with each other and all others they could find in their travels. A satyr, a lower deity that looked half man, half beast who sexually preyed on humans, drew the chariot he traveled in. In honor of both Dionysus (Bacchus) and Saturn, both Greece and Rome had yearly national celebrations where orgies went on for days on end in their honor. Saturn's festival was called the "Saturnalia" and began in mid-December. Dionysus' was called the "Bacchanalia." In fact, both Saturnalia and Bacchanalia have been passed down to today in the English language as synonyms for orgy.

The word orgy comes from the Greek *órgia* (although some argue that it derived from *ergon*, the Greek word for work.), which became the Roman/Latin *orgia* (which was later to be called *bacchanalias*), which evolved into the French *orgies*. Orgiastic is the word used to describe the present and ongoing "celebration" of or one who "celebrates" orgies, as *orgiatikós* was coined for its earlier celebrations in Greek society.[81] The terms go back no further in time.

In pre-modern European society, the European elite, as

controllers of both high culture and the presentation of reality to the general public, were the core, the source, the center, from which that tradition of perverted sexual culture trickled down. They were those whose privilege of time and money allowed for the constant pursuit of excess and extreme. Power and wealth permitted them to set the example of buying people for their seemingly unlimited sexual perversions. In European society today, this class still remains the primary carriers of perversions like homosexuality because of lesser opportunities for the general public and their concealment and protection by private forces.

Historically, however, orgies were in no way limited to the elite European class. As we noted before, in addition to orgies as fun and games which even precede the "Roman Holidays" where sexual depravities were openly practiced night and day,[82] the accepted number of partners for males in ancient European culture, which in so many cases also made it the acceptable number for females, stood somewhere around four, with the number of regular sexual partners increasing according to one's power and prestige. However, locating this pattern in ancient European culture does not negate its presence in traditional or contemporary European society.

Orgies, group sex, group gropes, chain sex (where each participant is in some way or another sexually linked to no less than two other participants, often referred to as a "daisy chain"), "circle jerks" (where a collection of homosexuals form a circle and masturbate each other and/or themselves), and the more formal "cluster" and "group" marriages of a number of couples who all have sexual access to each other, as well as open marriages and swinging, still frame the European sexual landscape. Open marriages and the like are no more than updated versions of the Roman policy that a bride was communal property, sexually, for all the other men in the group. It is a form of *pantagamy* where all of the husbands and wives in a group are free to sexually interact with each other. In other historical marital situations, brothers shared a single wife sexually. The Oneida community that existed in New York in the 19th century was an example of general sexual sharing among married couples. However, this society was even more bizarre. In order to promote birth control, barren and older women who had passed their childbearing years, willingly served as practice dummies for males coming of age to rehearse controlling their ejaculations once they married.

Then and today, orgies can basically be defined as sexual free-for-alls between three or more individuals. They know no age, place or time limitations in European society. And the participants start young.

Kissing and petting parties, long lauded by Western sexologists as a natural and necessary precursor to a healthy and productive adult sex life, where one experiments with kissing a number of other guests, provide one of the first places where our children, following in the footsteps of their children, are encouraged to entertain the idea of swapping partners. But even earlier in their innocence, we find parlor games like "Spin-the-Bottle," "Twister," "Special Places," "Doctor" and even "Truth or Dare." These games are foreplay. In the words of a European children's rhyme of old, "k-i-s-s-i-n-g" naturally leads to sex. Such play progresses into the teens to what have come to be popularly known as make-out parties. If not already mastered, advanced play begins here.[83]

And here, in these virtual orgies, sexual and gender confusion is initiated at a practical, personal level. Peer pressure is used to manipulate the minds of those who may think to question that there is any meaningful difference between the sexes. The idea that you are insecure if as a male you won't kiss another male is played on. And, once a male is successfully goaded into this test of his "manhood," the argument is then made that lips are lips as demonstrated by the victim's inability to distinguish the males' from the females' kiss. Therefore, if the kiss is no different, then the sex makes no difference.

Another common sex confusing agenda/theme at these parties is promoting the idea that having sex with someone is having sex with whoever they've had sex with. So having sex with a female who has had sex with a male is also having sex with a male. Such nonsense is cultivated by movies like *Being John Malkovich* and *Xchange*.

In order to progress, European sexual culture can know no age. It must make the young into adults so that their exploitable lifetime in the sexual market is extended. So, historically, wherever we find Western children at play, we find sexual play and abuse among them. As indicated by its continuity and pervasiveness, obviously neither parents in their nor our community really want to know how much sexual activity (consensual and imposed) occurs in their children's schools everyday. Trains, gang rapes, "2-in-1s" (an increasingly popular sexual perversion among youth, previously known as "sandwiching," where a female has her vagina penetrated by the penis of one male while another male enters her anus with his) and orgies are not unusual in the schools and communities among these children who time and time again bring their childhood practices into their adulthood. This behavior is not unusual in their society. It would only be unusual to find their media revealing the truth about themselves and their children to the world before it is time.

We must bear in mind that while our children play around with sex, a deadly game is also being played on their bodies, minds and lives. Sex is the main agent through which disease infects them. There is important history here that relates to our instructions that in order to know what is happening to us we must understand the history of our enemies. We must study the problem to know and distinguish it from the solution. There is a reason, based on the filthy and squalid conditions that prevailed throughout European society at all class levels for many centuries,[84] why as Europeans spread around the world they carried venereal and other diseases that contaminated and devastated so many of the world's people of color, but they received virtually no illness from contact with other peoples. Primarily, their infections outside the European continent came from contact with animals, plants, insects and other phenomenon in the natural environment that they had not previously been exposed to, not from other humans.

Filth and squalor harbor and breed disease. Tolerance levels for diseases are a function of exposure and biophysical adaptation to them. When a people's tolerance level for disease and filthiness greatly surpasses that of any other, as in the case of the European, it becomes a function of an unusually protracted and mass exposure. That was the condition of traditional culture for tens of generations before and after the Moors cleaned Europeans up.[85]

Today, so many individuals in our community have contracted sexually transmitted diseases (STDs) from each other as a result of the sexual invasion of Europeans that we have come to believe they originated with us. Like the roaches and mosquitoes that have continued to absorb, neutralize and become stronger because of decade after decade of Western chemical bombardments, the STDs spreading throughout our community remain immune, and apparently oblivious, to the assault of advanced European scientific medicine. AIDS (however defined or misdefined), herpes, syphilis and gonorrhea (which has become the CDC's second most reported of *all* diseases) have all demonstrated this resilient survival and killer instinct.[86] And, speaking of mosquitoes, there is no credible scientific evidence that AIDS, or other STDs that are in the bloodstream, cannot be transmitted via mosquitoes. By the way, since people can get gonorrhea and syphilis of the oral cavity (throat and mouth) through performing oral sex on an infected person, why would AIDS be exempt? Moreover, if one person's oral cavity is infected with an STD, why could it not be passed to another through kissing, especially kissing where the tongue is inserted into either mouth. In closing this point, it is worth mentioning that no less than one quarter of all people in this society are expected to be infected with venereal diseases during their lifetime. This statistic has increased with time.

The activities of today's youth continue into their adulthood as hobbies and games. Games enhance the unnatural excessiveness of sex. That wife swapping (renamed "swinging" to remove the sexist label implying wife ownership) and full-fledged orgies can be found everywhere attest to this fact.[87] While the movie *Eyes Wide Shut* was a box office failure, those with their eyes wide open could see its depiction of wife swapping/orgies as an historically normal sexual state of mind among many Western adults. Like organized orgies, wife swapping societies are found throughout time in European culture. The Agapemone are but one such group singularly committed to this purpose which thrived in the mid-1800s in England.

Games must be incorporated into sex because a constant and ever increasing state of hypersexuality requires an unnatural and excessive stimulation. Fantasy is very real in the world they have created. And games are one of the best ways of facilitating fantasy. The games people play have escalated, not in their actual historical presence but in their present rate of occurrence. Flirting, affairs, flings, liaisons, one-night stands, manstealing, mansharing, tallying conquests, these and innumerable other pastimes found at work, in neighbors' homes, on vacation, on business trips, in college dorms, at parties, clubs, bars and social events are all forms of sexual play which lead to increases in what should be considered the normal sexual appetite of individuals.

The *Kinsey Report* found that by the time they had reached their forties, half of all married men and a quarter of all married women had had affairs. That today nearly 20 percent of all married people admit to having affairs does not change this pattern. It only points to a greater European deviance from the human norm. It is in this context of willful sexual play that time and time again European psychiatrists are compelled to invent involuntary crises like the "seven year itch." Such scientific explanations are used to masquerade the continuous stream of sexual immoralities that create social havoc in the family institution as normally defined for humans. But, in truth, they are disproportionately the result of a culturally imbedded and reinforced lack of self-control among individual European adults who happen to be married.

Once surveys are performed that proportionately include married people who aren't European, the percent of *all* married people who have had affairs declines because there are more married people in the pool who don't act like Europeans in terms of disrespecting their marriage vows. As in the soap operas, everybody is expected to sleep with everybody, eventually. And, to bring this into historical cultural context, to watch the soaps is to read Greek mythology. There is no difference. Europeans are today as they were yesterday. And, then as today, they are as adults as they are as children. Only, in some cases, they play with bigger, more sophisticated and expensive habits and toys.

Their ritual ancient orgies have evolved into nothing more than the same old public "sex binging" celebrations. The Roman Holidays now come in the form of Mardi Gras, Oktober Fests and Spring Break beach parties. At one time, the Oktober Fest was notorious for its spouse swapping activities. Both husband and wife were considered free for the duration of the Fest to find other sexual partners. If the wife came home with her new partner and the porch light was on, she had to go elsewhere because the husband had already arrived and claimed the house for entertaining his temporarily new bed partner. It is believed by many that this "break" from each other is what kept Germany's divorce rates the lowest of any old European nation. During the Mardi Gras, which is internationally known for its sexual license and orgies, women "flash" (publicly bear) their breasts in exchange for colorful bead necklaces. Unknown to many, Mardi Gras celebrations occur in a number of southern coastal cities besides New Orleans including Mobile, Alabama. This French holiday is also found in Rio de Janeiro but, there, it is called "Carnival." Interestingly, Mardi Gras is immediately followed by Lent, a period when Christians seek penitence (forgiveness) for their sins.[88]

Bestiality

Bestiality and zoophilia are one and the same. They are terms used to describe those individuals who have sex with animals. It is a common perversion among Europeans. And, for obvious reasons, they most commonly practice it in their rural communities. Most of the domesticated animals that they favor having sex with are on farms. Among these preferences are sheep, goats, cattle, oxen, horses, pigs, turkeys, chickens and dogs. The shepherding tradition it strong with them. Their attempts to universalize bestiality has failed for lack of evidence. They were not the first people to domesticate and herd animals. Neither were they the only ones shepherding during or since they began. So why are these "shepherd kings" the first and, historically, only ones to make a practice of having sexual intercourse with members of their flock?

Evidence of the origins of bestiality can be found in the crude drawings of the most primitive Europeans. It is as much a part of them as an absence of melanin. Pictures of humans engaged in sex with at least a donkey and moose, as well as acts of homosexuality and orgies, go as far back as the Neolithic Age.[89] Mythologically speaking, it was Zeus himself who turned himself into a swan to have sex with Leda (he also had sexual relations in the form of a snake with Persephone and a bull with Europa). It requires a special imagination, and/or reality, to dream up and sculpt for public viewing the image of a woman having sex with a bird.[90]   That

European imagination is still actively and progressively at work. For these and other unnatural sexual acts have evolved down to this day as part of their rituals and traditions. It is consistently seen down through the ages as part of their normal interaction with their world. No recorded break from these practices can be found except when they chose to selectively exclude all or some of these activities from their public historical record.

> Part One of Richard Poe's *Black Spark, White Fire: Did African Explorers Civilize Ancient Europe?* makes note of many of these presumably primitive and extinct behaviors like "engaging in ritual sexual intercourse with a horse" and public performances of "intercourse with their mothers and sisters." These immoral and repulsive excessive extremes are still unquestionably evident throughout Western culture today....[91]

There is ample evidence in the literature that the European practice of having sex with every animal possible is an ongoing tradition. The *Kinsey Report* found that eight percent of all males, as well as four percent of all females, sexually interacted with animals. The percent of all males who lived on farms who engaged in such carnal activities was 17 percent. Bear in mind that the *Kinsey Report* is over a half-century old. And also bear in mind that no Afrikans were included as a part of the 16,000 individuals interviewed in the surveys. Almost all those included in his study were European.[92]

One animal in particular has dominated this perverse scene, almost from the beginning – sheep. Wool has been a vital element in European culture for nearly 12,000 years. Originally, it was essential for their survival on the glaciers. Without it, Europeans probably would not have survived the relentless cold. Out of that initial lesson, sheep (and goats) evolved into a major traditional European industry. The ongoing desirability of wool in a frigid climate have made these animals constant, valued and intimate members of the European family. Even today we see the remnants of this bond. Every major country that raises sheep for their fleece and meat, even those where sheep are not indigenous, is European or politically and economically dominated by them.[93]

The vocation of shepherding, therefore, carries a proud and unbroken narrative among them. Often for very extended periods of time, male shepherds are isolated in the company of sheep. Sheep graze over a wide area and prefer high, hilly areas which makes it necessary for their shepherds, who are almost exclusively males, to be alone with them and away from human females for extended periods of time. When this isolation, even if for only a few hours, is combined with the European sex imperative, boredom, their power and control as shepherds and the knowledge that sheep are sexually compatible, the outcome is fairly predictable. And this predictability of European males having sexual intercourse with sheep has been born out in the evidence of centuries of sheep herding.

Present day science has also inadvertently contributed to this evidence. They have discovered that the sheep's vagina is anatomically closer to that of the human female than any other animal, i.e., the sheep's vagina looks and feels the same as the female human's to the male human. Apparently long ago the question of the sexual compatibility of men and sheep had been answered by those experimenting on high and hilly laboratories. It only makes sense that the disproportionate number of these field testing sites, relative to those of other animals, had much to do with Europeans posing the question of anatomical compatibility in the first place. But what may be most damaging to arguments that this research is purely scientific and is not about the interests of European males in the sexual compatibility of sheep is that none of these "scientific" discussions inquire into the ram's (male sheep) sexual compatibility with the human female. It is only a discussion of female sheep. And most of us have not thought to question just what led these scholars to ask this question of compatibility in the first place.

This confusion provides a prime example of how they have made unnatural things appear natural. Because, initially, the sheep rejects the human penis but usually is in no position to argue. Over time, it comes to accept it as normal because it has no choice.

This is exemplified in the case of the European girl who took her sexual frustrations out on a horse. Her father noticed some unusual changes in the behavior of his horse when he approached. So he began to watch it. It was then that he noticed her twisted interaction with it. The child had developed the habit of thrusting her fist, up to her elbow as with homosexual "fisting," into the horse's rectum. Apparently, this had gone on for so long that the horse automatically spread its flanks as the girl approached in anticipation of reducing the pain of its violation. Obviously, when something is done to an animal long enough, it no longer distinguishes this "sexual" act from its normal sexual behavior or its role in service to humans. The same transformation applies to any other animal including humans, especially those who are slaves or otherwise under a planned and systematic physical and mental assault. For it is neither the sheep nor the sodomized boy who is in a position to define, or rather redefine, normalcy to its or his liking.

It should be noted, however, that modernity has somewhat altered the bestial diet of Europeans. Progress has occurred Domesticated birds such as chickens, ducks and turkeys (as well as wild ones such as turkeys, geese and ostriches when they can be caught) now seem to have assumed the lead in having the best sexual fit for their males' penises. The practice of breaking the fowls neck at the moment of orgasm is also very characteristic of these acts. The sex-pain connection is no less pervasive in perverse European sexual culture than in their general culture. One has to consider these facts when looking at the proportion of chicken in the average Afrikan's diet.

The *Hite Report* also showed years ago, seemingly to everyone's surprise, that the majority of cases where animals are sodomized by human males occur on farms and in rural districts. For us, this evidence is good. Afrikans are disproportionately urban in this country. And, some of the evidence of this, while a negative for our independence, speaks to who is most disproportionately committing these sadistic acts. Afrikans have and continue to lose their farmland at an unprecedented rate. Most surveys agree that the loss is at or above 3,000 acres per day.[94] Therefore, in terms of having and living on farms, because Afrikans only constitute a fledging one percent of all farmers, then, at most, we could only be accused of that percent of humans who have sex with animals in the rural setting. Given the still more morally conservative disposition of Afrikans than Europeans, and the fact that this conservatism is more pronounced in rural than urban Afrikans, this one percent guesstimate is, in all probability, very greatly exaggerated. Moreover, for those not living on farms where livestock is raised, very few rural Afrikans own animals. The same, of course, cannot be said of rural Europeans. In fact, their numbers in the rural setting and farms is increasing as wave after wave of young European males with newly acquired degrees in agricultural engineering go beyond this country's borders to steal more and more Latin American and Afrikan land for their personal farming ventures.

The latest fascination with lip-kissing, and even tongue-kissing, animals an interesting point when analyzed using the common knowledge that kissing leads to sex. In the borderless world where any and everything becomes a sexual object/toy and Europeans serve as the reference group, animals have been brought into the realm of possible sexual partners with nonEuropeans. It is not new to Europeans but it must be introduced to others in the degrees that will allow them to eventually accept it as normal to them. Kissing appears innocent but is extremely important for this discussion because it is evidence of a deeper agenda, reflecting thought and behavior historically hidden from others.

Animals appear to kiss humans on the lips only because that is what they are trained to do. Animals are animals. Any noninstinctual, unnatural behavior that they exhibit is a result of being trained by humans, and/or the intentional misinterpretation by Europeans of their imitative behavior as natural to them. They are imitating their trainers. They do not *understand* what they are doing. The answer to the question many may ask about these animals' sexual utility for humans is found in their instinctual drive to lick and, when constrained, wiggle. Kissing is not natural to them – nuzzling yes, rubbing yes, sniffing yes, licking yes, but not kissing and definitely not having sexual intercourse with other animal species. Animals whose lips touch each other's are construed in this classic European sense. So-called "Kissing Fish" are an excellent example of this form of warped personification. Animals' tongues are extremely important sensing organs. Their tongues give them an enormous amount of information about their physical environment and the things that they come into contact with. Semi or fully domesticated animals will sniff and lick virtually anything that is consistently put in their faces. They also can sense emotional states so that if the thing/person that feeds them is happy when they lick them on cue then they will begin to consistently do that so as to please the source of their food and comfort. Animals do not "kiss" humans. The concept has no meaning to them outside of being connected to the source of comfort in the way that source wants, and has trained, them to connect with them. If an animal, who had never learned or had been kept from learning how to provide for itself, learned that licking the penis or vagina of its caretaker would bring it food and comfort it would eagerly do it. It is called conditioning.

Of course, European animal psychiatrists and sexologists have their own political interpretations of the natural behavior of pets. They now selfishly see true conscious intent in the actions of the animals they once declared unable to feel pain so they would be comfortable in using them in perverted and commercial experiments. Today, if we were to believe them, dogs who lick their private parts to clean themselves are anal retentive.

There may indeed be a convincing reason why there has been a dramatic increase in the number of European females who own dogs that goes well beyond personal protection. Given the significant and growing shortage of available, qualified heterosexual men, dogs (as well as every other domesticated and domesticable animal including bears, pigs, snakes and mice) serve as surrogate sexual partners. It would not be reaching far to suggest that "family" photos of European females and their dogs often carry a much deeper meaning than meets the eye.

In addition, as people age, the number of males continues to dwindle, but at an even more dramatic rate than before. But the sex imperative does not. Therefore, we would expect dogs to become even more useful to European females as they grow older.[95]

As we've already noted, bestiality is one of the two most sought after viewing activities on the internet. And the internet is only one facet of a single-minded media. So one must ask if all the commercials, programs and media attention to loving relations between humans and their dogs, cats, pigs and other pets are a prelude to revealing the true extent of their zoophilia. Their true nature and intent are revealed in the symbolism and scenes from a new breed of movies like *The Animal* and *Little Nicky*. We also need to ask if these images, which are still read differently by Europeans and Afrikans, have a practical side? Is the explanation as simple as

Europeans see sex in this imagery, but Afrikans simply see an unnatural and excessive love for an animal?

We should also note that violent sexual perversion and bestiality are intricate parts of devil worship rituals. The fact that Satanism is apparent in a wide variety of forms throughout all levels of the Western community, especially the media, is clear evidence of a strong love of the most perverse of the baser desires. Rhetoric should never be confused with reality. No matter how disguised behind the rhetoric of Christianity, Europeans worship the god they made a pact with to give them power over others.

In Any Event

The extreme sex priority builds upon the cultural imperative of progress where you must always be doing something. What that something is, is defined and controlled by other more fundamental asilic imperatives. Boredom becomes the individual's worst nightmare. The time and quiet required to connect with ancestors and spirit become impossible because of the ever present fear of silence and stillness. Europeans feel that if something cataclysmic or phenomenal is not happening in their lives they are not living. They are driven by the need to continually make something happen. Whether that happening holds meaning or is meaningless is not of consequence.

Whether through ignorance or intentional betrayal, we are not blameless for allowing these imperatives to seep into our homes. We allow Europeans and their representatives into our homes to raise our children, children we have already allowed to feel that they must be constantly entertained. Our children cannot focus on one thing for long because they have only been trained to receive successions of rapid images. They cannot focus for long because we have based their success in European society upon getting a head start on their (social) integration skills and miseducation by the over visual stimulation of computer games and media imaging.

> The continuous display of babies as the center of attention can cause them to be self-centered and egotistic. They become conditioned to think that other people or gadgets

(toys) must entertain them. They also begin to develop the
idea that the absence of entertainment brings boredom.[96]

One of our children's favorite phrases, one that should
send shock waves through our consciousness, is "I'm
bored" or "that's boring." When that phrase is uttered, it
is an indication that we have surrendered some part of
their being and our collective souls to the clutches of white
western infamy.[97]

Although a steady diet of processed sugar heavily contributes to this
lack of focus, being raised in preparation for the European way makes
it easy to understand why they have attention deficits. They are being
torn from the Afrikan way and thrown into a ball of chaotic
confusion. Because our boys sit in front of computer games longer
they naturally have even greater attention deficit problems.

Never being able to get enough sex drives the need to have
every available second of one's time involved in sexual activity.
Within the European cultural context, whether or not one has money
or even a partner, sex is the most plentiful and pleasurable
method/tool for filling time; it is an activity whose quantitative
engagement indicates that one is progressing sexually. According to
the Western psychology, one can sexually progress even if stranded
by oneself on a deserted island.

In turn, being "horny" has become elevated to the status of a
most desirable quality. First, it slipped out of the mouths of brazen
individuals at opportune times. We snickered about it, thinking it
was rather forward, if not silly. Being horny progressively became
adopted as an acceptable orientation among those who had nothing
better to do with their time but engage in sex, or who simply lacked
self-control. And now, as if an accident without a history, being
incurably horny has become a popular precondition for dating and
marriage. Nymphomania has followed the same path to normalcy.
It has become a prized quality, particularly among females. Only a
couple of decades ago being "loose" was considered an extremely
negative quality relative to having a serious date or getting married.
Today it is an asset. Being on constant "booty call"[98] is no longer
something to hide. Extraordinary experience in sexual practices now

adds to one's dating and marriageability resume. What yesterday was classified as a whore qualifies as today's virgin before the alter.

This drive for a release from boredom is also visibly reflected in the club scene. Teen clubs are thriving, especially in Afrikan communities where youth are not afforded the same in-house privacy (because of their parents virtual absence) of their European counterparts. And the privacy of clubs is not an asset today. They are primarily places that encourage sexual play. Clubs are not conducive to lasting relationships, at any age level. The proliferation of clubs (and their growing membership) has helped to amplify a climate of one-night stands and extremely casual approaches to male/female relationships among youth. Long-term relationships have declined as clubs have proliferated. As another example of the love of profit motive in this capitalist system, clubs are very big business.

Although there is a drive to make everything today appear as if it has always been that way, we must remember that teen clubs are very new. No prior generation has had this experience so early in their lives. Every decade witnesses the introduction of clubs, like drugs, to a younger and younger generation. And each earlier introduction allows for the introduction of adult sexual behaviors and perversions at earlier and earlier ages. Those of us who allow our children to indulge neglect to ask about the cultural source of their growing and insatiable boredom. In not being responsibly oriented toward their future these parents do not think about what will be left for them to be exposed to when they turn 18 or 19 or 20 or 21? Following in the footsteps of their slave ancestors who learned never to ask questions for fear of the possible reaction, many among us do not want to look to see what European culture has waiting for our children in the wings after the dance and strip clubs loose their charm. And these same parents, drunk on European progress, dare not even think to ask what their children's children will be doing at 8 or 9 or 10 or 11.

Individuality

A   society   with   a   high   priority   (and   protection)   of individualism was/is necessary in order to provide free spaces for them to exercise and practice their perversions. Therefore, all nonessential social rules and guidelines of morality and ethics must be removed. You cannot be a freak in a sexually moral society. You must argue, and politically enforce in the media, law and educational system, that there is no moral base beyond individualism. Expressing oneself is seen as the preeminent individual function and singularly operates to benefit individualities, vis-a-vis the community/family, in the West.

In a society of individualistic psychopaths practically anything can be made sexually appealing, including being defecated on, urinated on or even having someone spit in your mouth.[96] As we will see below, these and other similarly perverse sexual acts, have been named by Westerners. It goes without saying that language speaks to culture. The words a people use, define and identity the material and immaterial evident in their society. Humans give everything a name. Language, the ability to verbally communicate thoughts and meaning, is central to the definition of humans. Therefore, if it exists as a part of your society, it has a name. If a thought, thing or act does not exist in your culture, you have no name for it (except as taken from others to speak of their thoughts, things or acts). This is a primary proof of cultural differentiation. When words, terms and concepts are found to have been born and flourished among a particular people, and not others, it gives us a cultural map into the uniqueness of that people. And so it is that many terms originating in European culture and society speak to the fact of a peculiar European sexual imperative.

Terms identifying and defining European people and their peculiar sexual interests and imperatives include, but are not limited to *coprolegny*, where people derive sexual pleasure from touching, licking or eating the bodily secretions of others, including feces,[97] and giving each other "golden showers"[98] with their urine and vomit as well as drinking one's own or other's urine; *vampirism*, which characterizes those who need to drink blood in order to become sexually excited; *saliromania*, attaining sexual arousal through looking at and smelling things abnormally dirty and grotesque such as pictures of deformed persons, watching mud-wrestling and wading through sewage; *klismaphilia*, which is the repeated use of enemas for sexual excitement; *necrophilia*, where individuals become sexually stimulated by and engage in sexual intercourse with corpses and *autonecrophilia*, where "being" the corpse, i.e., acting dead, provides the stimulation; *urophilia*, where people derive sexual pleasure from urinating on others or having themselves urinated on; *sadism*, where individuals are sexually stimulated by mentally, but especially physically, hurting others through spanking, paddling, whipping, beating, restraining, punching, gagging, blindfolding, electrically shocking, electrocuting, insulting, cutting, cutting hair off (or "braid cutting"), burning, raping, mutilating, fisting, starving, asphyxiating and other forms of excessive torture; its complement; *masochism* or *algophilia*, which is sexual stimulation by having these things, up to the point of death, done to self by others (*autopedophilia* is a very popular version of this where one becomes sexually excited by being treated like a child during sexual activities);[102] *pedophilia*, where children are ones primary sexual outlet; *homophilia* (*homosexuality*), when one seeks out sexual relations only with members of his/her own sex, of which *bisexuality*, sex being sought with both males and females, is a derivative; *coprophemia*, where obscene language is a essential for good sex; *autodermatophagia*, where a diet of one's own skin provides sexual excitement; *autoflagellation*, the whipping of oneself into a sexual fervor; *autoassassinatophilia*, where fantasizing about or staging one's own murder is erotic; *automutilation* or *autotomy*, collections of acts where sexual arousal comes from imagining or actually physically harming oneself (self-mutilation); *exhibitionism*, where people are sexually stimulated by exposing their private parts to, usually unsuspecting, others as in indecent exposure, "flashing" (or "streaking") and "mooning," which is related to *voyeurism*, where secretly watching others engaged in sexual activities, or just looking at other's body parts, is exciting sexually, as in the "Peeping Toms" who use telescopes, binoculars and holes in walls to invade others' privacy (*scopophilias* is a synonym which breaks this group of watchers into those who love to watch (active scopophilias) and love being watched (passive scopophilias)); *acrotomophilia*, where the fantasy that one's sex partner is an amputee is sexually stimulating;[103] *zoophilia*, which is virtually synonymous with *bestiality*, where one seeks to engage in sex with animals (*zoosadists* receive sexual gratification from injuring or killing animals); *frotteurism*, which describes those who become sexually excited by the actual or imaged experience of touching others without their consent; *secondarism*, which is when arousal occurs only because the partner just had sex with someone else; *kleptolagnia*, where stealing increases sexual excitement; *pyrolagnia*, where setting and watching large fires is sexually stimulating; and the classic *telephone scatologia*, or sexual pleasure derived from giving or receiving obscene phone calls. There are quite a number of other sexual perversions, including a whole host of fetishes including ones for shoes, rubber, leather, fur and underwear (often masked behind a childish game called "panty raids" among groups of undergraduate school males), but these stand out as the dominate types.

On the other hand, Europeans exhibit a serious collection of fears (phobias) related to sex. The scientific names for the most documented ones (with lay item of fear) are: *aichmophobia* (penises, pointy objects and symbols), *anal-rape fantasy* (being sodomized), *androphobia* (men), *coitophobia* and *genophobia* (sexual intercourse), *cypriphobia* (venereal disease), *eurotophobia* (female genitalia), *gamophobia* (marriage), *gymnophobia* (nudity), *gynephobia* (women), *haptephobia* (touching), *hedonophobia* (pleasure), *maieusiophobia* (pregnancy/childbirth), *parthenophobia* (girls), *spermatophobia* (semen), *teratophobia* (giving birth to a monster) and *traumatophobia* (sex after rape).

And before confusion sets in, these are not the psychological disorders of one or two strange individuals. It is not a case of the proverbial few bad apples. They are widespread enough in the population to be cataloged, form societies, be regularly portrayed in pornography and be common knowledge among Europeans and their closest admirers. All of these can be identified as to sources that impacted numerous individuals over extended periods of time in their sociocultural history. If nothing else, read Terence McLaughlin's *Dirt*.[104] We are dealing with some sick people here.

In this cultural context, any attraction within a society that is inordinately sex focused is deemed a natural, sexual attraction, no matter the object of desire or the act itself. None of the above sexual perversions had meaning in other traditional societies because such acts were beyond sane comprehension. Sex served a biological purpose and male and female mates were peaceful complements.

And, in relation to language as a direct reflection of material and nonmaterial culture, none of the above sexual perversions are found in any traditional Afrikan language group. And they are not part of the vocabulary of any other civilization prior to European invasion. That means that such thoughts and practices did not exist in our traditional places. That means that European culture is their origin. And any statement attempting to place them outside of and before it inevitably have a European origin and political intent.

Sexual perversion was inconceivable until brought by the "superior" intellect of the European. These are the unique historical practices of Europeans who feel it their duty to corrupt the world with a superior sexual psychosis. When there is no morality and the primary goal is to satisfy the desires of the individual(s) who has/have more power than you, anything goes. Morals establish limits. Cognitive dissonance,[105] or the contradiction between what you have and what you need, is easily alleviated in the weakened minds of those who accept the superiority of others' guidance and power while suppressing their own intuition.

Politics determine a behavior's acceptability. The degree to which we are willing to accept heretofore considered deviant and/or abnormal behavior largely depends on what Europeans sanction as acceptable. When sodomy becomes the norm, anybody and everybody with an anus becomes a target. When fellatio becomes the norm, anybody and everybody with a mouth is a potential sucker. Anal sex was introduced to Afrikans in the same way that oral sex was, by Europeans. And when you normalize sodomy, you sanction male homosexuality. Sodomy is disproportionately found in the homosexual, not heterosexual, realm of sexual intercourse. But regardless of where it is considered or is necessarily most essential to orgasm/sexual pleasure, the normalization of sodomy makes a person's sex irrelevant. Particularly among males, it makes no difference who you penetrate sexually. Whether the penis enters the female from the front or rear, the point of penetration, and interior beyond that point, is the same. Both sexes have an anus. In the end, any orifice will do. The same applies to fellatio. The focus is on the orgasm. Discriminating between oral and manual masturbation or vaginal and anal intercourse becomes a hindrance to reaching as many climaxes as humanly possible. They are simply various ways to the same end.

The explosion, not origin, of perversion in sexual behavior is largely the result of the anonymity that extreme individualism offers. In a world where individuals are made lonely and alone, and made to believe that without the "love" of another they are nothing, any love will do. But I repeat. The source of extreme and perverted sexual behavior is not the privacy afforded individuals but the nature of a cultural mentality which sees excess and degeneracy as normal and natural. Let us be clear that it is not that individuality did not exist before the European. Every culture promotes independent thinking or there is no growth or development in the solving of human problems or a philosophical understanding of the physical or spiritual universe. European culture brought about a change in emphasis from group priority to that of individual survival. No other culture had previously perfected and offered a chaotic and aimless helter skelter style individualism based on a normalized psychotic human model.

European scholars often accuse urbanization for the increases in immoral and socially dysfunctional behaviors/practices such as prostitution, strip clubs and pornography in an effort to, again, universalize their particulars. But, because immoral and socially dysfunctional behaviors/practices are also found in relative excess in Western rural communities, the argument does not hold. When looked at scientifically, this pervasive orientation toward an extreme sexual imperative among Europeans is based on a genetic cultural predisposition that has roots going back to their socio-cultural beginnings in the caves of the Caucasus Mountains.

The notion that "you just want me for my body" becomes unisexual and positive. To be unisexual dictates that you see male and female as no different except in the accident of having exposed or concealed genitalia. Otherwise, physically, psychologically, spiritually, you are told there are no meaningful differences.

The very nature of the European psychology encourages sexual relations with multiple others around you. Westerners operate at the same time within multiple sexual arenas which reinforce each other and magnify the normal human sex drive. Multiple, interlocking arenas include:

1. Fantasy (in dreams, daydreams, fiction, kwk....)
2. Subconscious (a constant stream of images and symbolism

in commercials, print advertisements, billboards, kwk....)

    3. Actuality (flirting, extramarital affairs and other activities, the dating game, kwk....)

    Sex has become life, not the procreation of life, but what one lives for. Sex has become the answer to all individual problems. The woman with the attitude, the tomboy, the male workaholic, all can be cured with an intense dose of good ol' down home sex.

Anal/Oral Politics

    William H. Masters and Virginia E. Johnson were not the first European "experts" on sex to believe both anal and oral sex to be unjustly condemned in the religious literature (Bible) and, therefore, unnecessarily prosecuted.[106] However, they are the most renowned and instrumental in making it into a modern, scientific statement. They used the science of statistics to show that these behaviors were evident and increasing among a significant number of Europeans, despite threats and, in some cases, actual prosecution by the state. Assuming the arrogant theoretical posture that what is natural for Europeans is normal for everybody else, they use European sexual history as a normative model. They saw in their own past and present a pattern of perversion that runs through all societies in the European nation. Still today, the Greeks are known for homosexuality and sodomy and the Romans for homosexuality, sodomizing males and females and orgies. The Italians are said to have perfected anal intercourse, the French excelled in oral sex (both fellatio and cunnilingus) and the British took a fancy to being spanked. But all European societies are known for their perpetual debauchery. From this Masters and Johnson could conclude that such thought and behavior were normal and natural for all humans. Then, as sex consultants to the world, they go on to explain the best ways for people to positively approach the idea of oral and anal sex. However, this was not something they had to work at. In a society devoted to hedonism any sensation that can in any way be associated with the pleasure principle fits what is normal and natural for humans. In the relentless search for stronger and stronger doses of pleasure there can be no natural or unnatural boundaries.

However, Europeans' lack of a sense of natural limitations should not signal us to be likewise. We should follow the lead of our own. Anal and oral sex are unacceptable practices for Afrikan centered individuals who study pre-European invasion sexual practices among Afrikans as the foundation of their thinking. It is understood that if the ancients did not practice it we should not. However, even the best of us become confused in the rush to professional recognition. Therefore, we must use caution at all times. We must question all inclusion of European ways in any discussion of our tradition. For example, it is utterly surprising and deeply disappointing to find the inclusion of oral sex involving the protagonists in the writing of Ayi Kwei Armah, one of our most profound and renowned writers.

> He slipped his tongue inside her from the clitoris, keeping the pressure light. A thought circled in her mind: He's sure in his movement, so sure, so light, so gentle. How can he be like this with me after so long a wait? He stroked deeper, then brought the tip of his tongue back right against her clitoris. She felt her hold on his head tighten as her body shook, and she couldn't let him go. Sensing her coming, he flattened his tongue against her clitoris. Now instead of resisting the pressure of her hands against the back of his head, he let her push his head against herself. At the same time he licked her in tiny vibrations that made her orgasm a long slide into pleasure.[107]

Deviation from the Afrikan sexual norm can be found earlier in his work in the inclusion of an act of postillionnage. In *Fragments* Baako inserts his finger into Juana's anus during sexual intercourse.[108] Even though it is not stated or implied in the above oral sex scene, one can but hope that these lines were designed to demonstrate the corruption that the West can have on the young minds of even the most committed Afrikan warriors. Regardless of why, when there is deviation from the Afrikan norm in the words of Afrikans it must be addressed. This must be so even with an elder as deservedly venerated as Armah. Though in *Two Thousand Seasons* he correctly describes these perversions as the acts of our destroyers, he must be challenged when he depicts Afrikans willfully participating in such acts. There can be no sacred cows on our journey to the Afrikan way.

It is enough that fellatio was historically introduced to a very limited number of Afrikans through forced encounters with Europeans. It is worse to glorify and advocate those sexually perverted behaviors which have become increasingly normalized for Afrikans through the media, especially through the new wave of Blaxploitation turned sexploitation movies such as *Waiting to Exhale, Belly, Don't Be A Menace To Society While Drinking Your Juice N Da Hood, Baby Boy, Love Kills, O, Two Can Play That Game, How To Be A Player, Sprung, The Best Man, Groupies, He Got Game, In Too Deep, The Players Club, 3 Strikes, Any Given Sunday, Trois, The Wood, The Brothers, Pandora's Box, Punks* and *Booty Call.* It is present or implied in virtually every other new age Blaxploitation film turned out. Throughout most of these movies, and more, the conversations outside of actual sexual activities were loaded with jokes and innuendo about sex and sexually perverse activities. Sex is entertainment in the West.

Parents also seem to be oblivious to the fact that their children have access to and faithfully watch X-rated videos (which they call flicks) like *Fuck with Friends, You and I, Jake Steve* (multi-volume), *Snoop Dogg Doggy Style* (multi-volume), *Elvis Goes To The Ghetto, Uncle Luke's Summer Jam, Cisco's Thong Song Uncensored* and *Too Short, Charge It To The Game* (multi-volume); mail order videos with oral and anal sex scenes like *Girls Gone Wild, Summertime Stick Up, Carribean Booty Call* and *Hoe Vibe* (multi-volume); and "BET Uncensored," an very late night program with implied or semi-concealed sexual scenes by artists like Uncle Luke, Little Joker and the Bomber, China Man, Vita, Too Short and N.E.R.D.S. These videos freely circulate among the youth in our community. It is the parents who are unaware or permissive. Most of this information came from surveys this author conducted among middle and high school students. Homosexuality has also found a normalized place in many of the films our children frequently view, such as *Set It Off, Players Club, Don't Be A Menace To Society While Drinking Your Juice N Da Hood, Baby Boy, Love Kills, Money Talks* and *Three Strikes,* to name only a few.[109] *The Wood* is but one example of the media gods making sexual perversion seem as if it were normal "back in the day." Nothing could be further from the truth. Neither oral nor anal sex was a significant part of the Afrikan community's sexual behavior two generations ago. Remember that even French kissing is relatively new to Afrikans.

Now we have Afrikan "experts" on Afrikan interpersonal relationships in New Europe who rubberstamp European habits as if Afrikans are Europeans. Many of these so-called experts call on us to introduce European-style play into our bedrooms as a means of making sex more exciting. Among other recommendations, they, too, advise the liberal use of aids such as strawberries and whipped cream and fruit flavored lubricants as well as wearing edible (candy) dresses and panties, encouraging us to engage in oral sex feasts.

Our children are the primary victims of this growing mass confusion among Afrikans. They are put on the defensive when they declare they don't "go that way," as if they are the ones who are wrong in their choice, as if they are abnormal and narrow minded. They, along with adults who refuse to bend to the European extremes, are labeled "sexually repressed" and victimized by Western sexual terrorism. Or, they are told, they are not enjoying life to its fullest, or they do not know what they are missing. And, as usual, traditional Afrikan culture is painted as being the greatest repressor of this individualistic spirit. European behavior is always the norm, the template from which others' sexual behavior is measured. Reflecting this universalizing arrogance, the classic response given by Europeans when questioned about their sexual perversions is "Don't we all?"

The fabrication that everybody, including the European, although less so, is sexually repressed, is a psychological ploy designed to help spread the European sexual priority among others. Others must be made to feel that something is missing from their lives. They must be led to experiment with the abnormal, perversions and deviance until they are addicted to the European sexual priority.

The Best Medicine

And all the while, many Afrikans have been looking at the comical depictions of European sexual imperatives on TV shows thinking they are funny and not sick. Too many of us have been laughing when in truth and reality we should be crying. Apparently hypnotized by the lessons flashed in our minds by the idiot box, fascinated by the perversions and moral disrespect lost/bought Afrikans take pride in parading across these stages, so many of us uncontrollably fall out laughing in celebration of our destruction. One of the 42 Negative Confessions states that, "I will not commit treason against my ancestors." To applaud and revel in another's way and dismiss our own as uncivilized and obsolete without any understanding whatsoever as to the meaning behind why it is necessarily different from the ball of confusion we currently subsist on is treason against our way. And, among any people, the penalty for treason is death.

If you let sickness create your reality, sickness becomes your reality. The solutions you develop and implement within that reality are based on the assumption that the reality you live in, the one created to order madness, is real, viable and meaningful. "The present is where we get lost – if we forget our past and have no vision of the future."[110] And we have invested so much of our energies fighting to be free to be *like them* that we have forgotten that we need to be free *of them*. That is why the solutions we propose for ourselves within this European reality have not, and will never, bring us peace or empowerment. They will not work for us. They cannot because you cannot design sanity within insanity without crippling or destroying the insanity. And Europeans have no desire to become sane.

Yes, laughter is a great medicine. But what about laughter that arises from and leads to greater illness? What about those acts portrayed as humorous that are designed to lower our defenses against our moral spirit? Of what issue is the programmed laughter given in response to unfunny words and behaviors that we laugh at because the cue cards say so, because we follow what make-believe and handpicked audiences find humorous? What is it about the star quality of those Afrikan male comedians, like their political, educational and business counterparts, that makes them so appealing to their sponsors and, in hypnotic turn, us? What makes for Afrikan stardom in European theater? We should know that the common display and vocalization of effeminate mannerisms and mentalities by the likes of Eddie Murphy, Jamie Foxx, Steve Harvey and Martin Lawrence, even when they are not playing comedic effeminate roles, is not without purpose for those who seek to destroy us by turning us into them. European culture and society use those images/idols, which are saying and doing things we would otherwise object to, to induce us into saying and doing them.

Ideas are subtly introduced through humor that have no place in sane minds. And once introduced, an enormous amount of conscious, willed energy is required to dislodge and eject them. The forces of peers, media and being socialized in a perverted, leisure society make individual acts of successful rebellion few and far in between.

The most important targets in this move to escalate the introduction of perverted, insane ideas into our minds are the children. You change who a people are through altering their children, gradually, generation after generation. And because of their innocence and impressionability, our children's minds are the most fertile soil for the introduction and successful implantation of perverted European ideas. As they grow, those insanities that they have assimilated as normal and natural becomes what they believe they are.

Laughter is the seed that enables confusion to take root. More often than not, it introduces the sexual perversions which individuals come to participate in and then develop a defensive appreciation of. Laughter makes the heart grow fonder of things that otherwise are not funny. Western media are acutely aware that if you can get people to laugh at a perversion they will eventually embrace and/or be accepting of it.

The female Russian TV news reporter who slowly stripped during the newscast in order to improve the program's ratings is an excellent example of this. This is an historical commercial tactic in European media. To boost ratings and profits, increase the level of violence and sex. We see this in Toni Braxton's return to center stage through wearing more and more revealing clothing. However, she is but one example of the norm. Sex sells any and everything in European society. As in the Cold War, we look at Russians as if they are somebody else because we believe in this New Europe called America. Russians, like Americans, are Europeans. They are family.

People found that striptease act during the reporting of the Soviet news quite humorous. It was not an extreme behavior, only a peek into what is to come in their commercial media globally. Laughter prepares us for their intensified assault on our moral and ethical sensibilities.

And we are preparing the next generation to be even more conditioned by the European way in their sexual orientation and desires. By exposing them to "R" rated movies (and even our small children to "PG," and "PG-13" ones where an extremely thin line exists between sex and sexual innuendo if it exists at all) we are helping them lose their minds before they even know they have them. Only those secure in their own miseducation could believe that, in their absence, their children are watching an educational channel on the cable hooked up to their bedroom televisions. Only those blind to the ways of the Western mind would leave "X" rated adult videos lying around, or even locked up, expecting children not to touch. Children are naturally curious and ingenious. They become even more so when prompted by adult secrecy in a society where they have been socialized to believe that they should see and experience all, regardless of their level of maturity. "X" rated media are no less dangerous to the mind of a child than loaded guns conspicuously left around, without discipline backed instruction, are to the body. Even allowing them to watch and be cued by the sex and sexual innuendo of family time media entertainment before they are even adolescents is destructive to their innocence and developing sense of humanity.

The conspiracy against their innocence pervades the media. Many children's movies are consciously made to seduce their subconscious eyes with images of sex.[111] The dust that Simba disturbs when he lays down on a cliff to stargaze rises to form the word "sex" in *The Lion King*. During a wedding ceremony in *The Little Mermaid* the minister's erect penis can be detected. The front cover of the original jacket that same video comes in also has a penis drawn in as part of the underwater castle. In *Aladdin*, during the scene where he is trying to get in the good graces of the princess but is cornered on the balcony by a tiger, a background voice, which is not part of the dialog, says "good teenagers take off your clothes." Listen carefully. A nude European female exposes herself in one of the windows two mice flying on the back of a goose pass by in the original version of *The Rescuers.* And sexual innuendo and confusion plague *A Bug's Life* and *Antz* as it does so many other children's movies where the characters are not animated humans. The bad part is that these are only a very small number of the motion picture industry's systematic efforts to implant the European sex imperative in those so innocent that they have not yet learned to walk or talk well.

And, again, these are neither unusual occurrences nor are they simply the neurotic or psychotic quirks of a few single individuals gone off the deep end. They intentionally destroy the minds of little children no less than those who put poisons and glass in children's Halloween[112] candy work to destroy their bodies. They just happen to be a little smarter and more legitimate. For this to occur requires a cultural framework which authorizes, fosters and excuses it. Whatever a culture does not tolerate will not be commonly found in it. Allusions to sex arouse the curiosity of the naive, impressionable, innocent, especially those, due to their level of personal development, who are still fixated on physical stimulation. And, children are naturally and intensively inquisitive and intellectually immature.

Equally important, children daydream. They spend an enormous amount of time in make-believe worlds. The backdrop for, and often players in, their fantasy worlds are most often created through the popular culture's literary, visual and oral media. And the popular children's culture, as the adults, is pornographic, either in direct images or through innuendo. In this reality, sexual obsessing and perversion have come to be the stuff that children's dreams are made of.

Neither the European presentation of fantasy nor reality contradict their intentions. Everything serves as a distraction from truth. And we, in following them, are caught in a culturally powered tractor beam of excessive sex and sexual perversion. We have become captives in a society of obsessions and insanities. This blind obedience to their way explains why many of the professional clowns and actors like Jimmie Walker of "Good Times" fame have suddenly been elevated to the status of experts on race relations, raising children and sexual behavior for our community on the talk show circuit.[113] As mentacidal captives, they speak in the slave's classic "we" mentality. They operate as if the master's interests are theirs, as if what happens to the master, his family and things happens to them. They speak out of the mind of their master. So, if the master does it, they have no problem in stating it as correct for them or us. That is all the proof they need.

Europeans have never stopped rewriting history in their favor. And we leave our children unattended in these theatrical classrooms as well as those ruled by the Ricki Lake's and Jerry Springer's of this world who are the queens and kings of sexual perversion. They promote every demented form of sexual orientation possible, except that between sane men and women. Whether their guests are real or fabricated is immaterial. And their closing apologies for their guests' insanities are of even less relevance. The way of the diseased mind has successfully been illustrated and promoted. The ideas are planted.

This tactic of meaninglessly apologizing after the fact is also found on commercial and cable television and in the theaters. The "Black" movie *Trois* is an excellent example. Here, a pornographic ménage à trois sex scene involving a husband, wife and another woman (along with other anal, oral and homosexual scenes) is firmly planted in the viewer's mind as a viable idea. It is then rationalized as a necessary part of a sorry story line to give the illusion that implanting that idea was not the prime motive behind the movie. Regardless of Hollywood's attempt at distraction, we must not forget, however, to always seek the source of deviance and perversion. The ménage à trois is a normal phenomenon in the ancient Greek and Roman world. Then, as now, it was the outgrowth of the relentless boredom that drives European progress. The unappeasable search is always for more because they can never be satisfied. Having wives to bear children and concubines and prostitutes to "play" with was characteristic of men of even meager means, as well, to a lesser degree, women. While it has remained constant in their history since then, those interesting in studying this phenomenon should take a close look at Italy from the 17th through 19th centuries.

We also are not thinking about the impact on our children of sex becoming a part of their daily thought pattern and routine at earlier and earlier ages. By the time most of our children reach the age of nine or ten "R" (and often "X") rated cable, rental and theater movies have already become a regular part of their commercial diet. Like European children go to parties specifically to get drunk, Afrikan children go to movies to begin witnessing sex. Most of today's movies have little value to audiences beyond sex and violence.

This is one way Europeans falsify and rewrite history, whether the pen is in their hand or that of their victims. While watching the performances of media superstars, whether news anchors or action heroes, we often forget that they are all just actors with an historical knowledge usually intentionally limited to what they read from cue cards, printouts or have memorized from their script. Even though we have the tendency to make them larger than life, attributing an objective human reason to their words of wisdom on and off stage, most musicians, actors and athletes are not experts. In most cases they have no more familiarity with the historical relations of Europeans with people of color than the Afrikans who measure European intent by the quality of the attention they receive from a best friend who "just happens" to be one.

Media backed research would have us believe that the parade of gratuitous sex and sexual innuendo poisoning virtually every form of media is innocent, natural and harmless. These political scientists would further suggest that continuously viewing sexual excess does little to nothing to increase the desire for inordinate and abnormal sexual activity among young and older viewers alike. They have said the same about violence.

Excessive sex is not natural. People are conditioned into it. They are socialized to accept it as normal in their thinking and then, through active participation, they develop the need of it by habit. Anything you constantly see remains in the forefront of your mind. Repetition is how most non-instinctual learning is reinforced and embedded in our memory. Why would we imagine this logic is fundamental to motivational affirmations, chants, mantras, creative visualizations and other forms of behavior modification but in no way applies to the baser desires which we are daily bombarded with and more susceptible to? Those of us who are unwilling to accept that their conclusions are valid are badgered into at least conceding that, on balance, the scientific findings are inconclusive. We are taught that absolute proof, not intuition or common sense, is what is needed for us to unilaterally decide to keep our sons and daughters away from the influence of morality corroding programming. What has worked for millennia no longer works. Suddenly, common sense is no longer valid.

Western sexual culture, with its extensive commercial counterpart, is a mentacide inducing social vortex. It operates as a cultural vacuum consuming then transforming then melding every being caught up in its corruptive path into a convoluted orgy of the dominated and exploited. Those daring to flirt on its fringes do so only at the risk of impending absorption. At every turn and in every place individuals interface with life in Western culture, every means is made to draw the curious and the lost deeper into its clutches.

4. Another World

"No one sends a child on a difficult errand and gets angry
if she does not perform it well."

Afrikan Proverb

Sanyika Shakur attempted to explain it, but too many of us refused to listen because we thought hard core rap/hip hop was confined to his "hood."[1] Most of us could not grasp the magnitude of what had been happening right before our eyes in order for his "hood" to exist. There is a another world out there. Invisible and unknown to most of us, it has grown right under our noses, the very same noses we turned up and away from our people in order to be recognized and validated by the European power elite and their liberal emissaries. It developed out of the decades-old intellectual, policy-validating, emphasis of class over race, of submissive integration over a self-determining empowerment, which progressively discarded an enormous chunk of our population confined to disrespected, disadvantaged, disenfranchised ghettos, slums, projects, hovels and cardboard boxes over grates in alleyways. It was a modernized version of differentially housed but equally enslaved Afrikans of the field and house. Only now we willingly help to finance the fabricated distances others have manufactured between us to serve them. Today, outside the occasional miracle story of some European's "self-sacrificing" effort to "elevate the helpless" or the no longer popular victim blaming and/or ineffectual liberal ethnographies like Elliot Liebow's *Tally's Corner*[2] or Elijah Anderson's *A Place on the Corner*,[3] mentally middle class Afrikans remain largely unexposed to the average economically disadvantaged Afrikan's mind, a mind denied humanity from our fear and others' benign neglect.

In that place, another set of rules and prizes and politics dominate. You see it in the stories selected by the producers of the local, national and international news. You smell it in the smog of urban decay. Some of us even hear it in the names the occupants of these "urban plantations"[4] call it and themselves.

In these places music is different, too. The problem is much deeper than most adults have ever thought to imagine and belies the even greater truths of what happens to mentacidal Afrikans lost in the wake of white supremacy. The themes in so much of this music subliminally attack and help suppress the common historical, cultural and racial memory of youth who are Afrikan but don't know it. They rob them of the probability of discovering and acting on their natural spirit. The Afrikan drum is compromised by the European word. Whereas music once informed and elevated our spirit it now serves only to degrade any higher consciousness and arouse and titillate the biological and material. They have changed our music to vibrate at a sexual frequency, a frequency and beat that create a mental sexual frenzy. The children call it basement or underground rap. I would prefer to call it subconscious *base bass* – it uses bass to feed into the basest carnal appetites pushed through the lyrics. The arrogance of youth in this cultural wasteland makes them blind to the fact that the lyrics that they write, record and spin are a tool that controls them more than they control themselves.

From these so called "sub"cultural centers, the music hypnotically emanates outward to the rest of the world's youth, sponsored, regulated, produced and distributed by power brokers cast in the matrix of the European asili. For the children of Europeans looking to find and define themselves as individuals, this corrupted form of rap/hip hop offers them the possibility of vicariously attaining soul. It naturally feeds their quest for the momentary pleasures of dominance through excessive, controlling sex, violence, things and power. It also marks and satisfies their inherited need for validation through acceptance and elevation by others.

Lesser Rap/Hip Hop

There are many levels of rap/hip hop. But, at any level, what most children are really listening to, most adults do not have the slightest idea. Most adults, if they know at all, are only slightly familiar with the superficial, "clean" level. Even the rap/hip hop radio stations do not go much deeper than this. But there is a hypnotic, programming level our children are drawn into that is characteristic of the cuts that never visit the public airwaves. And, this is the rap/hip hop music we should all be concerned about because it sells the sexual exploitation and distrust of women (and men), excessive sex and sexual deviation, violence and hurting others, money and the things it buys, death and using others and relishing it. It is the virtual laboratory within which the limits of Maulana Karenga's "connections" are tested. These are the cuts that rule our children's walkmans, car stereos, clubs and rooms once the doors are closed. These are the messages that dominate their conversations, thoughts and visions of success. Most parents who think they know what their children listen to have never heard of popular, gold and platinum selling songs like Adina Howard's "Do you Wanna Ride?," R. Kelly's "Bump and Grind" and "The Greatest Sex," Mannie Fresh's "Snake," Bigtymers' "Hello,"Dog Pound's "Bomb Pussy," Cap Posse -three 6 m's "Ass and Titties," Eightball and MJG's "Pimp a Bitch College," Snoop Dogg's "Pay for the .p." and "Wuff," Kilo's "Take|a|Dush," Tupac's "Me and My Girlfriend," Master P's "Killer Pussy," "Freeck Hose" and "Wabble Wabble," P. Diddy (featuring Jennifer Lopez)'s "I Need a Girl," Freak Nasty's "Down Low," 112's "Peaches and Cream," Lil Wayne's "Kisha," Sisqo's "What These Bitches want from a Nigger" and "That Thong Thong Thong Thong," Tru's "Freak Hoes," Luke's "Me So Horny" and "Pop that Coochie," Ludacris' "What's Your Fantasy," "Fat Rabbit" and "She said, Keep it on the Hush," Trina featuring Ludacris' "Everything Gonna be Alright," Too Short and T.I.'s "Hotel," UGK's "Let Me See It," Kilo's "Nasty Dancer," Hot Boys's "I Need a Hot Girl," Nitorious B.F.G.'s "Nasty Boy," LL Cool J's "Doing It and Doing Wild" and "Fatty Girl,"Neptunes' "Lap Dance," Camaflauge's "Let's Be Fuck Friends," DMX's "Fucking All Day and Fucking All Night," Lil Kim's "Queen Bitch," "Someone to Fuck

You" and "Don't Want Dick 2-nite," Old Dirty Bastard's "Girls Ain't Shit but Hoes and Tricks," Dr. Dre's "Fuck Shit," La Chat's "Slob on My Cat," Three 6 Mafia's "Slob on My Knob," Tweet's "No Panties, No Drawers," Mystical's "Dick on Da Track" and "Bumpin'," Jim Crow's "Holla at a Playa," Nelly's "Hot in Heree," Ying Yang Twins' "I Yi Yi," D12's "Bitch Pimpin'," RL's "Got me a Model," Khia's "My Neck, My Back," Cee-Lo's "Closet Freak" and, to take a half step back in time, R. Kelly's "12 Play."[5] Misogynous lyrics promoting violence like "Hit their heads in the wall till you hear that cracking sound, drown in the tub, rub-a-dub dub" in Eightball and MJG's "Mr. Big" and sexual exploitation and perversion as in "I like them hot, the ones that don't tell me to stop, eat dick, swallow the cum and know how to pop" in the Hot Boyz "I Need a Hot Girl" define the mentality advocated by this depraved side of rap/hip hop. It is also more than worth noting that the extreme and filthy perversion of coprophilia (defecating on another person for sexual excitement) is advocated in an interlude on Notorious B.I.G.'s *Life after Death* CD.

Do not be naive. Do not bet on the innocence of ignorance. Your children have heard these and more. Not only has the music "progressed" in its perversions, but also the portion of it that is so corrupted has increased dramatically. It is so plentiful that it is all many of our children listen to.

It should also be made clear that homosexuality is among these perversions. And homosexuality, as a message in the music of westernized Afrikans goes back most openly to the 1970s. The Village People modeled this with songs like "Macho Man," "In the Navy" and "YMCA." The YMCA song was about the normal meeting and hiding place for homosexuals in the 1970s when they could find no other places to live. "In the Navy" is a glorification of a modern, all male utopia where a large collection of males desperate for sex could find comfort in confidential homosexuality with a variety of partners, and heterosexuality was suppressed because of a virtual absence of female possibilities. Sylvester and, even earlier, Little Richard helped stage this sexual confusion. Even the group Fundakelic made a homosexual friendly song on their *Standing of the Verge of Getting It On* album titled "Jimmy's Got a Little Bit of Bitch in Him." Today, it has been taken to the next level by performers like

Luther Vandross, Meshell Ndegéocello and a very heavily promoted The Gay Rapper.[6] Whether the sexual confusion of the actors (because musicians on the stage or public display are actors) is real or imagined, whether they are only claiming sexual perversions or actually participating in them, whether it is a reasonable assumption by their audience or their complete misinterpretation of an act, these individuals are seen as the cutting edge in gender bending and sexual abnormalities. They have accepted payment for advancing European sexual interests.

The collection of extreme heterosexual sex focused songs listed above is only a *very* small fraction of the degenerate music our children are barraged with day in and day out. It is continuous in its effect, a tune they cannot get out of their minds. This is what most often seeps into their minds, sometimes with, most times without our knowledge. The lyrics are not simply the poetic license of artists trying to find themselves in and express themselves through their art. They are the systematic and selective injection of the individualized immorality of a corrupted culture. They act on the symbolism imposed on their minds by a foreign and enemy culture. They are the voices of singers and rappers bought by the wish to be rich and famous at any cost.

It is not without direction or purpose. It is taking us somewhere Europeans want us to be. Parents don't know because they don't listen to what their children listen to and often cannot listen because they are not with them on the playground, in the schools, at their friends' houses or in their rooms. Through their own complicity, they are not welcome in these spaces. But all it takes is to listen to the words of those who are and have been the number one sellers on the charts.

To grasp the normalization of disrespect and insanity in their world, one need only imagine that special night in the lives of a young couple. They have a candlelight dinner at a romantic restaurant. They uneasily pick at their food knowing what must come of the conversation. The stealing of glances at each other at every available opportunity through the lit candle, and the occasional touching as they laugh at an inside joke, have made the conversation unnaturally long. Anyway, the meal that their minds were never on has gotten cold. And the wine bottle is almost empty. Time will no longer wait.

He gently takes her hand and kisses it as he reaches in his jacket pocket with the other pulling out that classic, black velvet box. Slowly he slides it toward her, their eyes never leaving each other's. He opens it to show her his best effort at a symbol of their potential forever. He leans forward as if to whisper. She does too. And then, lovingly and with the tenderness and passion only a man who has made a final life's decision could have, he asks, "Bitch, will you marry me." With a tear of joy softly falling down her face, she responds, "Yes, forever my nigga." Something is wrong, terribly wrong with the language of our love. Something is even more terribly wrong with the relationships that evolve out of men and women who interact with each other in "loving" relationships bound by this hateful and dehumanizing language. As if visionary, the group War sang, "A dog is a man's best friend. But a canine can't be mine."[7]

To further understand the depth of this involuntary insanity, one need only visualize an actual interview with the popular rapper Lil Wayne, with Tommy Hillfinger appropriately draping his primary source of manhood in red, white and blue undershorts, and modeling the disrespect for Afrikan womanhood characteristic of too many entertainment superstars, who nonchalantly answer the question of "Whut's the first thing you do after a show?" with "Fuck a ho, slang dick." The interview continues with, "What's Turk doin' right now?" "That's my nigga; he chillin'. Probably fuckin' a ho' or somethin'." This interview was taken from the March 2000 *The Source* magazine. But he is not unusual. His childish fascination with physical gratification reflects the wishes of many of our sons and daughters who are no where near any stage. Read your children's magazines. This is truly an attainable reality in their minds, which makes the day-to-day world that they must live in now a momentary prison that must be tolerated until they are noticed and escape into the rapture of the entertainment industry.

The number of rap/hip hop songs where oral sex and sodomy is promoted is unbelievable. All forms of media are involved in this promotion. Oral sex and sodomy are served up on the same plate as Range Rovers, Hummers, Ferraris, Escalades, mansions, crosses bigger than their faith in anything spiritual and 14 plus karat diamond earrings for males as qualities characteristic of those on the cutting edge of cool. Those not going that way are considered backward, old fashioned, limited, closed minded and out of touch with reality.

The mentality that accompanies these lyrics causes real social phenomena. Images of being rich, famous and sexually over-satiated are not just blown about in the wind without effect. Just as with us in our time, they cause our children to act out those scenes, to fantasize and imagine themselves starring in those roles. For as hidden from public view as the homeless urban underground has been, we do not see the explosion of street hustlers, children pimping each other and prostituting themselves in malls, schools and the street,[8] a practice peculiarly reminiscent of the training and occupations available to many impoverished and discarded females in Greek and Roman society.[9] Today, however, we find these pursuits glorified in the minds of Afrikan children. A number of the songs our children are plugged into reflect and advocate prostitution (and pimping) as a viable "occupation" for them at their age. Just listen to *Trina*'s "The Baddest Bitch."

The numbers for these street hustlers have significantly increased since the mid-1980s. In an anti-family, immoral society, it should come as no surprise that children perform 40 percent of all prostitution done in this country.[10] Estimates range from 125,000 to well over 600,000 children under 17 being involved in prostitution and/or pornography in this country alone.

The media that concentrate on them glorifies and encourages this self-destructive behavior. *The Source* magazine, rap/hip hop's number one selling magazine to our youth (which incidentally was started and remains owned by Europeans), is one long materialism-sex commercial. Pimping is a dominant theme running through every issue's articles and ads. Although the December 2000 issue is unique in featuring a female homosexual pimp who is mentacidal enough to turn out her own younger sister for profit, it deviates little from its normal male pimping theme. Porno queens, the latest news on the blending of pornography with hip hop and, as best stated verbatim from the contents page, "Some women just wanna *fuck*" and "bisexual freak sessions and some lively S&M," are just a few of the pressing issues of "hip-hop music, culture & politics" highlighted in vivid detail for the responsive eyes of an Afrikan youth who yearns to play in that other world. Two of the more telling articles and pictorials in *The Source* glorifying pimping and related issues include

Dan Frosch's "Paper in My Pocket"[11] and Soren Baker's "Project's Chick"[12] (a discussion of the pros and cons of "chickenheads," another derogatory term of the magnitude of "bitch" which has expanded beyond its original definition of simply a "dumb blond" to a "dumb" Afrikan female who freely and eagerly performs fellatio on whoever). It is also interesting to note that young male prostitutes are called "chickens." Also scan the ideas and images promoted on pages 115-135 in the July 2001 *XXL*. For there are many more. Virtually every issue caters to this priority.

Vibe and *XXL*, *The Source's* chief competitors, are no better, although *XXL* will occasionally try to infuse a smidgen of positivity. For a relatively recent sampling, see the "Bedtime Stories" in the February 2001 *Vibe* for pictures of explicit sexual and female homosexual connotation,[13] displays of women in the June 2001 *XXL*[14] and numerous short discussions and articles dedicated to the promotional explanation of pornography in both the *XXL* and *Vibe* of July 2002. Parents waiting in line at the friendly neighborhood grocery store while there children rummage through the magazines racked to get their attention should also be aware of the pages of porno phone lines, videos and partial photos crowded into the back of these magazines. Often, the advertisements throughout them are no better. For example, see the "The Eckō/Playboy" advertisement in the December 2001 *The Source*.[15] The question is not only do we know where our children are, but also do we know what they are reading.

For those who question these changes in *The Source* because they stopped reading it years ago, it is not what it used to be. But, then again, what it used to be also pushed the European sexual priority, but only within the constraints of that time's limits on public displays of perversion and immorality in our community. Because this culture has convinced us that individualism extends to the point where we do not even feel comfortable looking at what our children watch and read, they are being brainwashed right under our noses in our homes, schools and grocery store lines. While we run from books with titles like Akil's *From Niggas to Gods*, which our sons and daughters need to read, we turn a blind eye to the magazines that turn them into sex-crazed consumer zombies. If they are listening to us, what are we really telling them?

Adult Afrikans are subject to the same sexual bombardment, just presented in a more mature, conservative format. We have not addressed those widely circulated magazines catering to the general interests of the Afrikan community like *Essence, Ebony, Jet, EM* and *Emerge*, but they should also be recognized for their contribution to this madness. None warrant our discussion at this point except to ask the readers who would study them for intent if, given their older audience, any of them do not promote sexual extreme/confusion/perversion as normative. In one way or the other they all do. Of these, *Essence* is by far the most aggressive in promoting a new world unisexuality and uniraciality among its readers.

We must stop closing our eyes and shaking our heads, hoping that the sky will open up and save us and them. This insanity is how our children have found a way to distance themselves from the pain of being Afrikan in a European cultural wasteland. They have learned to blend truth with fantasy in order to feel safe and alive without the protection of conscious parents or Afrikan centered institutions. We must be brave and wise enough to see what this progress will bring in the immediate and far future since it has already covered this much ground in less than thirty years. This madness must be stopped.

An Evolving Musical Tradition

When we criticize our children and their music, we speak out of an ignorance of historical context. We are blaming them for something we passed on to them. This insanity invaded our community years before they were thought of. It is we adults and elders who did not stop the invasion. In fact, our contradiction becomes more evident with every step they take into this sex and violence driven insanity. First, we let our children be conditioned into associating sex with violence. And, then, we condemn them for associating sex with violence. Although often out of ignorance, we welcomed European priorities into our homes as our hits "progressed" from love ballads to ballads of love confused by sex to sex ballads. What our youth listen to is only the next step "up" from what we listened to.

The moral corruption began a long time ago, with our first encounter with Europeans. Through our time with them, they have systematically promoted only those things which would eventually bring all others in line with their way. When these things were not clearly visible because of, or the potential of, open hostility due to an unobstructed recognition of their intent by others, they were encapsulated in the messages that gradually made their imperatives acceptable because these messages made Europeans acceptable. This is the greatest testament to the evil genius of the European – conscious and directed forethought. They know what they are and are determined to make everyone else into that so that they will be made normal.

As with so many other things, the use of the term "bitch" in the music promoted into our communities is not new. If we are to honestly identify sources that point to cultural origins of misogyny, then the earliest use of "bitch" to describe women was used by the Greek Hesiod to characterize the mythical Pandora.[16] We should be reminded that Hesiod was not the first to see women as only worthy of physical, mental and sexual abuse. He was only the first to articulate the European mind through putting these common thoughts into poetic myth.[17] His use of the term "bitch" shows much of the hatred for women that had existed from the earliest of European times. "Bitch," along with "funk" (which generally served as a euphemism and codeword for fuck), began its short road to popularity on our airwaves in the early 1970s. What we hear today is only the next stage in degenerative musical progress. And these stages are epigenitic, meaning each stage builds on the one that preceded it and lays the foundation for the next one. Outside of a mind numbing profanity and the creative manipulation of old and new language, one cannot morally or ethically say anything about our children's music. Given the progress of European time, we can barely distinguish between messages given in much of Generation X's music and songs from "back in the day." It only takes a minute to recall artists and hits like Prince's "I Wanna Be Your Lover," "Uptown," "Head," and "International Lover," Vanity's "Nasty Girl," Ohio Players' "Skin Tight," Cameo's "Single Life" and "She's Strange," Funkadelic's "(Not Just) Knee Deep," Commodores' "Brickhouse," Rick James's

"Super Freak," Mary Jane Girls' "Candy Man," Barry White's "I'm Gonna Love You Just A Little More Baby" and "What Am I Gonna Do With You," Mtume's"Juicy Fruit," Grace Jones's "Pull Up To The Bumper" (of which Juvenile's "Back That Azz up" is a direct descendant), Donna Summer's "Love To Love You Baby," Sylvia's "Pillow Talk," Jean Knight's "Rocking Chair," Anita Ward's "Ring My Bell," Diana Ross' "Love Hangover," The Bar-Kays' "Sexomatic" and virtually every song by Millie Jackson. We, their consumers, cannot claim innocence.

So many artists from the Afrikan musical community have contributed to the progressive popularization of themes promoting others' sexual priorities in today's music that it is impossible to name them all. At the same time, no one can or should be singled out for blame. Even if that were possible or productive, the success of any individual is dependent on the support of their group, even if it is a success based on the use of them to exploit their group. So, who are we to now criticize Barry White? We bought it. We thoroughly enjoyed "The Maestro." Especially among a group with relatively little power over the media's presentation of reality, stardom for any individual from the group is determined by his/her ability to outperform others in advertising the reference group's thoughts and behaviors. Artists never rise above the power and interests of the owners of their promoters, producers and distributors.

Our children's, as well as our own, sexual excesses and perversions were introduced from outside of our community. Our reference group showed us the way as you do children, with "how to" books, posters and movies like "Deep Throat." Many of us remember the black light poster introduced to the community in the 1960s of twelve, fully illustrated, male-female positions of sexual intercourse according to zodiac sign. Pisces, represented by the number "69" and illustrated by a male and female performing oral sex on each other, brought the most attention. ("66" and "99" later became popular symbols for heterosexual and homosexual anal sex.) In this way, perversion was introduced through a poster on a grand scale. The curious among us studied them. The progressive minded experimented. And those truly devoted to becoming European practiced these perversions until they became part to them.

The manufacture of successive and increasingly more divisive "generation gaps" between Afrikan youth and adults modeling their relations after the European way has allowed this intergenerational transformation to go on virtually unnoticed. Even the concept of "teenager" must be viewed as an important and divisive European invention that places our children under another's spell. It makes Afrikan, especially Afrikan centered, parents the enemy bound to keep Afrikan "teenagers" from a justifiable fun. It leads them to pull away from us to the all-embracing European playground of illusionary and empty personal freedoms. Europeans have equated individualism with personal freedom. And many of us have bought it for ourselves and our children. "How strangely slow we are not to connect the disassociated behavior of our young with our own misplaced values and our own willingness to adopt white parenting models."[18]

Any assumptions our youth may have had about having personal freedoms of expression in the Western capitalist system were shattered by *Frontline*'s "The Merchants of Cool." Whether pro- or anti-status quo, the political and economic marketplaces are ruled by corporate guidelines of profit. The idea of a generation gap, that parents and their children cannot understand each other because they come from different times and ways, falls in line with the illusion of European progress. Each generation aspires to not be their parents and not make the same mistakes their parents made with them, as if perfect parenting within this cultural context were possible. Like children, they seek a life freer of punishment and discipline.

The idea of a generation gap also supports the notion that European children, now mimicked by other children, are models of progress and that this progress is correct. In this context, every generation must progress (distance itself) from those who produced it and reinvent reality. Western "heroes" take after this model, being individuals who defiantly go against social norms and win. Even when meaningless and without direction, relentless change is a progressive orientation in Western society. Difference is new. And new is assumed to be superior. Today, this has assisted them usher in a more individualized individualism. As for Afrikan youth, the generation gap forces the individual to move further and further from his/her community with each progressive generation in the misguided attempt to truly become a new world individual completely independent of any traditions grounded in their people's history.

[T]he adoption of mainstream values coupled with an intensifying materialism have spawned subtle changes in the cultural attitudes of many Black youth who, although they are still hampered by racism, now embrace the values of the larger community. The effects of these changed conditions are best observed in the diminishing ability of the Black community to determine the meanings to be attached to particular events. This is a new racism which, though less explicit, is as virulent as the old one.[19]

And, even though generation gap is much too mild of a term to describe the splitting of our community into two, and now three and four, distinct age-based worlds, it can be a beneficial way of looking at ourselves in light of others' political and commercial divide and conquer exploitation of our age differences. The gradual but quantum change in the explicitness of our music's sexual lyrics from Billie Holiday and Nat King Cole to The Platters and The Shirelles to The Dells and The Stylistics to Prince and Barry White to Trina, Olivia and Gansta Boo is too detrimental to be left unnoticed. It is an unbroken and externally directed progression from an implicit to explicit focus on sex in our music.

Isn't it time for us to take on an active and central role in its correction? What lies for our next generation in this natural progression of "music?" In their confusion, Afrikan youth have inadvertently become the next link in a progressive chain of degenerative commercial consumption. And confusion is a necessary prerequisite for voluntary psychological slavery. We, their parents and elders, have allowed it because we felt secure in trusting the European vision. We bought the lie that this music was confined to adult bedrooms while they fed it to our young on the streets like cheap heroin. It is we who initially sponsored it financially and reveled in the sex driven beat and lyrics that are a natural extension of this permissive, hedonistic culture. We reveled in our newfound, assimilation-fostering sexual freedoms. We have voluntarily and quite heavily contributed to the evolution of the compromise of Afrikan beats with European lyrics. We must recognize our mentacidal error and speak to the deepest truth, no matter how compelled our heads feel to nod to the corrupted beat.

Now, we are talking about our children and their music as if they are not ours, as if they are not us, as if they are disconnected from any pattern we fully contributed to and participated in, as if children raise themselves, as if we are innocent of financing and sanctioning what we have come to call "trash." Or, as a least offensive surrender to what we consider inevitable in our drive to be and have them integrated/assimilated into European culture, we reason that they are temporarily lost in the European style in search of themselves. In error, we assume they will somehow return to us. Stop blaming the children. They have followed suit and bettered their parents. And, that skill and determination are not new to this generation.

Do not confuse the intent of this statement. There is much excellent rap/hip hop music that the minds of our children would gladly welcome. I could not agree more with Marimba Ani and Kofi Addae's assessment that music is the driving force behind our warrior class but that its force has been handicapped by the European puppeteers of the entertainment industry. There are ample Afrikan centered life's lessons our children can take from listening to Public Enemy, X-Clan, A Tribe Called Quest, Arrested Development, Professor Griff, D'Knowledge, Kam, The Last Poets, Common, Poor Righteous Teachers, Brand Nubian, Mos Def, Dead Prez, Talib Kweli & Hi Tek, KRS-One and Black Star.[20] For obvious reasons, they represent only a small fraction of that which European controlled distribution companies are willing to sell to the public. Long ago they learned the importance of keeping the minds of the children of their enemies from being empowered through knowledge of self.

And while we continue to be distracted by conspicuous pronouncements about how European youth absolutely purchase more rap/hip hop music than our children (obviously in an imitative effort to show in their own special way that they accept us and/or are at least trying to achieve rhythm), few ask, at the cultural level, why European children are so intensely and naturally drawn to it. As to the point of the intensity and naturalness at which European youth are drawn to negative rap/hip hop, as previously stated, there is a given connection between the imperatives of a culture and the desires of those who are the natural children of those who created it. Much too much rap/hip hop music glorifies the European lifestyle. It should be noted that even fewer broadcasts report that while their children as a group buy more rap/hip hop music that there are many more of their children and they have much more disposable cash to waste than ours. Neither do these reports mention that a larger proportion of Afrikan youth than European youth make these purchases. Equally obvious is the fact that Afrikan youth are not returning the favor by trying to mimic an absence of rhythm.

To the credit of the Afrikan sons and daughters who continue to dominate the rap/hip hop scene, the positive and negative music of this world can be credited with an intolerance for the production of effeminate and gender confused Afrikan males. The war against the homosexualization and effeminization of Afrikan males has many able soldiers among our rap/hip hop generation. Regardless of the positivity or negativity found in their lyrics, Black Star, Brand Nubian, Common, DMX, Goodie Mob, Ice Cube, Poor Righteous Teachers, Public Enemy, Ras Kass and Snoop Doggy Dogg are but a few of those who make a point of taking a stand against our emasculation. This is not so among the few European rappers who exist. Even *Eminen*, the most vociferous among them, had to at least symbolically bend over for his homosexual brethren or lose his stardom. Witness this in his much touted, symbolic embrace with Elton John during the 2001 Grammy Awards. But the Afrikan struggle to expose this threat is still but a drop in the bucket because the European controlled, produced and distributed rap/hip hop industry still favors the promotion of Afrikan male genocide at each other's hands and penises.[21]

> When a force is used against the people who create it instead of in their interests, the enemy is successful. This is the essence of good military strategy; the neutralization of the antagonist's force and then the use of that force to immobilize, to destabilize its source. That is what we have allowed our enemies to do. They study our tastes, create products which will appeal to us, then profit from our consumption of these products, and use them to retard the development of our consciousness, to keep us asleep...Our spirit is, in this way, used against us; its use is corrupted...Think of the confusion and illness that would result from bizarre images in music stamped on the minds of our children. Their development becomes distorted as

they learn to associate melodies with unhealthy Anti-Afrikan behavior which to them becomes not only "normal," but pleasurable.[22]

As reflected in the sponsored music programming that reinforces and enhances the sexual relations originally forced on enslaved and colonized Afrikans, the sex game is as strong here as elsewhere and it feeds our moral decay. To see our children at play, all one need do is attend the Bike Fest at Myrtle Beach, SC, the Spring Break and beach parties at Virginia Beach, VA, Cape Cod, MA and virtually every other beach that Afrikan youth frequent or visit some of their videos from Freaknik in Atlanta, GA.

Sex was made our priority during our enslavement and the colonization and subjugation of our people under European culture. It is not a priority indigenous to the Afrikan continent or Afrikans. This mindless groping for satiation guides us directly into the European way. Because Yurugu was unable to fit into the world he found himself cast into, he had to create his own. European's greatest efforts are in creating a fantasy world that forces everybody else into their insanity. Most of our greatest heroes/idols today are not real. They are manufactured by Europeans. They are a creation of imaginations bent on creating a reality that does not, and cannot, exist because it is diametrically opposed to the will of the universe. Sex is one of the most important playgrounds in this fantasy world.

5. The Language of Love

> "Hey baby won't you be my bitch and I'll be your tree and you can pee on me."
>
> *70's Funk Lyric*

The word "bitch" has become as common on prime time family television as sex. Of course, in the tradition of blaming its victims, the European media points to its usage among young Afrikan males as the origin and primary source of misogyny. The implication being that Europeans are simply copying us. Like so many other political oversights, they, of course, conveniently forget about the unique verbal demeaning of women that they originally passed to others. They have never stopped using these terms in their private circles in the same way that they have never stopped calling us "niggers" behind our backs.[1]

Wench, slattern, hag, harlot, prostitute, jade, rig, tart, trollop, slut, bawd, hooker, hussy, tramp, virago, moll, hex, grisette, cow, sow, termagant, bag, spinster, vixen, piece (usually "of ass/tail"), punk, demirep, cyprian, broad, minx, crone, trick, floosy, nymph, amazon, hen, nympho, nymphet, easy, slag, quean, doxy, frump, sloven, harridan, shrew, loose, beldam, streetwalker, butch, battle-ax, whore, strumpet, adventuress, bat, trull, baggage, floozy, jezebel, skirt, drab and bitch are but some of the misogynous terms European males have historically used to label and abuse European and other women.[2] They were alone in this verbal assault until other men and women came to see them as their language reference group.

Labels given to females in Western culture have consistently been more derogatory than those taken by males. No matter the media attempt to glorify it, even "dog" does not carry the aggressive, spiteful negativity of "bitch." The general thinking is that dogs have absolutely no self-control where sex is concerned. The damage they leave in their wake is a byproduct of this lack of control. It is simply a matter of having to move on to new sexual partners. Bitches, on the other hand, are specifically out to do serious damage. They are defined as mean spirited.[3] What is so important for us Afrikan parents is that, even though our sons may say that calling one of their sisters a bitch is "funny" or "a game," so many of them truly do see women and girls as simply bitches, as female dogs, as something in a constant "heat" begging for sexual intercourse (to be sexually assaulted), and see nothing whatsoever wrong with this misperception. It is not, and they do not see it as, a term of endearment.

It will shock some of us that many of them, unlike us, have no problem calling their mother bitch. The open disrespect for all women, including their mothers, has come full circle in European history, even though this affront to motherhood is nothing sudden or new in a large number of their families today. Their denial, or rather omission, of this fact is only the propaganda of a people trying to delay truth until others have accepted this practice as common, further lending it and them the illusion of normalcy and not oddity. Afrikans aping Europeans give Europeans the license to blame us for being them. And, it is only a matter of time before our children follow suit.

Afrikans cannot follow European traditions and expect their children to be anything but European. You cannot spoil children beyond control and then expect respect from them. You cannot raise your children as others raise theirs and expect them not to act like theirs. And, the situation is greatly complicated in Afrikan families because of our subjection to white supremacist society. For, as Afrikan children, particularly boys, come to increasingly see that the spoilage that, especially their mothers, have bestowed on them has further set them up for failure in this society, we will see their unconditional respect for them wane. It is only a matter of time before the illogic that "every female on the planet is a bitch *except my mother*" wears thin. Afrikan motherhood was not designed to remain sacred in Western culture.

English is such a vulgar language. It easily gives voice to the perversions of mind and body. It effortlessly gives way to disrespect and emotional bloodletting. Language reflects the person's unique personality which is a direct outcome of their socialization within a particular cultural personality. "The language that the individual speaks, which is the product of a particular people, plays an important part in the constitution of the individual's mental disposition and attitudes."[4]

Historically, Europeans are a filthy people.[5] And their way of being naturally cultivated a filthy language. Again, language is an important indicator of a culture's mentality. And, as the above words originate in the European language family tree and are found in no other prior to the European's cultural invasion of the world, the origin and source of misogyny must be sought at this root.

In keeping with Western political science, soon a great debate will be generated to support a genetic basis for cursing. In many ways it already has. Tourette's Disorder is but one example of how Europeans are making truth out of their political genetic arguments. Unlike nonWesternized offspring, many European children are naturally copying the cursing they hear their parents, older siblings and neighbors use as their first language. Not surprisingly, however, European political scientists have found a way to define this as a disease. Their childhood cursing spasms have become scientifically diagnosed as beyond their control. Imagine the scientific interpretation if this were a phenomenon of Afrikan children. Imagine what would be defined as natural if lice were characteristic of only Afrikan children, instead of a European problem. But even their own science contradicts them. For, like the children Emperor Frederick II murdered in his failed attempt to see which language they would utter first,[6] today's specially diagnosed Tourette's toddlers would have had to have first heard foul language in order to repeat it. They weren't born knowing language, less known curse words.

And there is yet another, more important proof of the discrepancy in their scientific evidence that cursing is natural to humans. If traditional Afrikan society is the true test of what is normal for humans, then cursing is not. For you will find in any rural Afrikan area relatively untainted by European culture that the people do not curse. Our most important lesson here, however, is to remember that using someone else's language to label our family defines it for us through their eyes.[7]

But, specifically, what does cursing have to do with their sex imperative? It complements the vulgarization and perversion of sexual intercourse. It helps make sex a violent, filthy act that must be taken to its lowest possible animalistic level in order to be fully enjoyed. By tainting what would otherwise be a sacred act with a profane and verbal abuse, the aggressions Europeans have naturally built into them feel more normal. Sex, accompanied by cursive language, enhances the intensity of these acts for Europeans and those who follow their way. Cursing at females (and males for that matter) makes them less than human and, therefore, more deserving of the ill treatment accorded them during whatever sexual abuse males mete out to them.

Even so, Western science again insists on giving their moral image a unblemished diagnosis, a pattern we historically find with the drug, alcohol and sex addicts, kleptomaniacs and liars residing in their homes. They know that you cannot, in good conscience, criticize that which has been defined and agreed upon as being beyond the control of individuals and/or normal for humans.

Other "uncontrollable" physical and verbal emotional explosions also find shelter in scientific euro-babble.[8] They are compelled to continue to manufacture scientific definitions and classification systems which fit their sanity. It would be unnatural for them not to. If you believe you are superior (i.e., most correct) and that your way is in need of no change, then you must look at the world and find only those answers which fit your reality, no matter how insane or illogical those answers may be. Others who have been immersed in your insanity follow suit blindly. Europeans do not, and cannot, look at spoiling or the permissiveness that comes as part and parcel of socialization into extreme individualism as abnormal or part of a cultural sickness. But it is insane not to be able to control your children. And it is an even deeper insanity for us to seek the solution to our children's problems, which are the direct result of us mimicking the childrearing practices of those without direct control over their own children, from them.[9] Spoiling is taking the easy way out. It is for parents who do not want to take the time to work at raising their children into conscious and empowered adults.

Behavior Modification

It makes absolutely no difference whether one takes the Skinnerian perspective that human behavior is a voluntary (conscious) reaction to rewards and punishments[10] or assumes the correctness of involuntary (subconscious) responses as modeled by Pavlov's proverbial dogs who were trained to salivate at the sound of a bell, even in the absence of food,[11] as one's guide for understanding. The European life force invariably conditions its aboriginal family and their colored neophytes to seek out sex and sexual symbolism in anything and everything. Any ting, ping, ring, click, tap, snap, zip, pop, bang or beat automatically elicits sexual urges. Everything possible becomes a signal that it's time for sex. Even the science that shows that the erection that males often wake up with is simply their body telling them that their bladder is in need of emptying is ignored in this single-minded pursuit of the orgasm. When scientific answers are filtered through the European culture's sex imperative, every erection is the result of a authentic sexual urge. We have learned to live for sex, to wallow in it.

People have come to associate more and more symbols, e.g., things, ideas, people, words, with sex. This means we more and more frequently, if not continuously, think about sex. We have accepted this conditioning to the point where anytime anything is stated, jokingly, flirtingly or otherwise, instigated in movies or on the idiot box, anytime a woman is raped, a man sodomized, a child is fondled in the media, anything that involves sexual conquest, we become immediately aroused sexually because we have been conditioned to do so at the slightest indication of the possibility of sexual contact. This is a world where every touch, every word, every look is interpreted as a prelude to sex.

In living for it, we are willing to die for it. It is nothing to risk our marriages, our family stability, for another chance at a difference in it, for just a piece of it. We are even willing to sacrifice the highest offices of the church and state in pursuit of it.[12] "A whore, male or female, is incapable of the focused and discriminating commitment to companion and children that viable families require."[13]

The sexual revolution of the 1960's had as its primary target/agenda changing the sexual attitudes and behavior of women, not men.[14] It was about increasing the level of conditioning among women and heightening the orgiastic frenzy through their voluntary uninhibited submersion. The sexual revolution that started in the late 1980s, which is still going strong today, was focused not on men or women, but children. The end goal is to turn everyone, at every age, into individuals whose main priority is sex.

From the attention given the Sex Revolution it might appear that sex has not always been a cultural priority in European society. The history of Victorian Puritanism and other extremist religious and political movements that forced individuals to abstain from the *public* glorification of sexual license leaves some of us confused. These religious complexes would seem to undermine arguments that identify the sexual revolution as simply a bump in an otherwise normal sexually overindulgent cultural personality. But Western puritanical movements crusading a chaste fidelity, in and of themselves, speak to how drastic the measures were which had to be taken in order to temporarily alter an overwhelming sex drive in the first place. Puritanical movements rose out of sexually extreme conditions. Of course, culturally, there is nothing unusual here. Europeans are constantly on the move from one extreme of control or release to the other.

If nothing else, Europe's extreme anti-sex politico-religious movements were and are central to their strategy of disarming others. Separation of church and state at the cultural level is impossible. Controlling the global image of their animalistic sexual urges directly coincided with and accompanied their imperialistic spread outside Europe because they needed to be seen as pure and divine. They had to appear God-sent for those they proselytized. But their sexual behaviors clearly demonstrated their inhumanity to each other and their backwardness relative to the world, so they were hard-pressed to give a more civilized image to their cultural elders. The many crusades galvanized by the ruling Christian Church and Puritanistic social movements all mark their imperialistic expansionism.

Cultures are self-serving and self-preserving. Therefore, Europeans consciously act on their own behalf based on their awareness of outsider's opinions and beliefs. They systematically sought to conceal their perverted sexual imperative at home. However, obviously, their behavior did not change even when their public image did. Punishments for almost every crime imaginable, especially against women, were imposed in sexually perverse ways to hide their sexual perversions and priorities. The types of punishments handed out served to satisfy the sexually demented priorities of the European males executing/performing the punishments. Remember that in European culture pain, in and of itself, is associated with sexual pleasure.

With an ever greater degree of sexual satisfaction their sexual perversions and priorities were punitively unleashed abroad. Punishment was constantly used against others in the name of Europeanizing them, as incentives against others retaining their "barbaric" ways. In the homelands of other people, Europeans were free from the restraint of keeping their unblemished image intact by blaming the victim for making them act in such sexually perverted ways against them. This is the same excuse used when they blame capitalism for their dehumanization of Afrikans. It was not their fault. The "devil" or other people or things made them do it.

In the final analysis they would vent their sexual frustrations on others using the excuse that it was necessary to violently oppress them in order to enlighten the natives. They knew that they had to minimize the incompatible differences between them and their victims in the minds of the victims. So, an acute awareness of differences in sexual preferences and priorities between them and those whose homes they violated would have been enough, combined with other significant cultural differences, to serve as another mobilizing force among indigenous peoples against them. It would have made the European wars to destroy their spirit and them physically even more difficult.

Negative Population Growth

Be that as it may, several factors contribute to an understanding of the unbroken continuity of the extreme sexual priority in European culture that flourished independent of the natural human drive to reproduce. As clearly evident by their longstanding, chronic negative population growth (NPG) rate, Europeans have found numerous ways to circumvent and suppress the natural process of reproduction among themselves and, increasingly, among their culturally dependent nations. Simply put, negative population growth occurs when a people are not producing enough children to replace themselves [which must be distinguished from zero population growth (ZPG) which means that a population is reproducing itself only enough to maintain itself at a constant number]. Over time, this trend is reflected in a decline in their numbers, which is especially noticeable when they were previously producing enough offspring for population growth and/or when other populations they are compared with have continued to increase or produce more than what would be needed to simply replace the adults who produced them. Considering this, both zero and negative population growth scenarios present the potential threat of the permanent disappearance of these people. In the case of Europeans, social behaviors molded by the cultural forces rooted deep in their individualistic survival thrust are the causal factors, not the environment or disease or other external biological or physical forces. Abortion rates are one of the best indicators that sexual activity continues unabated regardless of reproduction rates. And there are at least three important statistics about abortions in this society generally and those among Europeans and Afrikans that should be mentioned here.

First, the number of abortions per 1,000 live births climbed from 180 in 1972 to 312 in 1976 to 359 in 1980 but since then has steadily declined from 354 in 1985 to 345 in 1990 to 335 in 1992 to 311 in 1995, holding steady, but giving an indication that the thrill of infanticide is gone, at about 314 in 1996. In sheer numbers though, there are over one million abortions in this country annually which cannot be understood outside of the fact that over half of all pregnancies are unintended.[15] Apparently, the racial annihilation scare tactic has effectively shifted European attitudes toward favoring childbirth, regardless of the perception of children as liabilities/burdens. For it is only among Europeans that we find any real decline in abortion rates. This awareness is also reflected in the fertility research and multiple birth craze. Numbers are needed to prevent the disappearance of the "white" race in the same way as they were/are needed to fight wars against nonEuropeans and continue to occupy stolen lands. We should not interpret their growing desire to have more babies as a newfound appreciation of life. They are simply sterile numbers that physically and politically translate into racial survival.

Second, the percent of all abortions that Europeans have had from 1972 to present has declined while that of Afrikans has increased. In fact, since 1990, the percent of abortions that Afrikans have had has risen to more than half of the percent of abortions that Europeans have. This is statistically meaningful for racial politics because, relatively speaking, Afrikans represent much less than half of the population. Therefore, based on the ideal relative proportions model which states that

> Ideally, whatever proportion a group represents of the general population should similarly be reflected in its share of all the good and bad of society. For example, since Afrikan people are over 12% of all voters, we ought to have 12 times the 1% of all elected officials we now do. And, that 56% of all state and federal male prisoners are Afrikan and 27% are European becomes even more alarming when we see that they respectively represent 6% and 32% of all people in this country. To preempt those insistent on pushing self-serving diversity arguments it should be noted that, even though each group in society has its own historical backgrounds and unique characteristics, differences should not be so great as to negate this proportionate share assumption.[16]

the percent of abortions Afrikans have should be just a little above one-third of what it currently is while the percent for Europeans is much less than their population proportion. And, third, the rate of decline in the percent of abortions married couples have has been matched year for year with an increase in the percent of abortions by unmarried women.

The cultural drive that has led to ZPG among European populations worldwide is consistent with the social needs of reproduction in selfish, individualistic societies, not with real or meaningful declines in sexual activity. In the past, in traditional European society, changes in attitudes about and/or the outcome of sexual intercourse for the population in general have conformed to the limitations of the environmental, resource and spacial constraints of the European continent. Europe is small. It was no secret that producing more people bent on consumption and waste than the environment could sustain would have eventually brought poverty to most if not all. Thomas R. Malthus' theories and Jonathan Swift's "A Modest Proposal" are just two revealing sources reflecting these people's general apprehension about overpopulation and resource scarcity. That apprehension has not been lost with time. Their global population policy is still based on the memory of being without, the belief that resources are limited and that others are their enemy in the fight over what resources remain. They retain in their genetic makeup a collective historical memory of the impoverishment brought by their life on the glaciers.[17] What economists call the zero sum mentality (where resources are limited, and an inborn greed naturally causes fighting between people over these finite resources and constant scarcity) rules the historical and contemporary enactment of the European cultural memory.

Xenophobia and fear of genetic annihilation have provided the groundwork for projecting their childbearing practices on the world in order to control the feared onslaught of the world's growing majority of colored citizens. Europeans currently represent less than 10 percent of the world's population and are expected to control no more than 3 percent by the seventh decade of this century. Calls for a forced sterilization of undesirable populations to improve and control the quality of human (i.e., European) stock still resound throughout the scientific and political community today. Propagandic and tactical modifications designed to suit the times have in no way interrupted the flow of race-based genocide.

As we learned about ourselves through studying the relocations of Afrikans through the work of Chancellor Williams and others, it is very instructive to look at the migratory patterns of Europeans. For while now they are crying about the "colored" population explosion, they have already had their population explosion. They erupted like a volcano across the planet in torrents from the fourteenth through the nineteenth centuries, devastating everything in their path, suffocating natural cultures with an artificial one. By expanding onto the lands of people they conveniently defined as unworthy of the space they were accused of wasting, they resolved their population problem. Their expansion into others' spaces was only temporarily arrested by the Great Depression.[18] Imperialistic

European expansion resulting from the beginning of their population explosion and the limited resource capabilities of that continent, combined with a extraordinary talent for creating and abusing weapons of death and destruction, began in the sixteenth century (really the fourteenth if we can overlook a few internal setbacks in the form of a series of plagues, perpetual war, political-religious doctrines). It lasted, with increasing numbers leaving Europe to settle, colonize, dominate and explode elsewhere, until the third decade of the twentieth European century. For example, between 1650 and 1850 Europe's population had a faster growth rate, at 63 percent, than that of any other continent. Their population explosion happened when there were places to go, or rather, places they could "discover" and claim as their own through invasion, places other people could be genocidally removed from or at least segregated to the most unfertile scraps of land.

Scarcity, Surplus and Population Explosions

Of their need to spread out of Europe, history speaks for itself. Of the change that this move brought to their homeland we must now speak. The solidification of global control through malevolent and malicious military conquest exported their internecine (internal) aggressions through three millennium of concentrated resource extraction.[19] The relative barbarity and poverty of Europe which had nourished its naturally aggressive violence was replaced by a massive infusion of expropriated resources and technology. This transfusion helped bring the aggressive violence between Europeans under control. The generally elevated socioeconomic status for all Europeans fostered a decline in the perceived urgency and desperation millennia of resource scarcity brought.

Simply put, the infusion of surplus resources into Europe changed its class structure. In elevating more of those otherwise unqualified to rise, it lowered the visibility of the violent, aggressive, primitive type of crime disproportionately found in that society. Violent crime gradually became replaced by property crime as people generally became more affluent (and technologically serviced). Affluence provided for the circulation of goods through theft or barter without preserving the violent social atmosphere. The illusion of humanity became real as they could increasingly displace and point out their inhumanity in others whose societies they had destroyed or reduced to a relative poverty infested with violent interactions. They were able to effectively turn their frustrations outward.

In seeking historical understanding, we must again remember two very important variables in this equation of a then real scarcity. Europe was having a population explosion during its imperialistic expansion and Europe is a small place. It was unable to sustain the wasteful habits of large numbers of people without importing goods. And they needed to control the source of their imports to permanently free themselves from a not to distant impoverishment. Their population explosion gave emphasis and rationale to their imperialistic, expansionistic drive. We must always bear in mind that European expansion stunted, and in many cases completely eliminated, the natural population growth rates in other places due to the systematic genocide (murder, sterilization, imprisonment, colonization, enslavement, kwk.) of other people. Today Japan, whose contemporary culture is based on the European model, has the same fears over the availability of resources. They practice the same aggressive imperialism of the European. They, too, extract resources of already deliberately underdeveloped nations to the point of depletion.

Europeans now complain about the normal birthrates in nonEuropean nations because of their acute awareness of the drop in their own population. Due to a selfish individualism that places the idea of family and community second to that of selfish, personal wants, their abnormally low birthrates have resulted in a devastating negative population growth rate. They have not been producing enough babies to replace themselves for the last forty plus years. And, this, accompanied by the realization that they are becoming a smaller and smaller global racial minority which disappears when amalgamated with others, has significantly increased their already chronic fear of racial annihilation.

Their reaction to other's birthrates comes with absolutely no concern or any selfless understanding that the population explosion that other peoples are now experiencing they already went through when there were places to invade and remove the indigenous inhabitants from. Most of these people have little choice except to circulate themselves around other satellite nations dependent on Western charity. They exist in a world that often appears as little more than disorder and turmoil. Their trust for each other and their traditions have been almost destroyed while a determined appreciation for Europeans and the European way has been instilled.

The globalization of disorder and turmoil can only be explained in terms of its psychopathological origins. A practical understanding will only come through facing up to the truth and depth of the infusion of a devastating zero sum cultural framework into the captured minds of Afrikans who continue to fulfill their function of harvesting their land's wealth for the European while destroying their own spiritual being.

Logically, the enforcement of chaste initiatives in European society should have declined if not disappeared, when the floodgates to the "new world" opened as a result of "discovered" surplus land and resources. With more space, food and things, they could have moved to promote having more and more babies to fill in the spaces they stole from indigenous peoples. But that policy did not change significantly. The extreme fear of want forged during their socialization on glaciers and the fully matured culture left in its wake still direct the Caucasian spirit of xenophobia, selfishness and infertility.

That antiquated, but real, fear molded from a necessarily aggressive survival in an openly hostile environment still compel individual Europeans to callously calculate the outcomes of their actions if the result were to be childbirth. Ideally, in a moral, family oriented society, this outcome would force individuals to hold themselves accountable to the offspring and that society. So a memory preserved in ice for every descending generation made it easy to implement social policies of abstinence from procreation. But it did nothing to lessen the occurrence of sex. For sex had produced heat and entertainment in the cold. Bearing that in mind, sex has not decreased. Procreation has.

Historically speaking, in European society, sex and reproduction are considered distinct. So the result of social trends advocating the need to curb the reproductive process do not affect the nonstop engagement in sex. The point to be made here is that the

West has done well at controlling reproduction, not sex. It has been good at concealing its sex imperative (as measured by the number of childbirths) but not controlling its sexual activity (as measured by the number of abortions and birth control products as well as sexual practices that do not lead to pregnancy). As a telling indicator of the rationalization of the sex-reproduction disconnect in the European mind, those considered least likely to engage in sexual intercourse, those who vowed fidelity to divinity, monks and nuns, were quite active participants.[20] In the remains of traditional society of 7th century Europe, scientists have found the bedrooms shared by these two groups of sworn abstainers at the center of underground tunnels leading from monasteries to nunneries and vice versa. Obviously, even Europe's most sacred institution succumbed to the sexual imperative.

> Many [monasteries] had drains of a sort, and often these were tunnels which served two or more buildings – hence the tunnels which, to the delight of the anti-clerical or romantically minded, seem to connect monasteries with near-by nunneries. Obviously access could be had from one to the other through the sewer, but it would have taken quite a lot of the amorous charm out of the situation.[21]

Of course, this infidelity, along with a clerical history of rampant pedophilia, among the supposedly most religiously pious is being used to support the theory of an uncontrollable, biological urge for sex. But all it really does is further expose the moral weakness of even Europe's most gifted celibates and, therefore, the cultural genetic basis of their sex imperative.

Unknown to most today, for centuries these literal dens of iniquity, their monasteries and nunneries, were places where priests and women of the church who had been publicly caught in homosexual or other perverse sexual acts were imprisoned as the sexually insane or incurable romantics. Many of Europe's sexually confused and deviant civilians were also imprisoned in monasteries and nunneries. One of the most famous sexual deviants to suffer this fate is Pierre Abulard. He was a French philosopher who eloped with his 17 year old student and sired a child with her. He was castrated and confined to a monastery. She was forced to become a nun. Incidentally, the rooms in monasteries were called cells. It may also come as a surprise that, in 17th century Europe, whorehouses were called nunneries.

Obviously, committing the criminally perverse to the watch and care of monks and nuns was a major contradiction in thinking. Because, of all places, it would make the least sense to send the accused to a monastery or nunnery if the goal was punishment or rehabilitation. These places were where homosexuality, pedophilia and just normal heterosexual sexual intercourse thrived. This hypocrisy did not bypass the church leadership who proselytized and forced a religious abstinence on others. And that remains so to date. So, it would be unreasonable to expect more from the religiously unrestrained commoner bent on carving some pleasure out of their painful existence. In fact, it was the religious extreme of sexual repression mandated by the European church that ran many of its congregation away. It has only been the loss of revenue that has forced it to alter its attitude toward the unremitting sexual imperative of its clients.

Of course, none of this is to say there were no voices other than those which advocated sexual "freedom" in the 1960's. But it does say much about a social movement which carried virtually everyone regardless of their disapproval. It is not a question of how many other dissenting voices were out there screaming in the wilderness of Western political culture. The point is of which voice dominated and continues to do so in spite of those other voices, and why.

Sex is indeed a drug, an opiate. So many of us could not even live for a day without it, without going into severe withdrawal.[22] In the tradition of European style progress, individuals are driven to experience orgasms or cease to exist as an emotional being. This constant need would drive anyone crazy. Yet insane activity, if possessed and unchallenged long enough, becomes normal. We are in the midst of a people who cannot stop obsessing. Excessive compulsion is their natural means toward progress.

There is never enough. One can never be satisfied. Even if you just had sex, when the next potential sexual act approaches or an offer is made, we must jump at the opportunity. Just like the hold of alcohol, drugs, food, money, TV and religion on some, sex is increasingly craved more, constantly more. If sex is your ultimate focus, then anybody and everybody becomes acceptable and desirable targets and the ultimate high.

Nuclear Nightmare

The forces of production also guided the Western family's linear movement toward obsolescence and the accompanying rise of unisexualization. A statistical history of declining birthrates in this society during the last half-century looks something like this. While remaining relatively constant for the previous fifty years, with the exception of the second European war on the world, the birth rate of children born per 1,000 people dropped from 25.0 in 1955 to 18.4 in 1970. In 1975 it was at a 20th Century low of 14.6. Despite, and including the "baby boom" years, no yearly rate since has surpassed the 1970 low. Here is where Western individuality can be seen at its most intimate and personal, if we only choose to look. Nothing stops the selfish gene. The European family has systematically progressed from its small community origins to its extended family to its nuclear family to the self-sufficient, encapsulated "I don't need anybody" individualism.[23] This process is as natural to them as the incredibly rapid climb in destructive technology from fists to knives to revolvers to automatics to bombs demonstrates. European culture quite clearly remains indifferent to humane needs beyond that of acquiring bodies.

Initially, nuclear and extended family forms served the decentralized cottage industries of agrarian and feudal society well. However, as material invention brought the development of more mechanized modes of production, concentrating and consolidating them and their human operators in factories away from rural communities, the extended family became an even greater hindrance. Extended families not only worked to the disadvantage of industry but also against the very people forming them. They all were bound by a legacy of real and imagined perpetual scarcity and extreme individualism. In fact, the extended family only survived because of the homesteading demands brought about in "discovering untamed frontiers in the new world" and a medical science promoting childbearing because it did not yet feel confident in its ability to "control" death. Again, extended family, the production of children, was not for love. It was purely for genetic survival.

Nonetheless, it is clear that a major factor pushing potential workers from an underdeveloped rural Europe to its capitalist based industrializing urban manufacturing centers was the absolute power of the Western patriarch who dominated his mates and offspring no matter their age or ability. These personal kingdoms where fathers exercised an absolute dictatorship over all others were discussed earlier in the book.

Now, the nuclear family has become expendable. It burdens the increasingly smaller number of globalized corporate structures which need workers relocated at their whim. With steadily declining worker power, these corporate entities feel no need to deal with family encumbrances. The demise in the application and enforcement of those aspects of industrialization which are important for humanely determining both family stability and occupational security are progress related indicators. The cyclical return and rationalization of orphanages, homeless children, massive impoverishment and the death of welfare (except for the privileged and politically organized), for those who in paying more for cheaper goods and services finance it,[24] signal the need of European society through its business elite to once again more tightly control the opportunities and perceptions of the labor pool and increase profits for the few.[25]

The explosion of baby and child care interests and products is unquestionably the direct outcome of the statistical realization of the impending extinction of the European population as a distinct racial identity globally. It is not the result of any love of children. As previously stated, that Europeans are experiencing negative population growth, where they are not reproducing enough to replace themselves, is not new or news to their community.[26] The whitening process, especially in Latin America, and particularly in nations with heavy Afrikan concentrations like Brazil and Argentina and throughout the world of color, is indicative of this fear.[27] Europeans now represent much less than ten percent of the world's population they claim. And, using the best estimates, this will decline to three percent before we are three quarters of a century into this new millennium. As a supremacist culture, their fears, not their love of life or family, compel them to increase their own and move to reduce the population of peoples of color. In some ways the oppressed come to know their oppressors better than themselves. So, it is meaningful that Afrikans have always realized that "white women have a hard time giving birth. They don't like it."[28] You have to imagine the fear of a people who believe both that they have been the only ones blessed with the natural ability to elevate mankind and that touching any other people can erase them. Their record in working toward the removal of other populations is clear.[29] The explosive force behind increasing their numbers continues unabated, gaining more momentum with each new day.

In traditional Afrikan society, children are the priority. This priority is evident in how people marry families not individuals. That is not to say that individuals do not live as husband and wife. It is to say that the priority is extending and strengthening the extended communal structure that is family. It is even more appropriate to say that families marry families. Children are central to this process/arrangement because they are the basis of family. Men and women come together as a married couple in order to procreate to extend the family outward and from the past into the future. Children are the wealth that are the family's primary source of self-esteem in the group.

This Afrikan priority stands in direct conflict with contemporary moves to curb birthrates among Afrikan populations on the Continent and its Diaspora. When left on their own, populations grow exponentially. That is, they increase by multiplication, not addition, because parents tend to have more children than are required to simply replace themselves. But the Western initiatives promoted for people of color focus on genocide through birth control,[30] incarceration and success (only when childless) while fertility for genetic survival is heavily emphasized in European society. Over the years, Afrikans have increasingly become the targets of more sophisticated and unsafe birth control technologies. Sisters are now assaulted with everything from five year time release patches placed under the skin for disadvantaged to monthly contraceptive injections for sisters attending historically Afrikan colleges and universities. What is most interesting about the latter solution is that the advertisements are primarily directed at the male students and located where they are most likely to encounter them. Such strategic moves help the irresponsible among them apply pressure on females to remain solely responsible for preventing pregnancy with scientific backing.

Do you really believe all the research, promotions and development in baby/child seat equipped cars and vans, new fangled baby strollers and carriers, walkers, bottles, diapers, the baby fairs, "Baby Depots" and "Baby's Rooms," cover photos and glorification of pregnant European women's stomachs, the scientific discoveries of early pregnancy tests, fertility drugs, sex aids, a sudden return to breast-feeding and natural childbirth, test tube babies (the first, named Lucille Brown, was born in 1978 in London [31]), in vitro fertilization, legislation on renting ones body to gestate another's child (surrogate mothers), male impotence therapy and drugs, male and female sexual enhancement drugs (like "Viagra" and "HerTurn"), penile implants and splints, concern over women's biological time clocks, the television shows, magazines and newspapers where every European imaginable is "celebrating" their pregnancy, company sponsored childcare and maternity rights on the job has anything to do with Afrikans? The saddest part for Europeans easily deceived by this is that the main extrafamilial force keeping their birth rates low is still blocking their dreams of population superiority. "Mounting evidence shows companies are not adopting changes widely touted as key to helping workers balance work and life."[32] One major reason for this is that "employees are reluctant to demand more in an age of frequent layoffs."[33] The saddest part for Afrikans so easily deceived into believing that this is "our" agenda is that "[they] are caught in the discussion and [they're] not even relevant to the discussion."[34]

If memory serves me correctly, according to European cultural propagandic stereotyping, Afrikan women have never had a problem having children. They are still the butt of jokes about promiscuity and infidelity, no matter the excuses of Afrikan males trying to rationalize their desperate search for nonAfrikan females that European girls "give it up" more easily.[35] To the best of my knowledge, the media have never portrayed baby making as an Afrikan problem, and especially as one needing incentives. So, who is the target audience for this ongoing media blitz? Europeans are.

Survival of the Fittest

Once the population problem is resolved in their favor, the door will be open for Europeans to take male-female relations to the next level. Understanding the internecine nature of European culture, the argument could be made that unisexuality is the compromise of women attempting to destroy men and men attempting to destroy women. This movement has been guided and facilitated by waxing and waning cycles of male-female political power in the West where the drive to destroy each other remains constant. In Western realism it is possible to destroy one sex and still survive. The science of artificial reproduction – sperm banks, egg banks, a desire for male impregnation, kwk. – openly speaks to this. Survival of the human species through natural reproduction has never been a problem. The historical pattern attached to their survival of the fittest philosophy, with them of course being the fittest, applies here no differently. The difference is only a matter of level. In their eyes, now that the problem of who among humans will survive, it is time to finally and forevermore determine which sex will. The basic antagonism and hatred Western men hold for their women and vice versa is viciously written throughout their history. The compatibility today remains based on sexual satisfaction. Once that "problem" is alleviated, they will no longer need each other. The burden of compromise will be lifted. It is down to the great race to see which sex will survive.

> The mode of determining structure of the western world view is that of power, control and destruction. Realities are split into pairs of opposing parts. Conventionally, one of these becomes valued, while its converse is understood as lacking value. One is "good" and the other is "bad." It then becomes necessary (valued behavior) to attempt to destroy one (the "bad"), while the other ascends to supremacy.[36]

The struggle for absolute survival and dominance, given the availability of all of life's necessities, lends itself to the removal of all nonessential entities, human and otherwise. The battle among Western sexes is, like all other forms of human interaction in the

West, one of extreme competition – a fight to the death. The only logical, peaceful compromise that will insure the survival of both groups is the unisexualization of both into one. Only gender "synthesis" enables compromise. negroes seeking to survive in this chaos use this same logic to advocate for the total absorption of Afrikans into Europeans through amalgamation. negroes validate our mentacide.

Whatever gender or sexual insanity Europeans place before our eyes confuses our subconscious into accepting excessive and distorted definitions of gender and sexuality. Whether consciously or not, under the guidance of their cultural aggressions, we follow their cultural lead. They, of course, remain true to their own cultural heritage. In order to create a permanent balance between a persistent feminism and a sexist, patriarchical culture, every effort was, and continues to be, made to unisexualize every aspect of life. In order for men to keep their power and women exercise power of equal force, they must be made to appear the same. So, everything from clothes to shoes to purses and pocketbooks to jewelry to hairstyles and head wraps to cologne/perfume to eyeglasses to makeup, kwk., takes on a unisexual role. Everything becomes "designed for a man or a woman." This asexuality includes many of their names, which have a history of unisexual application. Names like Artemis, Francis, Chris, Pat, Sam, Sandy, Randy, Andy/ie, Nicky/i, Ricky/i, Tony/i, Terry/i, Jimi, Johnny/ie, Morgan, Carrol, Tracy/i, Marion/an, Courtney, Adrian, Stacy, Bobbie/y, Tommy/ie, Lynn, Alex, Jamie, Abbey/y, Dana, Dale, Jan, Jean, Robin and Seven have been given to male and female alike.

6. The Games People Play

"It takes a fool to learn that love don't love nobody."

The Spinners

In order to expand and thrive as the dominant consumer market on its "global plantation," Western culture must keep all individuals under its sway in a state of childishness. In addition to drugs, media and money, people must see sex as a primary defining characteristic, as one of their most important reasons for being. They must constantly seek to engage in sexual play. Play is the center of a child's world, whether that child be one or a hundred years of age. And, children are very impressionable and easily excitable. Maturing in such a world, adults, like little children, remain immature in their relationships with other adults because they have learned to look at everything as a game. They know no other way than to selfishly seek out physical gratification and to deal with each other on a manipulative basis in order to gain the greatest rewards with the least effort. Adult games, whether expressly sexual in content or simply limited to the over 21 market, are designed to make physically mature individuals comfortable with their uncontrolled drive to seek pleasurable physical stimulation, and the often deceptive manipulation of others to that end. It allows grown children to see themselves as adults. This chapter is a discussion of some of those games and the ways they are played out.

Tremendous Trifles

There is a sociological concept called "tremendous trifles" which helps conceptualize the chronic weaknesses that plague primary interpersonal relationships in Western culture. It helps us see through the distracting logic proposed by a confusion creating science where incompatible sexual appetites and other personal problems are blamed for the difficulties males and females in intimate relationships experience. By example, tremendous trifles would be defined as difficulties between intimates created over nothing. One partner, whose pet peeve is finding the cap off of the toothpaste finds it off for the third time in a month. In a rage he says that he cannot take it anymore, has had enough of her disorder and is leaving to find someone who understands his wants and needs. Beyond the fact that other issues are probably really at the core of the dispute, they separate over what, to the average observer, would appear to be nothing more serious than a breach of one's habit by the other. But when individuals are raised on selfishness, and struggle with another into higher levels of relationship is not part of their social training, any problem can easily escalate to a terminal situation.

Europeans are a people with no patience. Their life is the hunt for instant gratification. Except when violence or the threat of it checks them, they spend their days and nights searching for new and unique conquests because they are driven to continuously experience difference. Change, to them, is the primary indicator that they are alive. Because of this shortcoming, individuals involved in interpersonal relationships who have been socialized in the Western way go on these fault finding missions against their "partners," which mask their own often subconscious true drive to constantly embrace change (boredom avoidance) and an inability to handle the most simple things which could call their fragile individualism into question. The common denominator for virtually all such problems is a socialized selfish individualism.

In this selfish, materialistic culture, things are your primary symbols. This is no less so for those who are lost in love. In such a cultural environment, it is no wonder that things have evolved as the primary method of keeping peace between the sexes. Love, as every other state of mind, is best expressed through things. It is true that it is the thought behind what you give that is important, as long as what you present gives your lover cause to be impressed with its monetary value. Things have become love. In this mental/cultural context, the size of the diamond has become the definitive measure of a man's love for a woman. Yet, we would be foolish not to see that relationships based on materials are only held together by the material. This is one essential key to understanding the exceptionally high divorce rates in this society. More than fifty percent of all divorces are over money or some other problem directly related to the personal and/or family economics.

Over and over we hear that "diamonds are a girl's best friend." There is a reason as powerful for that saying in European culture as the European maxim that "dogs are a man's best friend."[1] Quantity overrides quality, materially and otherwise. The quality of a relationship is based on quantitative measurements. And, that simple fact, which recognizes the intricate tie of cultural imperatives to individual thought and behavior, makes it possible to understand the flawed thinking where sexual satisfaction is a measurement of a sex organs' length, width or depth.

> And while we recognize that anything fitting European cultural imperatives can easily become "fact" in their think tanks and talk shows and evening news, even their science finds no correlation whatsoever between the overall physical size (height and/or weight or hand or foot size) of the participants in sexual intercourse and their physical fit, satisfaction, or anything else for that matter. No credible evidence exists relating penis size with vagina fit and/or satisfaction. Absolutely none.[2]

Even though the seemingly attention/sex starved participants on talk sideshows would have us believe otherwise, studies and common sense show that no accurate or mature measure of manhood can be found in the length of his penis.[3] The same truth applies to women. Womanhood cannot be meaningfully gauged by the depth or breadth of her vagina.[4] Tallies of sexual encounters are equally sorry indicators of one's human potential.

The trends that speak to the progression of singlehood are phenomenal. Young people have come to adopt more detrimental partner arrangements because they see that the long-term relationship practices of their parents do not work. They do this without historical awareness of why. We must also remember that dysfunctional families and divorce were the norm among the gods and goddesses of Olympia which modeled thought and behavior for mortal Greeks who served as the model of their European children. Zeus and Hera, king and queen of these ancient deities, had the worst marital record of that family. And, yet, Hera served as the deity ruling over marital relationships.

Without a working knowledge of the probable outcome, young couples elect to cohabitate without obligation.

> In 1970 there were 533,000 couples who cohabitated without being married. And remember that people who live together before marriage have a higher divorce rate than those who do not. In 1993, there were over 3,000,000 couples (a 600 percent increase).

"Renewable marriages," where marital contracts are renegotiated or dissolved after about three years and what are called "starter," "practice" or "trial" marriages, where the connection is for less than five years and no children are produced, are unproven arrangements that sit somewhere between "shacking up" and marriage as a Western solution to this problem. What has been proven, is that these temporary couplings are rapidly increasing in popularity among today's youngest marriageable cohort.[5]

What youth see all around them naturally gives them the impression that their options are limited. A culture negating self-control combined with laws enabling easy instant divorce (another European practice that goes back to their traditional societies[6]) has kept divorce rates in Western society inordinately high. And, as every other social pattern in culture that is inevitably passed down through the generations because of asilic forces, there is a continuity of high rates of divorce among Europeans. Greece's dismal record on divorce and remarriage from the fourth and fifth centuries B.C.E. place their male-female antagonisms in historical context.[7]

Divorce has increased as women, dominated by men who believed that they knew everything including the role of women, became politically organized to understand that they could survive independent of the physical and mental abuse of these men. Divorce rose not only as a result of economic problems associated with the uncontrolled conspicuous consumption of wants turned needs (as would be indicated by money being by far the preeminent reason for divorce). And it rose more than just from an increasingly more independent thinking, politically organized adult female constituency's exertion of influence over politicians. It rose and continues to rise as the result of those reasons as well as Western women flaunting the same selfish, self-centered hedonistic "I know everything," "I must always have my way" attitude Western men have historically exhibited. Incompatibility was inevitable. There is a reason Afrikan ancestors passed down the wisdom that complements (Western opposites) attract, that no one person can contain all knowledge, that men and women were intentionally made different. Difference was not created so that one sex could dominate the other.

Because we often forget the universal nature of male/female complementarity, our scholars must constantly remind us that stable nurturing and lasting relationships are abnormal in the psychopathic racial cultural personality, the individualistic state bred by European culture. They are imaginary and without substance. It is the facade, the illusion, the image of stability and mutual love that is most important to a wholly political culture. It is the fabrication of a deliberate and calculating cultural mindset. And, in the attempt to appear normal, they try to write their behavior as everybody's. This initiative is found in the assumption that spouses naturally cheat on each other simply because they have excessive infidelity rates. Those thoughts and behaviors which they apparently cannot stop or control in themselves they have declared normal in their excess. Unlike the mind of the traditional Afrikan, the European has always sought to blame his thoughts and behavior on forces beyond his control.[8] Bobby E. Wright naturally included this glaring problem with the stability and longevity of nurturing relationships among Europeans as one in a collection of the qualities characteristic of *The Psychopathic Racial Personality*.

The psychopath is usually sexually inadequate with a very

limited capacity to form close interpersonal relationships. The European's sexual inadequacy psychologically explains why there is a constant projection toward Blacks as being super sexual beings and as having no sexual inhibitions. Yet, it is the Europeans who "streak," "mate swap," participate in orgies, etc. All of their sexual behavior is a desperate attempt on their part to achieve meaningful relationships which constantly, due to their psychopathic make-up eludes them. Whites' sexual dysfunction has produced tragic consequences in the Black community. They have attempted to achieve sexual gratification by such methods as raping Black women with the rationale being that Black women were oversexed and invited their attention. Black men were castrated with the explanation being that their "animal passions" had to be contained...The sustained sexual atrocities committed against the Black race by the White race has no parallel in history and there is no scientific explanation except under the rubric of psychopathology.[9]

In contrast to universal laws of complementarity, European culture creates a social atmosphere where women can justifiably say, "I don't need a man," and men can effortlessly respond with, "I don't need a woman." It creates an environment where extreme individualism drives individuals to claim expertise in all areas so sharing is not a necessary option for male and female adults. When females can fully provide for (and protect as well as men) themselves and males can "safely" with tender sensitivity raise children from conception, neither will need each other.

Divorce rates used to be higher for Europeans than Afrikans. That is no longer the case.[10] Along with living in a racist, white supremacist society, the change can directly be correlated with Afrikan "progress" and our ability to more closely approximate or, rather, ape the European interpersonal reality. As we have moved farther away from our culture and the traditions it fostered, we ignore evidence of those traditions. Just as there was no word for orphan, "step" family members, kwk., in tradition Afrikan society, as indicated by the fact that there were no words for them (and every people label their social, cultural and spiritual activities), "[t]here was no word in the Africans' languages that meant divorce."[11] As we more completely divest ourselves of Afrikan conceptions of love, and embrace theirs, we surpass their negatives in the same way that women are now "outdoing" men.

However, the higher rate at which Afrikan couples find themselves in divorce court leaves some of us bewildered as to why this would be the case.[12] Afrikans' divorce rate has stood at double that of Europeans for at least the last four decades.[13] Marriage statistics tell all.

> Only 36.3 percent of Black women are married, according to the U.S. Census Bureau, and only 41.4 percent of Black men. Compare that to 57.4 percent of White women who are married – and 60.2 percent of White men.[14]

Further, only one in four Afrikan women can expect to find a mate/get married in their lifetime. The statistic is nine out of ten for European women.[15]

The problem is that we cannot see how Afrikan's special relationship to racist oppression creates more substantial stress and strife on "loving" relationships among subordinate group members. Many of our scholars point out that the problems within intimate Afrikan male/female relationships, which we disparagingly point out in contrast to those among couples in other groups, are in no way unusual. The proportions of these problems for Afrikan male/female couples have, however, reached such a disruptive level in our community that, if not corrected, they will be our ruin. As the ancients understood, "The ruin of a nation begins in the homes of its people." Nations come to be destroyed from within.

> Finally, it is of equal importance to realize that any criticism of Black male/female relationships is at the same time and in equal measure a criticism of U.S. society which has shaped them to fit and function "properly" in it. For social conditions create both social consciousness and social conduct and failure to recognize this can lead one to see racial defects where social ones are more real and relevant....It is this final contention that serves as a key point of departure for any serious analysis of Black male/female relationships. For to say we are products of

our social conditions is to say the same thing about our relationships. Analyses of the major defects in Black male/female relationships clearly reveal their social rather than genetic or purely personal basis. Thus, to understand the negatives of our relationships we must understand the negative characteristics of society which have shaped them.[16]

Even so, the point of bringing up the generally disproportionate divorce rates in European society is not to say that, historically, males and females in intimate interpersonal relationships in other cultures did not have disputes that developed to the point where settlement required the counsel of and/or resolution by an agency outside the married couple. In fact, traditional Afrika had an elaborate justice system to handle such unpleasantness in all areas of interpersonal relationships. It, as grounded in the universe of Ma'at,[17] was the basis, the example, upon which morals and good speech and conduct were written, explicated and taught. The books of Ptah-Hotep, Ani, Kheti and Khun-Anup, as well as the *Book of Coming Forth by Day*, which guides the justice administered by a higher court, are primary examples of these decisive moral codes and institutions among our ancestors.

The point to be made here is that mutual and violent antagonisms between spouses was not a way of life among our ancestors as it is for Europeans. Humans quarrel. Disagreement is in the nature of intelligent relationships. The question is of the degree to which these disagreements escalate, dominate and are institutionalized into intimate, interpersonal relationships.

Deceit

A people's myth defines their tradition. Even though social practices come into being before myth, because myth requires a conscious, intelligent interpretation of one's environment as well as the possession of language, myth explains social practices by locating them in a supernatural origin and order. Both the supernatural origin and order, however, are identified and defined by the words of the individuals who speak for their people.

> Every self-conscious nation, race, or people will identify that creator as a paramount idealization of that people's concept of themselves. If they conceive of their ideal selves as characterized by truth, justice, propriety, harmony, balance, reciprocity and order; their self-reflective creator will manifest the same. If they should conceive of themselves as being in competition and conflict with the given natural order, as destined to reconfigure that order, and then dominate that transformed order, then their creator will manifest the same unifocal and vengeful character.[18]

European myth is located in the personalities and experiences of the gods and goddesses of ancient Greece and Rome. Only because they were the last of the two standing, the names of the Roman gods and goddesses are the ones most remembered. They are the ones whose names Europeans have attached to the planets, their companies and other things they hold in highest esteem. They are the ones who still give sense to their world.

The traditions that myth explains are practical. They evolve out of as well as update the myth that tell a people who they are and explain why they are how they are. Myth as a creation of the worldview out of which tradition evolved does not die even when a people is in public denial of their traditions because of the need to promote a seemingly directionless progress. European creation myths see evil, vengeful and unforgiving deities as the source of universal law and view "man" as naturally and necessarily sinful because he is no better.[19]

As Afrikans, we must see inside a mind that is so fragile and afraid of others that it imagines monsters that kill just to kill, and believes that others must be made to participate in this insanity. Many of us now believe in and are afraid of their monsters. These imaginary monsters make it possible and necessary to create, follow and aspire to be tyrants to secure a semblance of personal freedom and joy. Afrikans must look into the mind driven to produce this "horror of reality." For, out of its asilic roots, it has created a whole culture within a social climate of fear and power and death and, in natural reaction, the individual drive for excess and power over all things in order to achieve a momentarily fulfilling sensational happiness before all is gone.

These are their personal monsters. They are intimate with these beasts. But this insanity is not the product of a set of psychotic or insanely genius or mad scientists created or creating within a vacuum. As a people, together, they are the "genius" playing with a cultural imagination and dream of reality. The dream is to live in a world like Beowulf or Madd Max. The dream is to be them, to be bombarded with sensation, to finally feel alive. It is a mind that has created the devil and wishes that power for itself.

Social trends are the most effective and meaningful way of recognizing and gauging the permanency of behaviors that myth has produced. Infidelity is one of these social trends reflecting "competition and conflict" that forms a rich tradition in European culture and society. As measured in European myth, infidelity is a normal and inevitable original sin.[20] The highest of the European gods, Zeus, stands as the prime example. He had affairs and/or children with a number of goddesses and mortal women. They include Leda, Io, Aegina, Callisto, Alcmene, Semele, Danaë and Leto. Students of Greek mythology estimate that during his reign of womanizing Zeus fathered more than 45 children.

Zeus is also known for his bestiality, symbolic or otherwise, when he would use his power to transform himself into an animal when he wanted to have sexual intercourse with humans or other animals. No matter the form he took, he was still Zeus. Therefore, he committed acts of bestiality. We find these acts and mentalities among none of the ancient Afrikan deity. Among the lesser gods, goddesses and humans of Greek myth infidelity and perversion were also quite common. Phaedra was madly in lust with her stepson, Thyestes with his brother's wife, Pelop with Princess Hippodamia, Queen Clytemnestra with an unnamed lover, Hercules with numerous males, Oedipus with his mother and poor Pygmalion with a sculpture. Aphrodite worked hard to earn her name as the goddess of love through multiple immoral and perverse relationships. But Zeus was the original womanizer. And, as myth, Zeus is every European male. As the European man-made god, he is the creation of their mind as it reflects itself. He is their heart and soul. Roman myth was an extension of Greek myth and, accordingly, the characters followed suit.

Today's trends among the mortal European population continue to reflect this historical absence of any conception of natural boundary and an absolute lack of self-control where morality is concerned. In 1991, the percent of all people admitting to having an affair while married was 14.6. In 1998 it was 16.5 percent.[21] But even though these surveys are designed to keep the respondents nameless, clearly, many people remain very unlikely to admit to something as personal and telling of their character as an extramarital affair. Because of the social and economic ramifications, many married individuals are more likely to report a criminal act, that is acts outside of the crime of adultery, than of having an sexual encounter with someone outside of their spouse. Moreover, upper class (where European history tells us we would expect to find more infidelity because of resources, access and propensity) and lower class individuals are much less likely than middle class individuals to respond to surveys. This aversion toward giving out personal information also disproportionately applies to professionals and persons with higher education, individuals who are better able to conceal their illegal sexual activities.

Nonetheless, regardless of the flaws and undercounts in reporting, general trends in extramarital sex are quite interesting.

> "When it comes to cheating on your spouse, women are catching up to men," says Judith Slater, Ph.D., a clinical psychologist practicing in Buffalo, New York. 'One reason may be that with the majority of women in the work force, they have more contact with men and therefore more opportunity to engage in extramarital affairs.'[22]

In a society geared toward the equalization of power, i.e., the ability of males and females to exploit the baser desires to the fullest possible extent, women have been as eager to jump on the bandwagon of men's bad habits in the areas of sex and marital infidelity as they have been in those practices that more rapidly produce diseased states such as alcoholism, drug addiction and cancers.

Not surprisingly, as with virtually every other negative in

European culture, music generates much of the interest in illicit sexual affairs. It is the medium through which ideas are transferred and embedded in our minds through catchy lyrics. Even when we are not consciously paying attention to the background music, the lyrics continue to pull us along the European way long after the music stops playing.   And like the negatives generated through European produced, promoted and distributed music, there is an unmistakable history of songs glamorizing infidelity in westernized Afrikan music. Through the years we have been lulled into immoral thought by The Manhattans - "Kiss and Say Goodbye," Atlantic Starr - "Secret Lovers," Joe Tex - "Who's Making Love to Your Ol' Lady While You're Out Making Love?" Mtume - "You, Me and He," Billy Paul - "Me and Mrs. Jones" (one of the biggest selling "love" affair songs of all time), Whitney Houston - "Saving All My Love for You," The Soul Children - "I'll understand," Luther Ingram - "(If Loving You Is Wrong) In Don't Want To Be Right," Dexter Wansel - "Holdin' On," and Johnnie Taylor - "Somebody's Gettin' It."

Our children have not missed the boat. Songs with themes of infidelity and deceit have exploded on the scene in the last decade. Most of our sons and daughters are familiar with the lyrics of Carl Thomas - "I Wish," Master P - "That Nigga Got A Bitch I Like," Jay-Z and Foxy Brown - "Bonnie and Clyde," Ja-Rule - "The Freakiest Things That We Do," Shaggy - "It Wasn't Me," Eight Ball - "My Boyfriend's Girlfriend," Jermaine Dupri - "Jazzy Ass Hoes," Ludacris and Timberland - "That Rabbit," Memphis Bleek - "Bounce Bitch" and "Is That Your Chick," No Question - "Want It All," Three 6 Mafia - "Let Me Hit It From The Back With No Kinds Of Strings Attached, What You Think About That" Joe - "Stutter" and Master P and Mia X - "Ghetto Relationship."

This ongoing rash of affairs is the inevitable result of the belief that the rush of adrenaline that accompanies contact (visual, olfactory or physical) with a member of the other sex is driving one's sexual desire. It is first assumed that the individual is correctly interpreting these biological functions. What follows is the belief that the biological force is beyond a man's or woman's ability to practice self-control. In this society, an individual's "given" ability in interpret these social stimulants correctly is seriously manipulated by Western culture. Those in doubt must remember that a significant number of

Europeans even see pain as a natural sexual prompt. Many others in that family seek out their sexual stimuli from a variety of members of the plant and animal kingdoms, as well as from material things. As with Pavlov's dogs, the lack of self-control and the misinterpretation of sex as love is the conditioned response. For individuals socialized in this culture of personal irresponsibility, to deny any and every sexual interest or "invitation" is unnatural and inhuman. And, again, the animalistic interest and invitation are interpreted as love. So every time you experience these physical signs and submit to them (whether you are intimately involved with someone else or not psychologically), you are correct to give in to these urges because to not do so would be self-repressing. You may have missed your one final chance at true love. To not be allowed to do so due to some moral obligation would, according to the logic of the Western/westernized mind, be an infringement on your natural self-expression.

The Meat Market

The "meat market" approach to mate selection is as faulty as the "cash" approach. They are really one in the same. Both make for relationships built on quicksand.   Just as reckless eyeballing, separation and divorce result when economic resources wane or the romance and/or sex is no longer exciting for one or both members in those relationships built on "cash" or "flesh" connections, when the outer beauty of bodies on display fades so too does the attention. Moreover, there are obvious limits to how much can be displayed before nothing is hidden. Seeking to attract sexual partners through the seductive charm of revealing more and more flesh is no longer reserved for street corners.   It is in the schools, malls, homes, churches, kwk. Who in the audience is not familiar with the nipples of virtually every known and aspiring female actress? Is this really the expression of sexual freedom by women or a commercial offering specifically designed to sexually tease/excite male viewers? Even so, blind criticism at the individual, personal level would be unfair. Extremely seductive dressing has not gone beyond reason, at least not European reason. It is culturally guided for oppressor and mentacidal alike. That many of Afrikans are buying the thongs advertised for our little girls speaks to how a majority of us have fell for this reason. That some of our youngest daughters have sought out this and other sex-focused fashions in petite women's departments, even before they were targeted by the media, speaks to their inheritance of an intergenerational cultural insanity.

The extremes we now see expressly fit the intense nature of the competition of those immersed in the sex imperative. When the mental and spiritual are lacking, the physical is overemphasized. And when no more questions exist about someone's financial or physical assets, westernized individuals are driven to find even more ways to measure. When all other competitive avenues are covered, it comes down to who can sexually perform the best.

Multiple tactics have been implemented to visibly seduce potential partners. Again, image is everything. When it's a guessing game because all else is constant, individuals must find ways to out advertise each other. They must make themselves appear to be more sexually capable or accomplished than the others in their pool. What they use to attract must also inform.

Tattoos have become one in the collection of symbols used to inform potential partners of one's sexual preferences and potential for excitement. It's no big secret. People have tattoos and other brands placed exactly where they want others' eyes to fall. Males overwhelmingly have their arms, biceps mostly, branded. Females prefer showcasing wherever men are known to shop for sexual arousement, their thighs, buttocks, calves, ankles, breasts and cleavage, lower backs, back of shoulders and lower stomachs. Although, these standards are changing and females are coming to gape at males in places where they are usually lustfully scrutinized. Many women, now, have become preoccupied with men's buttocks and pride themselves in being "crotch watchers." Accessories ranging from titanium covered teeth to pubic wigs (called "merkins") help accentuate this display of epidermal art.

Another example of this hunt for tactics that project sexually enticing images is plastic and/or cosmetic surgery. In spite of the health threats, "the number of breast implants among teens has risen 89 percent in the last six years."[23] Along with the over 75,000 surgical breast augmentations performed annually, breast enhancement and enlargement products such as creams and "bloussant" pills, and falsies, "push up" and "wonder" bras, have found an eager and desperate clientele among women and girls who want to increase their competitive edge in the meat market. In the year 2000 alone, over 17,000 had elective plastic surgery performed on themselves. Less than half of that 75,000 women have the size of their breasts surgically reduced which, assuming similarity in size after operation of reduced and enhanced breasts, still leaves an increase in the size of some 40,000 women and girls. Surgical breast lifts add inches to another 1,000 bustlines.

Howard Hughes is known for having invented the bra to enhance Jane Russell's cleavage. Remember that European females like Mae West, Marilyn Monroe, Raquel Welch, Zsa Zsa Gabor, Barbara Streisand, Barbara Eden, Pamela Anderson, Linda Carter, Bernadette Peters, Dolly Parton and Bo Derek, as well as the many like them who became overnight sensations because of their breasts, were called "sex symbols." They did no more or less than symbolize sex. Seeing someone as "sexy" carries the same connotation. And, bear in mind, that the European mind makes a subtle distinction between being sexy and being good looking, although one can be both. Seeing someone as sexy simply means that individual is someone who you want to have sex with based upon their appearance. Yet, and usually because of knowing this, many females specifically seek out this kind of degrading attention. Not a week goes by without sexually born again females flaunting their newfound breasts down the runways of the new breed of gawk shows. Obviously, they know what works. Their self-esteem, as limited and misdirected as it is by their sex imperative, is affirmed through the applause of boys.

It is a game of sexual overemphasis. Any body part that is or can be construed to conduct sexual energy and appeal has to be made larger, more visible. The overly conspicuous display of flesh at any cost is designed to gain control of the presentation of individual sexual imagery. The body becomes more than just a natural art form to be admired and respected by members of the complementary sex. It becomes a material instrument corrupted in service of the single-minded pursuit of sex.

Self-Test

Is this an exaggeration or just my imagination? Am I stretching the power this game has over the brothers? Let's follow Cheikh Anta Diop's example and adhere to the rigors of objective science. Try an experiment. Stop looking. Stop lusting. Stop coveting for 24 hours, just one day. Whether you are on the street, in front of the idiot box, at the movies, the park, in the grocery store, the library or church, stop your brain from watering over the sounds, smells and appearances of women. Stop your eyes from even going in that direction. For the next 24 hours, one day out of 365, stop planning your next sexual "conquest." See if you have a semblance of self-control in this matter. This is increasingly becoming an "experiment" that sisters need to try, too.

If, through this self-evaluation, you come to realize the depth of your lack of self-control, and the living potency of culture over individual restraint, and you really want to do something that will give you some breathing time while you mend your mind, visualize an Ankh, the Afrikan symbol for family and intergender respect, every time you feel compelled, drawn, forced to "chase the cat."[24] Do not misunderstand. The problem is not seeing. That is the eye's purpose. The problem is with the subconscious (often conscious), incessant surveying for prey. The problem is with a needful visual hunt. The problem is with what we do with the thought of what we see.

Natural Born Liars

It is the cultural nature of Europeans to live in a fantasy world. Natural reality, like nature, scares them, dulls the hyper-anxiety they have grown accustomed to. That is why the practice of sexual covetousness is so important to them. Lying facilitates this process.

Lying is essential to the acquisition of money, sex and any other commodity in Western culture. The cause of so much failure in male/female relationships can be found in the simple acts of lying to each other. Although not new, the mushrooming business in private investigative background checks before and undercover surveillances during relationships is a telltale sign of lying's pervasiveness.

There exists a general/overall deception in interpersonal relationships. Image, or rather having an ongoing control over others' impression of you, is the overriding priority in primary as well as secondary relationships between individuals. Lying is fundamental to all personal relationships, be they between classmates, business associates, family members, neighbors, friends, kwk., in a society where an urgent sense of antagonistic, zero-sum competition pervades all aspects of life.

However, individuals cannot be singled out to blame for these hedonistic, self-serving, highly individualistic behaviors. As is the culture, so is the individual. And, more often than not, truth is irrelevant in Western culture.[25] It fluctuates from day to day. Lying is considered a viable means to an end. Lying facilitates power by manipulating information. And it is the end which justifies any means to achieve it. The extent to which conquest and control are an important measure of an individual's self worth is a culture specific phenomenon. And, as such, they are socialized into the personality of the individuals raised in those cultures where these imperatives dominate.

That truth is political for Europeans is absolutely attested to by the historical consistency in their *rhetorical ethic*. This is what Marimba Ani exposes and defines as their shameless, systematic, historical use of lies (false words) against others. These lies are intentionally designed to destroy others (true intent) through using their belief in the humanity of all humans to manipulate them into believing that Europeans are not trying to destroy them.

It is the politics of morality, not universal morality, which rules. And in the Western cultural context, morality is purely political. Because of a deep history of immorality in Western society, there is an abhorrence of any identification or definition of that which should or should not universally be considered as morally correct. Hence, those driven to extremes in sexual perversion, attack any person, organization, thing, society and culture that promotes a moral order. Extreme individualism removes the possibility of a moral base, especially in Western culture, because anything that produces a profit or physical pleasure is morally correct.

Regardless of the truth of an individual's statement, convincing others of its truth is what is most important. Skill at manipulating others' minds is the ultimate priority. Truth itself is irrelevant. It is set by the winner. So rules are meant to be broken. And because winning is everything, and deception the easiest and surest way to winning in Western society, there can be no moral rules except those arbitrarily given by the winner. It is the master of the lie who wins. For a lie is only a lie when one is caught. As the pathologically lying character George of *Seinfeld* convinces his audience, "It's not a lie if you believe it." And as further evidence of this fact, regardless of profession, excellent liars seeking public acclaim tend to have the largest followings and coffers.

If nothing else, the pervasiveness and magnitude of lying among Europeans and their followers are demonstrated, as with all of its other related peculiarities, by the intensive efforts to make its excess among them appear normal for all humans. Lying is "proven" by their academicians as a genetic and uncontrollable urge individuals feel compelled to engage in. Divine evidence of its innateness is even shown by its classification as another of their original sins by the church. And original sins are proclaimed to be characteristic of all humans. So, even if we say that way is not ours, according to the Western church, we are lying and are aware of it. This imperialistic mentality is reflected in the rhetorical ethic commonly utilized by natural born liars in their dealings with others who are naturally seen as mental inferiors who must be manipulated as children in order to be optimally exploited and kept powerless. Their intelligence and glorification are shown in their ability to manipulate others into doing their work for them and in having these others accept that their lies were indeed the harder work.[26] Using children as the analogy,

> The European is a spoiled child caught up in a lie, a grand lie, built upon a foundation of lies that has required innumerable lies to corroborate. In fact, this brat is entangled in the mother of all lies. His lie is the compilation of generations of impacted lies. There are so many lies, in fact, that it would require a new beginning to clear the original lie. And, even then, the memory would, and should, continue to taint new beginnings until truth tellers prevail. This collection of lies are bound to each

other to the point where truth is indistinguishable from lie. And that becomes the purpose for the lies as the child seeks to survive in the world of lies it has created. With so many lies on the table, and more issued daily, it becomes nearly impossible to tell truth even when the child admits it, for that truth is usually a means of sustaining other lies that insure his privilege. The child is also quite aware that, for those who are not deceived by his lies, to admit that even one lie is a lie is to initiate the dreaded process of unraveling all the others. The spoiled child is caught, alone and afraid, trying to garner allies of true believers willing to be friends if he will continue to let them play with his toys.[27]

As stated, this clandestine way of relating to each other is quite unlike anything found in traditional Afrika where the social and cultural "Order" of Ma'at promotes and rewards truth.

In African tradition, speech, deriving its creative and operative power from the sacred, is in direct relation with the maintenance or the rupture of harmony in man and the world about him. That is why most traditional oral societies consider lying as an actual moral leprosy. In traditional Africa the man who breaks his word kills his civil, religious and occult person. He cuts himself off from himself and from society. Better for him to die than to go on living, both for himself and for his family...When a man thinks one thing and says another he cuts himself off from himself. He breaks the sacred unity, the reflection of cosmic unity, creating discord in and around him.[28]

Of course, in a society where individuals only form it because it is an umbrella protecting their rights to selfishly pursue their individual rights at the expense of social order, there is no regret in being cut off from that or any other society.

7. Boys to Boys

"You can't think easily if your life is a social thing."

Ivan Van Sertima

Western society intentionally raises us into childhood. We are socialized to remain permanently children. We seek a life of play, no matter the sophistication or cost or risk of the toys. That's why the highest level, outside of being a superpredator in violence or business, that boys aspire to is that of a playboy or player or some derivative thereof, and girls want to be romanced forever.

Western science's move away from their misconception of children as simply short adults was not only a function of an evolution in purely scientific thought. It was also driven by the need to move even farther away from the conclusions that would logically come from that assumption that might agree with the Afrikan circular understanding of spirit. In the Afrikan understanding, the child is the adult. The child is part of the ongoing cycle of life from physical birth to adulthood to physical death and a return to pure spirit followed again by physical birth and on and on and on. Children bring the wisdom and mission of the ancestors into the physical plane. So, in that sense, they are born as adults who, through the guidance of community, have to responsibly mature into this world/reality.

However, the point of all of this is not to underscore another basic Afrikan-European difference in the interpretation of reality. It is to make a completely different contrast. In terms of the level of maturity, self-control, vision, kwk., the reverse of what was said about children according to Western psychologists applies to adults. Adults reared on a strict diet of Western culture *are* simply children who have gotten taller.

If we note the difference between Western (and Westernized) and majority cultures in the ages at which the roles and responsibilities of adulthood are assumed, the depth to which immaturity is misdefined and glorified in European society becomes obvious. Childhood is clearly a permanent condition in Western society. They, and those of us who play the game along with them, wish to have their cake and eat it too. Any mature form of commitment except those which have the capacity to produce cash money are outright rejected or approached with extreme trepidation. Fear of marriage, "flying"(standing on our own two feet), revolution, kwk., are rampant in the little minds that animate Western society.

Sex *is* play in the West. And, children love to play. In fact, this claim is pretty much validated by the Western media's presentation of the overly excessive practice of sex in European society as little more than an interactive game. And like the selfish, self-involved child who wrests power from others by threatening to not be their friend if they don't play the game his way, Afrikan "children" as adults want to be allowed to play in the European kid's sandbox, too.

There is much more evidence driving the argument that Europeans are willing to do anything including dying to stay forever young. Note their problems with aging and trying to control nature (i.e., what is natural).

We have now reached the point of absolutely blaming raging, uncontrollable hormones for the youth's sexual license. Again, others' immorality is the European's disease. Again, this has no historical basis in fact. The rage of hormones is restrained or unleashed by the social will. It is the choice, the will, of the group. What has happened is that this individualistic culture will not allow forces external to the individual to create the internalized guidelines to modulate a productive expression of youth's natural hormonal development. It promotes an uncontrolled, aggressive venting of those biopsychological changes. It naturally promotes the natural expression of the European way. Social regulation is absent outside that of the media which reaps extreme profits from its deregulation and manipulation.

Consequently, it was easy to draw us into the 1960s and 1990s sexual revolutions. Three specific reasons stand out. First, we were oppressed in every way and assumed the European sexual way to be a part of an overdue freedom. Second, we wanted to be Europeans and our children wanted to "find themselves" in European ways as we had taught them to aspire to be Europeans. And, third, we had been bred to value our sexual prowess, which during our enslavement was all many of us had beside our backs/muscles.

Men and Boys and Women and Girls

Women have been taught to think of themselves as girls and men as boys in a world where they must act as adults. And the resultant confusion often leads to misdefinition and misinterpretation of each other. This is why the clothes that women (and increasingly men) wear creates and feeds discord between the sexes in the Afrikan community. An incident involving one of my former female students at "Freaknik" a few years ago exemplifies this dilemma. A sister who wore a cut off T-shirt barely concealing the bottom of her breasts and "daisy duke" style shorts out to the activities felt she was wrongly hassled by a group of males. In righteous indignation she stated that she should be free to wear what she wants without being disrespected. My response to her was yes, you should be free to wear what you want whenever you want and wherever you want to wear it. But you must bear in mind that this is a society where the conspicuous display of human flesh has meaning. It is actually and imaginarily bought and sold in a 24 hour meat market. So, what you wear is not neutral. It is culturally connected to visions of exploitation and conquest. Clothes send signals. Clothes have become flags signaling the possibility of sex. They are intentionally designed and worn to do so. Especially in well established societies with stable cultural cores, what you wear becomes a very sophisticated way of communicating who you are and what you're about.

I also told her that she must realize that there is a distinct difference between men and boys in the Western cultural context. In it, boys have no self-control. Neither do girls. So, if you act like a girl around boys, they will act with the level of immaturity and lack of internal guidance that should be expected of boys. The mistake would be in assuming you are dealing with men. A *woman*, of course, recognizes that even when she appears and behaves as a woman, boys will still act like boys. She refuses to corrupt the potential men in these boys by acting beneath herself because she is keenly aware of the Afrikan woman's role in the development of powerful, self-respecting Afrikan men. She knows that "a man's mind is elevated to the status of the women he associates with."[1]

That well worn adage, "boys will be boys," holds true. The priority in life for boys is still play, no matter their age, income, educational level or job. The same applies for girls.

8. Fair Game

Expansionism is the projection and imposition of the
cultural ego onto the world...It is the expression of
arrogance, greed, and an obsession to consume all that is
distinguished from self...In European ideology the cultural
other is like the land – territory or space into which
Europeans expand themselves. The cultural other is there
for Europeans to define, to "make over"...it is their role to
impart definition to the world. People of other cultural
traditions and "persuasions" are part of the world to be
defined; it is a European world.

Marimba Ani

The Western sex game was designed to make anybody and
everybody a target. The goal is to make people into whores, walking
slot machines which are readily open to unrestricted violation and
unobstructed access, clear of moral obstructions to any new- (or old)
fangled sexual violation, denuded, laid bare, receptive and exposed to
the sexual whim of others, naked without protection or places to hide,
within easy reach, easily available and accessible, unimpeded,
prostrate, breached and spread eagle. Western men, women and their
victims become any given combination of walking vaginas, penises,
fellating, anilingusing and cunnilingusing mouthpieces, anuses and
givers and receivers of torture.

All of the sexual confusions nonEuropeans imitate help feed,
justify and normalize European sexual perversions. When people
have no practical and functionally operating model of their traditions
operating around them to follow, they mimic whatever is available
and advertised as correct, no matter how self-destructive, corrupt

and/or abnormal it may be to humanity. Unless taught to do otherwise, Afrikans brought up in European culture imitate Europeans. Just as family structure, economic relations, religious doctrine, the educational system, political arrangements and military preparedness and operations have all been molded to fit the European asili's imperatives, those wishing acceptance in the European global world order must modify their sexual appetites and practices to fit Yurugu's norm. Those hypnotically drawn toward inclusion are compelled to adapt and adopt the reality of others. In other words, the more willing Afrikans are to participate in the European's perversions, the more willing Europeans are to (pretend to) accept Afrikans.

So the seemingly random changes in the number and type of sexual practices, partners and encounters are not arbitrary. All of these sexual and mating confusions contribute to the end result of making any and everybody a legitimate target for European sexual conquest and exploitation. We say European because this process has been initiated by them and on their behalf. Every person dying to be let in the gates of privilege adds to the layers of clothing that shields European sexual anomalies against any rigorous, unemotional critical study and analysis. Everyone forming the crowd outside the inner circle is an imitant, a virtual practitioner, a vicarious participant in a mentality that they are driven toward but can never attain because they don't have the cultural genetic heart. And, because European culture teaches others that they, alone, are the sole creators and determiners of their every thought and behavior, except those conveniently defined as natural, they must actively and zealously defend their European way.

Just as Europeans do not now and never will have rhythm, Afrikans do not now and never will have the real subconscious drive to kill or destroy or exploit for no reason. We will always fall behind in the race to deliver the most unwarranted and perverted "death, destruction and domination." But by disconnecting ourselves from our culture we can be made to believe that what we are doing is really us. The outsiders that make up the bulk of this multicultural crowd of aspirants to the European sexual way stand as monuments to confusion. Because of our unquestioning dedication to another's sex imperative, they/we are left unable to see the trees for the forest. It is becoming increasingly more difficult to distinguish Europeans from their cultural clones. Like in some abstract artwork where one thing is a part of one or more others to the point where the two or more things appear both separate and indistinguishable at the same time, the real perverts become hidden in the crowd. The more imitative people there are in the crowd, the better Europeans become concealed. If everybody becomes part of this crowd, or at least everybody is presented as being so in popular media, then the real operators become indistinguishable from everybody else. Once they make their way everybody's way they become indistinguishable from the crowd. Only the patient, keen and knowing eye can tell the wolf from the sheep.

This process is fundamental to mentacide. First, you remove people's cultural moral grounding, sympathetically offering them salvation through the gift of your immoral one to replace the cultural vacuum every living human will seek out when dispossessed of culture, and then make your immorality natural to them. Without a correct cultural grounding, reality and fantasy become confused. The Afrikan comes to see European culture as his/her way. Successfully acculturated/assimilated Afrikans become a defensive camouflage for Europeans who remain busy about the business of pursuing their unnatural and unique perversions, no matter how universalized they become through the contagion of Western culture.

> Though the appearance of this non-Afrikan commenced a period of violence and barbarism on a scale unmatched in known human history, this being – Yurugu – is in fact an opportunistic, parasitic entity. Like a marauding viral disease, it senses the internal weaknesses and self-compromised defenses of a possible host. It then infiltrates, neutralizes the host's defenses, camouflages and multiplies itself, and finally overwhelms the host in a feeding frenzy. In its greedy, blinded engorgement, it eventually exhausts itself. A weakened host galvanizes heretofore unrecognized resources and mounts a renewed offensive that facilitates its own recovery and expulsion of the disease. It is not enough, however, to merely arrest or contain the disease. It must be expelled. [1]

THE SEX IMPERATIVE

Manifest Sexual Destiny

There was no limit to the sexual exploitation of enslaved Afrikans by European males (or females). There were few things to stop them. So it is illogical to assume that they would have. If anything, they would have taken their perversions to even greater extremes. Moreover, the "mulatto thesis" provided scientific reasoning as to why their acts of rape were necessary evils required to fulfill the divine responsibility of their manifest destiny. It proposed that any European genes/blood added to an Afrikan through sexual reproduction improved the quality of the Afrikan line. This was supposed to be made visible through a lightening of the Afrikans skin color. If not in word then deed, this misconception is still common among many Europeans and Afrikans alike.[2]

Speaking racially (with reference to everybody being fair game and the need to cloud their sexual agenda by drawing as many others as possible into their perversions), the unnaturally induced sex drive among people of color is a vehicle for global whitening. This whitening is already a process well into development as long evident in places like Brazil and this country and is gaining momentum in places like Azania and most other sub-Saharan Afrikan nations. It is no secret except from those whose denial forces them to cry out that their physical mutilations are only cosmetic. The waves of interracial interbreeding are again producing a pastel, multicultural raceless "race" for the express purpose of protecting a pale core. Only this time, the global nature of European imperialism has required the melding of Europeans with every possible racial and ethnic group in order to fully buffer itself from the unprivileged hordes.[3]

We must think clearly. If the pious chastity of the publicly enforced Protestant "ethic" was unable to stop their rampant and wanton sexual exploitation, then why would anyone believe that the privacy of a personal kingdom could have? If anything, slavery would have exacerbated the prevalence of such perversions on a captive audience. Because there is no yet discovered written record, what would make us blind enough to believe that pedophilic and homosexual behavior stopped at slavery's door? If anything, it would have literally been a smorgasbord of sexual perversion for Europeans.

Homosexuals (whether heterosexually married or not) and

pedophiles (adults who exercise their perversions on children, whether they be adult males who prey on boys, adult males who prey on girls, adult females who prey on girls or adult females who prey on boys) have never disappeared from the European social landscape. They did not remain in Europe as Europeans invaded the world. They were the Europeans who invaded the world. Homosexuality and pedophilia spread along with European imperialism, as a natural expression of the unbound aggression of missionaries, traders, diplomats, and military personnel who already embraced that sexual persuasion. It was not limited to a particular group of the invaded countries or kept away from certain continents being overrun by the European hordes.   During our enslavement in this society, homosexuals were as much present with the "liberal" North as the "conservative" South.   The difficulties of travel and battle did not keep them confined to the comfort of European lovers or imported "specials." They spread across this planet along with every other face of European tyranny. They too sought out new victims.

9. A Tradition of Purpose in Order

"We must look at the psychopathology of everyday life
and must recognize we cannot have it both ways. We
cannot talk about a people who have enslaved us, who
discriminate against us, who insult us, who do all manner
of other things against us, and then use them as models of
normality...And yet, these people are held up as normal,
and are used as the standard against which we measure
ourselves as a people, and are used as models for us to
determine the way we wish our children to behave."

Amos N. Wilson

    Traditional does not mean archaic, outdated, outmoded,
primitive, backward, useless. In the case of the Afrikan, however, it
unequivocally means nonEuropean. Tradition symbolizes that which
has come to work. It speaks to what has come to work successfully
for a people through extensive intergenerational trial and error and
communion with the universe. This means tens of thousands of years
of deep thought among Afrikan people. Only that which is tried and
true stands the cultural test of time.
    Knowing this, we must remove this notion of traditional as
out of step with reality. We must stop this equation of civilization as
advancing with European progress. We must stop our equation of
our europeanization with Afrikan victory. For, "[w]e are following
a people who do not know where they are going."[1] This is the world
we have been reduced to, not the one we consciously made.
    In the cultural wasteland we struggle in we must remember
this. We must see that this reality has very few traditions worthy of
our respect and/or imitation, except those that rise out of the

struggles of people for their humanity that have been relegated to this society's subbasement storehouses. At this low point in the history of humans, Europeans must make the very idea of tradition seem to be as the polar, undesirable opposite of a future utopia or, they, as a power hungry people, will be reduced to dust. Their idea of progress necessitates the dismissal and decline of all traditions. Only those thoughts which are newly manufactured to insure the continued forward motion and direction of European style progress are worthy of life. This obsession is marked by what Michael Bradley termed the "chronus complex" – an all consuming obsession with time as if it is running out. As a fundamental human idea it is flawed.

For progress, in the European way, often represents an absence of any discernable direction. In fact, direction appears to be defined on the cuff and is determined by the accidental nature of European invention. But there is a method to their madness. Progressive change conforms to the European asili's parameters. Progress is the ideology of a culture bent on defining itself as comparatively more advanced than all others based on its technological lead. In fact, the definition of "technology" itself becomes confused as being a European creation/quality in the same way that "civilization" does. European progressions distinguish them from so-called past civilizations and makes them the culmination and cutting edge of human civilization. They help Europeans maintain their sanity. The illusion of cultural/technological evolution keeps them superior by consistently leaving them in the position of defining what is correct.

> The white self-image requires an "inferior" to which it relates as "superior." The idea of progress helps to explain to Western-Europeans in what way they are "superior." They believe, and are able to make others believe, that since they represent the most "progressive" force at any given moment, they are most human and therefore "best." Others in the world represent varying degrees of inferiority....In other words, the idea of progress provides a scale on which to weigh and by which to compare people via their cultures (their group creations). The Western-European ethos requires a self-image not merely of superiority but of *supremacy*, and the idea of progress

makes white people supreme among human beings...Without the idea and this conceptual sleight of hand, cultures would merely be different; Western culture would merely be intensely and obsessively rational. *With the assumption of the idea of progress, the West becomes "better."*[2]

Based on this observation by Marimba Ani, eurocentrists feel confident to offhandedly label her a misonegist, one who is fearful of and against change and/or innovation. But it is their myopic perspective which should awaken us to the fallacy of such a predictable accusation. She is all for change. In her written and spoken word, Ani makes it crystal clear that she supports any and all change that moves us toward a clearly defined and empowered Afrikan way that is thoroughly grounded in the tradition of our ancestors. Progress for our people has the specific purpose and intent of developing and protecting the global Afrikan nation.

Need we remind ourselves that the European conception of progress arose out of their conception of man's creation in chaos, out of their presumption of ceaseless "problems" and constant tension. It presupposes disharmony, disequilibrium, imbalance.[3] Everything is approached as a problem to be solved. Problems are never ending. And change, in and of itself, becomes a prerequisite for civilization. Progress is seen as advancement because new equals better in the European mind.

This ruse is easily dramatized through the gullible consumerism it engenders. For example, if an underwear company came out with a new pair of shorts advertising them as better than others because it had one piece of fruit as the logo on its label people would rush to buy it. If, shortly thereafter, they advertised a "new and improved" version which now featured two pieces of fruit on the label (even though no change whatsoever had been made in the quality or appearance of the shorts), consumers would again feel compelled to make the purchase. If this were repeated, each time adding more varied fruit to the label, an escalated degree of consumer self-satisfaction would again be felt through this purchase. When sober minds deeply analyze this example, they will find that the same blind consumerism is exploited by virtually every product on the market. Advertising is the mastery of deceit for profit.

As long as Europeans remain the primary political and economic imperialists of "global culture," they will command and control all definitions and images of reality, worth and beauty. Until they have been removed from this position of authority and ultimate validation, our children will continue seek to assimilate into them by attempting to emulate their image and cultural imperatives. Only when we are again an empowered global nation, defining reality, worth and beauty for ourselves, based upon our own natural appearance and ancestral definitions of universal law and order, will our children see themselves as Afrikan and dismiss Europeans for what they are to us.

We are wrong to assume that what we see and hear about us is a natural human progression. This is not the way the world would or can naturally progress. This is especially not the way it would progress without them. The world has only "progressed" in this fashion because this is the way they are.

To add to the confusion, people are talking about going back to the "good ol' days." People speak of going back to the good old moral base in Western society. That, in and of itself, is a fiction. There never was a moral base. In fanatically grasping at some mythical ideal past, we are inevitably confronted with the fact that constantly searching backward for solutions to today's chaos means that things have progressively gotten worse.

For a long time after overcoming our enslavement, Afrikans considered themselves to be the moral superiors of Europeans in every area, especially those involving sexual behavior. We took great pride in knowing that, even in their insult, we were not them. But that has rapidly changed over the last three decades. We have moved from being models of morality to modeling the morally wretched of the Earth. So many Afrikans are unable to recognize that we have become involuntary participants in a perversion-dependent culture, compelled to commit unnatural sexual acts on ourselves and others. As pseudo-Westerners, we have adjusted to solely operating on the plane of the physical pleasure principle in order to become indistinguishable from them. And so many of us think it's funny. But the joke is always on people who have no sense of history.

It is imperative that we teach our children correct morals and our moral history if we are to remain Afrikan. They need to know that we did not do these things before others corrupted our "Afrikan Self Concept."[4] They must be kept from accepting the propagandic claims of Western media that this is how it has always been. We must use our critique of their propaganda as a means of developing the critical thinking our children need to combat cultural imperialism. We are not being close minded or judgmental. We are being Afrikan. Our children must be taught that Afrikans are not Europeans.

First we, and then our children, must be made to understand that the sex imperative in European society reduces interpersonal relationships to their lowest common denominator – sex. When their imperative is spread globally via cultural imperialism, it reduces humanity to this lowest common denominator. Excluding a state of cannibalism, sex is the only thing that every individual can be exploited for. Crudely put, for the European mind, everybody has an exploitable hole or orifice. The sex imperative is a central European tradition. And, in order to implant their way as normal and natural for all humanity, those aspects of other ways that conflict with their sex imperative must be destroyed or reduced to insignificance in the minds of people who have not yet been able to make themselves into Europeans.

The method by which Western science assaults traditional Afrikan thought and behavior is by extracting and eurocentrically interpreting each tradition singly, in isolation, and outside of the traditional Afrikan context. If these practices, which obviously worked for progressive Afrikans for many thousands of years, do not seem to make sense now, it is because the cultural context has changed. Practices that develop into traditions only make sense and remain effective in the whole and natural cultural context in which they were created and nurtured. Transplantation to other cultural contexts render them useless if not destructive to the people who thrived in their original culture but who are now, out of blind fear and confusion, caught up in trying to blend them into another. And, as we know, Afrikan and European cultural imperatives are incompatible. Unlike the extremely individualistic, God-vying European personality, a natural, universal order defines the Afrikan worldview.

Afrikan cosmology is then a spiritual, Creator-centered science that guides every institution and every facet of life. The use of the understanding of the natural order as a guide to human life is universal among indigenous Afrikan cultures.[5]

The ancients did not practice sexual restraint due to some religious fervor or because of some masochistic calling to punish themselves for being born in sin. They understood the importance of self-control for the development of individual and group character. In fact, using the word "restraint" to describe their behavior is incorrect in the traditional Afrikan cultural context. Because restraint is relative. To those steeped in sexually perverse European culture, anything less than what is correct for them is restraint. So it is not our ancestors and those who still operate on an Afrikan principle who are restrained. It is Europeans who are excessive and extreme.

Sex served and serves a procreative purpose for Afrikans.

In Africa, rigid sexual intercourse codes (laws) were in all wholistic cultures and religions...sexual intercourse occurred three to four times in a wholistic woman's lifespan...A woman would have between one to four children because sex was abstained from while pregnant (10 months) and while breastfeeding (three to five years)...Sexual intercourse was indulged in from one to four times in a monogamous man's lifespan and 12 or more times in a wholistic polygamous man's lifespan (based on number of wives). In the case of a woman with two or more husbands, the sexual intercourse was from one to four times in a lifespan.[6]

Sex was not a game or play. It is serious. And being serious, it must conform to the universal model of order and morality. Our ancestors exercised control over baser desire in order to uphold and stand right in the order of the universe. Their pressing cultural need was to elevate the spirit and mind through the cultivation of balance. Adopting the so-called greater intelligence of the European forces us to assume that when our ancestors ruled the world they just had no idea what they were missing by seeking to align themselves with the higher power of the ordered universe. Excess, in whatever form and direction, is characteristically European. It insures an imbalance throughout one's mental, physical and spiritual systems. Malcolm X taught that, "History is a people's memory, and without a memory a man is demoted to the lower animals." In terms of the ancient moral discipline advocated by this discussion and the immoral disorder packaged as a desirable reality by European culture, his words ring true in more ways than one.

The general level of accepted discipline required for such a state of mind in Western culture is beyond most of our imaginations. It would be unbearable because of how we have learned to think, what we have learned to think and what we think we are. Such spiritual focus would necessarily be considered a backward form of sexual repression.

Most Westerners who are able to play the game could not imagine a fraction of that time without sex, without an overpowering reason for denial or "abstinence." Abstinence in a culture prioritizing freedom over social order implies a cruel and unusual punishment in the minds of its citizens. It implies a denial of what is natural or desirable to the degree of self punishment. For some it would mean a powerful, psycho-physical withdrawal mimicking that of seasoned crack addicts denied their fix. We say we are not animals. Yet even animals have mating seasons with abstinence in between. So who are the real animals here?

Sex must be redefined as having the purpose of cementing love. And love must not be confused with sex. Sex serves a purpose in the order of things. It is not the order itself. And love must be defined in the Afrikan context of sacrifice. Love means being willing to die for someone, to be willing to kill to save one's own family and nation, to accept the responsibility of dying for one's people. The higher purpose our ancestors gave their intimate relationships indicates the low priority sex was given in their day to day effort to become godlike.

This higher calling of relationships for Afrikans has not changed. Relationships must have spiritual and political foundations well beyond those developed simply to solve the immediate, ephemeral problems of the individuals involved. The reason the relationship exists must be grounded in a cause, a mission, a purpose that embodies yet transcends, combines and utilizes the life purposes of the mates. For Molefi K. Asante, Afrocentricity is that reason.[7] The elevation of our people should be basis of choosing mates with compatible purposes. The needs of the community are assessed to determine the purpose of any male/female union. There is no contradiction here. We fulfill each other by strengthening the community that gives us life. A community builds a community. "I am because we are" does not stop at the couple level. The couple becomes almost as minor as the "I" when the "we" are Afrikans.

In an earlier essay, Asante listed four reasons making for viable matings of Afrikan souls.[8] In each case, the priority was the social context, the family, the community, the village, the nation, not individual fantasies. Afrocentric relationships work when the mates choose to *sacrifice* their relatively insignificant wants for the needs of their people. They thrive as both participants are *inspired* by seeing and feeling each other's commitment to a higher cause. Respect grows out of witnessing the active involvement of another through internal motivation. It is a beautiful sight indeed to be awakened to your mate's power.

Vision is belief in the possibility of an Afrikan world. *Victory* is knowing it already exists. Both are necessary to act toward its fulfillment. The former facilitates continuous and consistent planning. The latter enables active engagement in a struggle to bring that existence into being. Afrocentric soul mates must have both together or antagonism will prevail bringing further confusion and damage to an already battered and scarred "we." Sometimes I believe that Asante listed these four reasons in their inverted order because an acceptance of *victory* usually precedes the actions that ensure it. And *vision* is the reason people become willing to *sacrifice* as well as put away the antagonisms that allow their eyes open to the *inspiration* of others. No matter. His point is solid.

It is also interesting to note that traditional society recognized that the ultimate warrior refrains from sexual intercourse.[9] This form of meditation serves to conserve and focus his energy in order to remain in readiness for war. And we are at war. The elite, and sometimes all, soldiers in the royal guard and armies of many Afrikan empires were eunuchs for reason. If nothing else, for the warrior, sexual activity should not be his/her primary or even secondary expression of power.

* * *

We had their language forced on us, their labor, their religion, their children, their miseducation, their psychosis, their frustration. Now we are walking around in a daze, volunteering to claim their sexual perversions as our own. We want to become them. We pigheadedly believe that if they cannot distinguish us from them they can no longer see us to harm us, that they will blindly love us. But they move forward with a clear vision. Europeans know that regardless of how fully they are aped, they must *never* share power. There is no "we" in them.

The sexualization of everything and everybody has worked hand in hand with the drive toward a progressive, antagonistic individualism of the European asili. This makes it difficult for people to communicate, to be honest with each other, to develop trust. It is so sad that Afrikan men and women are becoming increasingly more reluctant to sincerely and selflessly compliment each other's appearances and intellect for fear it will be misinterpreted as a "line" portending some sex game. Solidarity is based on trust. Truth is based on the experience of trusting. As fundamental to egalitarian nationbuilding, truth requires conversation between workers that does not naturally connote sex.

Social and cultural priorities determine the direction of a people's aspirations. "[W]e take on the form to which we submit our consciousnesses."[10] If we wish to guide our children in the direction they need to go, we must control our and their desire and access to the European sex imperative. If they are not guided in our way, they become others' children. They belong to whoever is distracting them.

ENDNOTES

Introduction

1. Larry D. Crawford (Mwalimu A. Bomani Baruti), *Excuses, Excuses: The Politics of Interracial Coupling in European Culture*, Atlanta, GA: Ankoben House, 2000, pp.6 and 7.

2. Other excellent definitions of culture can be found in Marimba Ani, *Yurugu: An African-Centered Critique of European Cultural Thought and Behavior*, Trenton, NJ: Africa World Press, 1994, pp.10-23, Amos N. Wilson, *Afrikan-Centered Consciousness versus The New World Order: Garveyism in the Age of Globalism*, NY: Afrikan World InfoSystems, 1999, pp.112 and 118 and *Blueprint for Black Power: A Moral, Political and Economic Imperative for the Twenty-First Century*, NY: Afrikan World Infosystems, 1998, pp.56-63 and Kwame Agyei Akoto, *Nationbuilding: Theory and Practice in Afrikan Centered Education*, DC: Pan Afrikan World Institute, 1992, pp.12-15 and 31-32 and Akoto and Akoto, *The Sankofa Movement*, p.78.

3. This is the translation of an Afrikan proverb by Kimbwandende Kia Bunseki Fu-Kiau (*African Cosmology of the Bântu-Kôngo: Principles of Life & Living*, Brooklyn, NY: Athelia Henrietta Press, 2001 (first published in 1980), p.111. He translates another proverb to say that "societies, like human beings, have their own identities/personalities, be they open or hidden (p.103).

4. Carl Sagan, *Cosmos*, NY: Random House, 1980, pp.24-26.

5. Ani, *Yurugu*, p.12.

6. Paulo Freire, *Pedagogy of the Oppressed*, NY: Continuum Publishing Company, 1996 (1970), p.134.

7. Ani, *Yurugu*, p.4.

8. London: Karnak House, 1989 (first published in 1963).

9. More than anything else today, this is reflected in the European's pride in Nordic, Scandinavian purity. Those said to be most European, to best epitomize those qualities most closely associated with the pure European individual are considered to be those of the northernmost old European nations, countries like, but not limited to, Sweden, Norway and Finland. The people in these places remain most unchanged by time in terms of the archetypical European cultural personality. The July 4, 1999 episode of *60 Minutes* was most revealing of this Nordic, Scandinavian personality in its look at the people of Finland. Finns have the lowest birth rate of any European nation and the highest suicide rate. The people "brood" and even describe themselves as brooders. They seldom speak to other Finns, less known strangers. They stare down as they walk.

10. Cheikh Anta Diop, *Civilization or Barbarism: An Authentic Anthropology*, Brooklyn, NY: Lawrence Hill Books, 1991 (first published in 1981), pp.13-16.

11. Charles S. Finch easily explains away one such exception to Diop's theory in his *Echoes of the Old Darkland: Themes from the African Eden* (Decatur,

GA: Khenti, Inc., 1991, p.91). A small sampling of our scholars who have much more fully explained Diop's model are Ani, *Yurugu*, pp.171-173, Kobi K. K. Kambon, *The African Personality in America: An African-Centered Framework*, Tallahassee, FL: NUBIAN Nation Publications, 1992, pp.1-21, V. Wobogo, "Diop's Two Cradle Theory and The Origin of White Racism," *Black Books Bulletin*, Vol.4, No.4, 1976, pp.20-29, Jacob H. Carruthers, *Essays in Ancient Egyptian Studies*, Los Angeles, CA: The University of Sankore Press, 1984, pp.15-18.

12. Crawford (Baruti), *Excuses, Excuses*, p.9. Kobi K. K. Kambon points out the logical sequence for arguing "race as culture" in both his *The African Personality in America* (pp.2-4 and 6) and *African/Black Psychology in the American Context: An African-Centered Approach* (Tallahassee, FL: Nubian Nation Publications, 1998, p.124).

13. Diop, *Civilization or Barbarism*, pp.16-17.

Chapter 1. A Sexual Framework

1. Na'im Akbar, *The Community of Self (Revised)*, Tallahassee, FL: Mind Productions & Associates, 1994 (first published in 1985), p.3.

2. *Focusing: Black Male-Female Relationships*, Chicago: Third World Press, 1991.

3. "Materialism and Chauvinism: Black Internalization of White Values," in Nathan Hare and Julia Hare (eds.) *Crisis in Black Sexual Politics*, San Francisco: Black Think Tank, 1989, pp.49-56.

4. *Introduction to Black Studies*, Los Angeles: Kawaida Publications, 1982, pp.214-219.

5. Karenga, *Introduction to Black Studies*, pp.215-216. Aldridge wholeheartedly agrees:

> An ideological institution is a codified and long existing set of social arrangements that forms a basic element of a given society. It follows that such institutions share the distortions inherent in the rationale for their existence (*Focusing*, p.20).

6. Jawanza Kunjufu, *Black Economics*, Chicago: African American Images, 1991, p.57.

7. John Henrik Clarke, *Who Betrayed the African World Revolution? and Other Speeches*, Chicago: Third World Press, 1994, p.25.

8. *The Falsification of Afrikan Consciousness*, NY: Afrikan World InfoSystems, 1993, pp.44-45.

9. *Extra Tonight*, October 21, 2000. This number would make the BBC Video, *Intimate Universe: The Human Body*'s statistic of 2,580 times over a lifetime a serious undercount. Since the average lifespan of European females in this society is 80 years, they average 10,560 sexual intercourses over their lifetime, not merely 2,580 times.

10. Elleni Tedla does a superb job of showing the fundamental differences between the individual in Afrikan and European thought and behavior in *Sankofa: African Thought and Education* (NY: Peter Lang, 1995).

11. The principles of Machiavellianism have been passed down through Niccolò Machiavelli's *The Prince* (NY: The New American Library, 1952 (first published 1903)).

12. Paul Hill, *Coming of Age: African American Male Rites-Of-Passage*, Chicago: African American Images, 1992, p.45.

13. Amos N. Wilson, *Blueprint for Black Power: A Moral, Political and Economic Imperative for the Twenty-First Century*, NY: Afrikan World Infosystems, 1998, p.229.

14. Akbar, *The Community of Self*, pp.72-73.

15. *TV Guide*, "African-Americans' Viewing Habits on the Rise," March 26, 1994, p.36.

16. July 3, 2000.

17. *From the Browder Files*, DC: The Institute of Karmic Guidance, 1989, p.47. Of course, we might even want to consider even Browder's estimate an undercount because many of us sleep with the television on. Its messages are still invading and adhering to our minds. If nothing else, this is obvious from the practice of sleep learning. It is also obvious from the fact that many people will instantly awaken the second the television they have been sleeping to is turned off. Also see Mark I. Singer, et al., "Contributors to Violent Behavior Among Elementary and Middle School Children," *Pediatrics* Vol.104 (October 1999) No.4, pp.878-884.

18. *Africanity and The Black Family: The Development of a Theoretical Model*, Oakland, CA: Black Family Institute, 1985, p.83.

19. "Black TV Shows Contain More Junk Food Commercials," *The Atlanta Voice*, May 5-11, 2001, p.3B.

20. *TV Guide*, "New Violence Survey Released," Atlanta Edition, August 13, 1994, p.37.

21. Gerrie F. Finger, "Campus concern: Problem drinking," *The Atlanta Journal/The Atlanta Constitution*, August 31, 1997.

22. Toni Morrison, *The Bluest Eye*, NY: Holt, Rinehart and Winston, 1970, p.95.

23. Sonbonfu Somé, *The Spirit of Intimacy*, NY: William Morrow and Company, Inc., 1999, p.96.

24. Asante, *The Afrocentric Idea*, Philadelphia, PA: Temple University Press, 1987, pp.6-7. This same point is made by W.J. Hardiman in "The Nature and Elegance of Ancient Egyptian Literature" (in Maulana Karenga and Jacob Carruthers (eds.), *Kemet and the African Worldview: Research, Rescue and Restoration*, Los Angeles, CA: University of Sankore Press, 1986), pp.167-172, esp. p.172).

25. Nernasengers A. Mutota, of the African Spectrum Bookstore, brought this to my attention.

26. C. High Holman and William Harmon, *A Handbook to Literature* (6e), NY: Macmillan Publishing Company, 1992, p.413.

27. Larry Williams and Charles S. Finch, "The Great Queens of Ethiopia," in Ivan van Sertima (ed.), *Black Women in Antiquity*, New Brunswick, NJ: Transaction Publishers, 1997 (originally published as the April 1984 (Vol.6, No.1) edition of the *Journal of African Civilizations*), p.19.

28. Ibid, p.20.

29. "African Warrior Queens," (in van Sertima (ed.), *Black Women in Antiquity*, pp.127-128).

30. Somé, *The Spirit of Intimacy*, p.74.

31. It is important that we make the distinction between *slaves* and people who are *enslaved*. Slavery is a mental function where individuals see themselves as property of those who control them. Slaves believe in the correctness of their oppression and exploitation and are often willing participants in it. Enslaved individuals understand that they are only physically bound. And they are constantly at war against those who capture and detain them. Afrikans were not slaves. They were enslaved.

32. Karl Marx and Friedrich Engels correctly defined the class relations that remain a constant in European society. They used the terms "false consciousness" ("a class-in-itself," where complacent workers are tied together simply because they have similar wages) and "class consciousness" ("a class-for-itself," where workers are politically united into revolutionary action against their wage exploitation) to describe stages in the political development of members of the European working class. See their "Manifesto of the Communist Party," in Robert C. Tucker (ed.), *The Marx-Engels Reader*, NY: Norton, 1972 (first published in 1848), pp.331-362 and *The German Ideology*, NY: International Publishers, 1930.

33. Group dating is also part of this trend where one male goes on a date with multiple females, or vice versa, presumably, in the end, to select one of the females as his (sexual) partner. We also find multiple males and females electing to compete for each other on the same date..

34. We will use "kwk" throughout instead of "etc." Kwk is the Kiswahili abbreviation for "katha wa katha" which means "and so on" (Kwame Agyei and Akua Nson Akoto, *The Sankofa Movement: ReAfrikanization and the Reality of War*, DC:)yoko InfoCom Inc, 1999, p.283).

35. Michael Bradley, *The Iceman Inheritance: Prehistoric Sources of Western Man's Racism, Sexism and Aggression*, NY: Kayode Publications LTD, 1978, pp.129-130.

36. Ibid, pp.132-133 and 146-148.

37. "Real Times, Real Times" (*Dateline* special) July 28, 2001.

38. October 2001, p.143.

39. Sarah B. Pomeroy, *Goddesses, Whores, Wives, and Slaves: Women in Classical Antiquity*, NY: Schocken Books, 1995 (first published in 1975), p.6.

40. BBC Video, *Intimate Universe: The Human Body*.

41. *48 Hours*, April 5, 2001.

42. Ra Un Nefer Amen, *An Afrocentric Guide To A Spiritual Union*, pp.63-67.

43.   A person who is desperately drawn to sexual activity is in a lot of ways a person
who is desperately trying to break into the spirit world. He thinks that the more
he involves himself in sexual activity, the more he will find himself or find
spirit.(Sonbonfu Some, p.94)

44. Somé, *The Spirit of Intimacy*, p.20.

45. Mary B. Morrison (DC: Booga Bear Poetry Group Publishing, 2000).

46. Zane (Silver Spring, MD: Strebor Books, 2000).

47. Magdalene Breaux (Fairburn, GA: 2000).

48. Of course, a homosexual presence is not new to fictional or nonfictional
literature written by and about Afrikans. For example, see James Baldwin's
Giovanni's Room (NY: The Dial Press, 1956), Gloria Naylor's *The Women of
Brewster Place* (NY: Penguin Books, 1983) and Alice Walker's *The Color
Purple* (NY: Washing Square Press, 1983).

Chapter 2. The Safety Valve

1.   John Henrik Clarke, as quoted in Marimba Ani, *Yurugu: An African-
Centered Critique of European Cultural Thought and Behavior*, Trenton, NJ:
Africa World Press, 1994, p.xvi.

2. A small fraction of the evidence of the systematic rape of indigenous
populations by Europeans can be found the *Surviving Columbus: History of the
Pueblo Peoples* video, Gloria Jahoda, *The Trail of Tears*, NY: Wings Books,
1975, pp.137-138, Jan Carew, *The Rape of Paradise*, Brooklyn, NY: A&B
Publishers, 1984, Runoko Rashidi, "Black War: The Destruction of the
Tasmanian Aborigines," *Global African Presence*, www.cwo.com/~lucumi. An
extremely important children's book on this topic we need to read to and/or with
our youngest warriors is *Encounter* by Jane Yolen (NY: Harcourt Brace &
Company, 1992).

3. This behavior is flawlessly depicted in the Arab sex feasts described by Ayi
Kwei Armah in *Two Thousand Seasons* (Oxford: Heinemann, 1979, pp.20-24).

4.   S.E. Anderson, *The Black Holocaust for Beginners*, NY: Writers and
Readers Publishing, Inc., 1995, p.33.

5. As Runoko Rashidi summarizes this research on his *Global African Presence*
website in "The African Woman as Heroine: Great Black Women in History,"
"There is not a single recorded incident of sexual assault or domestic abuse
against   an   African   woman   in   the   entire   history   of
Kmt"(http://cwo.com/~lucumi/women.html).

6.   As we see the world today, it is upside down according to the cardinal
directions known to the ancient Ethiopians and Egyptians. Just consider the fact
that the Upper and Lower Nile are contradictory to the "modern," European
directions of north and south. Jacob H. Carruthers, *Essays in Ancient Egyptian
Studies*, Los Angeles: University of Sankore Press, 1984, pp.19-20.

7. As a reflection of this, many Afrikans seeking European ancestry will not be able to grasp the historical magnitude of Abbey Lincoln's statement in the PBS documentary *Jazz* that "They'll steal your ancestors if you let them."

8. Kobi K. K. Kambon, *African/Black Psychology in the American Context: An African-Centered Approach*, Tallahassee, FL: Nubian Nation Publications, 1998, pp.72-73, 76, 81 and 84. The movie *Uncle Tom* (not *Uncle Tom's Cabin*) brings this psychologically devastating tactic to life.

9. Chancellor Williams, *The Destruction of Black Civilization: Great Issues of Race from 4500 B.C. to 2000 A.D.*, Chicago: Third World Press, 1987, p.253. And European Jews were as much a part of this systematic rape of Afrikan women and girls as every other European ethnic group (The Nation of Islam, *The Secret Relationship Between Blacks and Jews*, Volume One, Chicago: The Nation of Islam, 1991, pp.196-201).

10. In *Of Water and the Spirit* Malidoma Patrice Somé gives a personal, contemporary example of a European tradition on the Afrikan continent (NY: Penguin, 1995, pp.108-110).

11. Before the Europeans changed it to suit their politics, the Atlantic Ocean was called AEthiopicus Oceanus (observe the map in Yosef A.A. ben-Jochannan, *Africa: Mother of Western Civilization*, Baltimore, MD: Black Classic Press, 1988, p.681 and read John G. Jackson, Introduction to African Civilization, Secaucus, NJ: The Citadel Press, 1970, pp.82-83 and Richard B. Moore, *The Name "Negro": Its Origin and Evil Use*, Baltimore, MD: Black Classic Press, 1992 (first published in 1960), p.38). The same applies to so many other places such as "North" and "South" (Jacob H. Carruthers, *Essays in Ancient Egyptian Studies*, Los Angeles: University of Sankore Press, 1984, pp.19-20) and Mwanza Nyanza which they renamed Lake Victoria.

12. Cambridge, MA: MIT Press, 2000.

13. Jacob H. Carruthers, "Science and Oppression," in Daudi Ajani ya Azibo (ed.), African Psychology in Historical Perspective & Related Commentary, Trenton, NJ: Africa World Press, 1996, pp.185-191, esp. p.188 and Wade W. Nobles, *Africanity and The Black Family: The Development of a Theoretical Model*, Oakland, CA: Black Family Institute, 1985, esp. pp.14-15.

14. Paulo Freire, *Pedagogy of the Oppressed*, NY: The Continuum Publishing Company, 1993 (first published in 1970), p.37.

15. *The Psychopathic Racial Personality and other essays*, Chicago: Third World Press, 1984, pp.1-15.

16. Bureau of Justice, *Criminal Victimization Statistics Bulletin*, DC: U.S. Government Printing Office, 1997.

17. Patricia Tjaden and Nancy Thoennes, *Extent, Nature, and Consequences of Intimate Partner Violence*, DC: National Institute of Justice and the Centers for Disease Control and Prevention, 2000, p.4.

18. Wayne B. Chandler, *Ancient Future: The Teachings and Prophetic Wisdom of the Seven Hermetic Laws of Ancient Egypt*, Baltimore, MD: Black Classic Press, 1999, p.170.

19. "Ecstacy" is one popular drug that is not classified as such because it is knowingly and voluntarily ingested. Its popularity lies in its hallucinogenic effect of making everybody "love" everybody. Ecstacy removes the inhibitions to sexual intercourse, orgies and homosexuality. It is a commonly found at "rave," "circuit" and "block" parties where there are no real physical or sexual boundaries.

20. Bridget Freer, "The Dominatrix," January-February 2002, pp.102-103. Do not limit your reading to that one article. The entire issue is dedicated to European sexual mind games.

21. Afrikan proverb.

22. Jacques Rossiaud, "Prostitution, Sex and Society in French Towns," in Philippe Ariés and André Béjin (eds.), *Western Sexuality*, NY: Barnes & Noble Books, 1997 (first published in 1982), pp.84-86.

23. Assata Shakur, *Assata*, Chicago: Lawrence Hill Books, 1987, p.116. In my estimate, though, very few writers have taken us inside the mind of the participants, both victims and victimizers, better than Gloria Naylor has done in *The Women of Brewster Place* (NY: Penguin, 1982, pp.168-171).

24. Scott Henry, "Swing Shift: A New Generation Discovers the Lifestyle," *Creative Loafing*, June13-19, 2001, pp.29-30 and 33-34.

25. *Frontline*, "Lost Children of Rockdale County," October 19, 1999.

26. There are thousands of Rockdale Counties all over the Western world, communities of privilege where bored, highly sexually excitable children seek ways to satisfy their urges based upon the images they are fed by the media and their own parents' bedrooms. There are also thousands of graduation (and other) parties every year in thousands of communities where students gather and celebrate by disrobing themselves and having mass orgies as was evidenced on the July 10, 2002 *Oprah Winfrey Show*.

27. *20/20*, Special entitled "Drugs in Black and White."

28. Andrew Hacker, *Two Nations*, NY: Charles Scribner's Sons, 1992, p.35.

29. Ibid, pp.147 and 151.

30. Bart Landry, *The New Black Middle Class*, Berkeley, CA: University of California Press, 1987 and John H. Franklin, *The Color Line*, Columbia, MO: University of Missouri Press, 1993.

31. Llaila O. Afrika, *African holistic Health* (3e), Beltsville, MD: Sea Island Information Group, 1989, p.191.

32. Michael S. Kimmel, *The Gendered Society*, NY: Oxford University Press, 2000, p.254. Also see Erriel D. Roberson (Kofi Addae), *Reality Revolution: Return to the Way*, Columbia, MD: Kujichagulia Press, 1996, p.36 and Federal Bureau of Investigation, *Uniform Crime Reports: Crime in the United States 1996*, DC: U.S. Government Printing Office.

33. Patricia Tjaden and Nancy Thoennes, *Extent, Nature, and Consequences of Intimate Partner Violence*, DC: National Institute of Justice and the Centers for Disease Control and Prevention, 2000, p.2. *ABC World News Tonight* reported that the domestic abuse of women married to military personnel is even more extreme. With one out of every three of these spouses physically abused,

they experience violence at the hands of their husbands at a rate that is twice that of the general population (August 8, 2002).

34. Marvin E. Wolfgang, "Husband-Wife Homicides," *Journal of Corrective Psychiatry and Social Therapy*, Vol.2, 1956, pp.263-271. Today, those percents nationally stand at around 30 and 3 percent, respectively.

35. Suzanne K. Steinmetz and Murray A. Straus (eds.), *Violence in the Family*, NY: Harper & Row, 1974. Also see Richard J. Gelles, *The Violent Home: A Study of Conjugal Violence*, Beverly Hills, CA: Sage Publications, 1974.

36. U.S. Federal Bureau of Investigation, *Uniform Crime Reports for the United States 1996*, DC: U.S. Government Printing Office, 1997 and Jan Pahl, *A Refuge for Battered Women*, London: HMSO, 1978.

37. Gelles, *The Violent Home*, Dianne Herman, "The Rape Culture," in John J. Macionis and Nijole V. Benokraitis (eds.), *See Ourselves: Classic, Contemporary, and Cross-Cultural Readings in Sociology* (4e), Upper Saddle River, NJ: Prentice Hall, 1998, Anson Shupe, William A. Stacey and Lonnie R. Hazelwood, *Violent Men, Violent Couples: The Dynamics of Domestic Violence*, Lexington, MA: Lexington Books, 1987 and Richard J. Gelles and Claire P. Cornell, *Intimate Violence in Families* (2e), Newbury Park, CA: Sage, 1990.

38. This mentality, although of the same cultural source, should not be confused with the mob mentality exhibited during events such as "Freaknik," Spring Break, the New York park incident in June of 2000. The movie Zooman dramatizes this "bystander apathy" which has, as its most famous example in the social sciences, the Kitty Genovese incident.

> In 1964, a woman named Kitty Genovese was murdered outside her home in New York in the early hours of the morning. Her assailant took half an hour to murder her, and her screams were heard by at least thirty-eight of her neighbors. These people watched the entire scene from their windows, but not one of them came to her aid or even bothered to call the police (Ian Robertson, *Sociology*, NY: Worth Publishers, Inc., 1977, p.129).

Haki Madhubuti's "Rape: The Male Crime" is a must read for Afrikan men who want to actively stand up against the rape of Afrikan women (*Claiming Earth*, Chicago: Third World Press, 1994, pp.111-126).

39. Linda L. Lindsey and Stephen Beach, *Sociology: Social Life and Social Issues*, Upper Saddle River, NJ: Prentice Hall, 2000, p.396 and Murray A. Straus, Richard J. Gelles and Suzanne K. Steinmetz, *Behind Closed Doors: Violence in American Families*, Garden City, NY: Anchor/Doubleday, 1980.

40. Rodney Stark, *Sociology* (3e), Belmont, CA: Wadsworth Publishing Company, 1989, p.383.

41. Palmer and Thornhill, *A Natural History of Rape*.

42. Robert A. Hill and Barbara Bair (eds.), *Marcus Garvey: Life and Lessons*, Berkeley, CA: University of California Press, 1987, p.317.

43. *Yurugu*, p.xi. In an interview with Meter Unnerta of the *Metu Neter* journal, Marimba Ani sufficiently clears up the insignificant problems that others seek to find in her using the Dogon myth of Yurugu to explain the European (Vol.1, Issue 2, January 1998, p.18-19).

44. Bradley, *Iceman*, p.130.

45. Ibid, p.131. From the personal to the societal level, this quote is a perfect analogy of the historical development of the European people relative to the world's other peoples.

46. Bio-psychological theories point to the left brain dominance of the European brain as a primary source of this imbalance. See Richard King, *African Origin of Biological Psychiatry*, Hampton, VA: U. B. & U. S. Communications Systems, Inc., 1994 and Ra Un Nefer Amen, *Metu Neter: The Great Oracle of Tehuti And the Egyptian System of Spiritual Cultivation*, Brooklyn, NY: Khamit Corp., 1990, pp.9-19.

47. Bradley, *Iceman*, p.130.

48. Bell Hooks, *Black Looks*, Boston: South End Press, 1992, p.23.

49. Ibid, pp.24-25. The use of the Afrikan female model Sebastian is a more blatant example of this. Not only has she served to push their unisexual agenda but she was used to promote the continued sexual exploitation of Afrikan females by European males. A photo of her posing in the nude sandwiched between two nude European males, one embracing her front and the other clinging to her rear, is found in Barbara Summers *Black and Beautiful: How Women of Color Changed the Fashion Industry*, NY: Harper Collins, 1998, p.174.

Chapter 3. Superfreaks

1. Ra Un Nefer Amen, *An Afrocentric Guide To A Spiritual Union*, Bronx, NY: Khamit Corp., 1992, pp.68-69. That Europeans historically consider their peculiar kissing tendency natural and essential to their children's socialization is reflected in its unique and excessive presence as a dominant theme in their children's stories, fables, fairy tales and nursery rhymes. In them, kissing does everything from waking the dead to changing animals into humans.

2. French kissing is also known as "tongue," "deep" and "soul" kissing. As in all things that we practice in ignorance and to our detriment, we should understand the source of all contemporary practices that began as, and continue to honor, oral rituals among traditional Europeans. For example, Ishakamusa Barashango informs us that the "harmless" game of *Pin the Tail on the Donkey* our children play at parties evolved out of a Halloween ritual for Europeans. In order to save themselves from deceased ancestors who came back from the grave to physically and mentally haunt them they had to be saved by Satan, i.e., be inducted into Satanism/satanic cults. A key ritual in this induction was to be blindfolded and French kiss a donkey's anus. This act evolved into the game of *Pin the Tail on the Donkey* (Lecture at the Fihankra Cultural Arts Center, Atlanta, GA, December 21, 2001).

3. Amen, *Spiritual Union*.

4. *A Saintly Switch*, featuring an Afrikan cast, is a watered down version of this same gender bending theme.

5. Brian Skoloff, "Lawyer Describes Boy's Rape, Murder," *Associated Press*, March 15, 2001.

6. Also search the cannibalistic and homosexual exploits of Nathaniel Bar-Jonah, in Bryan Robinson, "Cannibals' Recipe: What Would Make Someone Kill, Then Eat, Their Victim?," *ABCNews.com*, May 22, 2002, and note the Sawney Bean family's appetite for hundreds of their fellow men mentioned in the same article.

7. Lawrence Morahan, "Mass media coverup?: Death of a young boy at the hands of a homosexual couple ignored by media." *www.capitolhillblue.com*, November 10, 1999, pp.1-2. Also see Michelle Bradford, "Inquiry into death of boy, 13, expands," *Arkansas Democrat-Gazette*, 12/11/99 ("Carpenter, 38, and Brown, 22, his roommate, are both charged with capital murder and six counts of rape in the Sept. 26 death of Jesse, a middle-school student from Lincoln in Washington County. Jesse was found near death in the men's Rogers apartment bound with belts, gagged with his own underwear and strapped to a mattress. He suffocated, an autopsy found.")

8. According to an ABC special titled *Vanished* (July 25, 2001), approximately 100,00 people are officially listed as missing in this country alone.

9. Hannibal Lecter is the cannibalistic feign (where his every cannibalistic act carried sexual innuendo, sexual conquest, the sexual submission of women and children and perverted masochism, just as Dracula's every mortal seduction and bite did) who is the "protagonist" in the movies *Silence of the Lambs* and *Hannibal*. Evil can be, and is increasingly becoming, the protagonist model in European film. We should note that next to cannibalism, vampirism is considered in the European imagination to be the most civilized and refined form of sadism.

10. Wade N. Nobles, *African Psychology: Toward Its Reclamation, Reascension & Revitalization*, Oakland, CA: Black Family Institute, 1986, pp.3-5. Also see Marimba Ani, *Yurugu: An African-Centered Critique of European Cultural Thought and Behavior*, Trenton, NJ: Africa World Press, 1994, p.377.

11. *What Your Mother Never Told You About Sex*, NY: G.P. Putnam's Sons, 2002. Sadly, Rosie Milligan does the same thing by using the logic of dozens of European psychologists, psychiatrists and sexologists to create eurocentric definitions of sexual behavior for adult Afrikan men and women (*Satisfying the Black Woman Sexually Made Simple*, LA: Professional Business Consultants, 1990 (revised 1994) and *Satisfying the Black Man Sexually Made Simple*, LA: Professional Business Consultants, 1994).

12. *Chosen People from the Caucasus: Jewish Origins, Delusions, Deceptions and Historical Role in the Slave Trade, Genocide and Cultural Colonization*, Chicago: Third World Press, 1992, p.5. This genetic connection of a people to their past, however, brings up a very important political question for Afrikans. If we are going to argue that theirs is a genetic aggression, then cultural context becomes irrelevant in producing a more humane change in their collective

personality. Their excessive aggression will show itself no matter the humanity or passivity of the culture they find themselves in. This fact, in and of itself, changes the nature of our options and relations to Europeans. It defines Afrikan-European culture differences as irresolvable outside of the context of war, however defined.

13. Fox Channel.5, *Extra*, "Sex in the Sky," July 23, 1998.

14. Although a very common theme on every popular talk show, *Sally Jessy Raphael*'s "Stop Exposing Yourself"episode, which aired on September 7, 1998, is quite thought provoking as to the extent of the progression of sexual extremes displayed in public. In connecting sexual excitement with these extremes we must also be able to see the relationship of *speed* to venting. Speed enhances extreme sexual gratification. Sex is venting for Europeans and those socialized in their way. And speed is an exhilarating way of venting. The more accelerated and extreme, the greater the release. Speed adds measurably to this release. Therefore, sexual activities involving great risk and speed are not for the challenge, as propagated in Western media. They allow for a greater release of tension, for sexual excitement, for venting.

15. Chancellor Williams, *The Destruction of Black Civilization: Great Issues of Race from 4500 B.C. to 2000 A.D.*, Chicago: Third World Press, 1987, p.41.

16. Dona Richards, "European Mythology: The Ideology of Progress," in Molefi Kete Asante and Abdulai Vandi (eds.), *Contemporary Black Thought*, Los Angeles, CA: Sage Publications, 1985, pp.62.

17. James M. Henslin, *Sociology: A Down-to-Earth Approach* (4e), Boston: Allyn and Bacon, 1999, pp.629-630. The European male's sexual connection with cars is well brought out in *TNT*'s "The Life of the Car."

18. Robert E. Lerner's article "The Life of the Urban Working Class," in Robert E. Lerner, Standish Meacham and Edward M. Burns (eds.), *Western Civilizations: Their History and Their Culture* (13e), NY: W.W. Norton & Co., 1998, p.516.

19. Also see *Pride and Prejudice*, *The Magnificent Ambersons* and Stephen King's *Sleepwalkers*. There are literally hundreds of actual and fictional books written of by the victims, and those sympathetic to the victims, of incest and even more dealing with helping the victims, victimizers and family and friends of victims of incest. There is nothing new here.

20. Some of the cultural politics of this are alluded to in Raymond A. Winbush, *The Warrior Method*, NY: Amistad, 2001, pp.119-121.

21. Zondra Hughes, "Risky Business: What's Behind The Surge In STDS," *Ebony*, January 2000, p.116.

22. Our participation in nudist activities, to the delight of Europeans who dominate these places, is being advertised as a means to gain, and as evidence of our further, acceptance and integration into European society and culture (Afton Alexander, "Sex Tales: Taking a Walk on the Wild Side at Hedonism II," *Pathfinders Travel*, Summer 2002, pp.36-41). Because of the drive among many Afrikans to be accepted and integrated into Western society and culture, combined with a socialized, extreme focus on continuous individual sexual

gratification, we cannot see that the "delight" Europeans feel is stimulated by the sexual variety our presence provides for them

23. Terence McLaughlin, *Dirt*, NY: Dorset Press, 1971, pp.36-37.

24. Ibid, p.137.

25. Larry D. Crawford (Mwalimu A. Bomani Baruti), "The Cultural Continuum," in *negroes and other essays*, Atlanta, GA: Ankoben House, 2000, pp.33-74.

26. *The Hartford Courant*, February 19, 2000.

27. Daniel S. Campagna and Donald L. Poffenberger, *The Sexual Trafficking in Children: An Investigation of the Child Sex Trade*, Dover, MA: Auburn House Publishing Company, 1988.

28. Karen Auge did an interesting story on this in *The Denver Post* of February 26, 2000 about "involving children in sexual techniques that involve near-asphyxiation..."

29. Murray Kempton, "A New Colonialism," *New York Review of Books*, November 19, 1992 and Campagna and Poffenberger, *The Sexual Trafficking in Children*, esp. pp.146-147 for statistics and ethnographic data.

30. John J. Macionis, *Sociology* (7e), Upper Saddle River, NJ: Prentice Hall, 1999, p.300 and Joan J. Johnson, *Teen Prostitution*, NY: Franklin Watts, 1992, pp.27-31.

31. *ABC News*, July 8, 2002. *The Atlanta Voice*'s report that "some 4.7 million South Africans - one in nine - are HIV positive, more people than in any other country in the world" is not unrelated (David Bauder, "South African version of 'Sesame Street' to introduce series' first HIV-positive character," July 27 - August 2, 2002, p.15). And while these are for the entire population, and not only children, the spread of disease in Azania speaks to the tourist invasion, and the sex market it creates, not any change in the sexual practices of Azanian Afrikans.

32. UN – Refugee Sex Abuse, *The African Shopper*, May 2002, p.29.

33. *Pornography and Obscenity*, NY: Alfred A. Knopf, Inc., 1930.

34. Sarah B. Pomeroy, *Goddesses, Whores, Wives, and Slaves: Women in Classical Antiquity*, NY: Schocken Books, 1995 (first published in 1975), p.192.

35. Betty-Carol Bender, *Feminism and the Law*, Free Press, 1992, p.148. An excellent historical discussion of the industry is provided in the Frontline video *American Porn* which aired February 7, 2002.

36. One can get a bird's-eye view of the illegal market through books like Yaron Svoray with Thomas Hughes, *Gods of Death*, NY: Simon & Schuster, 1997 and movies like *3M*.

37. Scott Henry, "Booty Call: How the world's oldest profession became Atlanta's newest growth industry," *Creative Loafing*, January 16-22, 2002, pp.29-30 and 32-34.

38. John W. Wright (ed.), *The Universal Almanac*, NY: Andrews and McMeel, 1990, pp.243-244.

39. Anne R. Carey and Suzy Parker, "Trends in New Magazines," *USA Today*, May 5, 1998, p.1D.

40. Scott Henry, "The Girl Next Door," *Creative Loafing*, October 10-16, 2001, pp.29-30, 33 and 35.

41. Crawford (Baruti), "The Cultural Continuum," pp.54-55.

42. The *AUC Digest*, August 25, 1997, p.5.

43. "Online sex addiction on the rise, specialists say," *Boston Globe*, May 6, 2000, p.A12.

44. As a nation of people, we must realize that right under our noses the exposure of Afrikan children to pornography has taken on global proportions. Wherever our children are with a computer hooked up to the web, and driven by European cultural imperatives, we will find them subject to such exposure by force of conscious deception or the choice of curiosity. An example in Barbados where "four students...will face disciplinary action for using their laptop computers to access porno sites on the internet" should suffice to prove the point ("Net Lock in Barbados," *The Caribbean Star*," May 2002, p.8).

45. Erriel D. Roberson (Kofi Addae), *Reality Revolution: Return to the Way*, Columbia, MD: Kujichagulia Press, 1996, p.31.

46. This characteristic tradition of excess and waste apparently dates back to ancient European culture where Romans
> had their palaces built with a special room in which to take "upward purges." Such rooms were called "vomitories." In these vomitories there was a marble rail, where, after they had eaten a feast, the Romans would go and lean over and have a slave tickle their throats, after drinking some warm water or decoction. Then they would go back and finish their feast (Jethro Kloss, *Back to Eden*, Twin Lakes, WI: Lotus Press, 1999 (first published in 1939), pp.79-80).

No accepted mentality, no matter how its behavioral manifestations or the reasons given for them have become mutated, is without origin.

47. Pomeroy, *Goddesses, Whores, Wives, and Slaves*, p.192 and Timothy Taylor, *The Prehistory of Sex*, NY: Bantam Books, 1996, pp.205-207.

48. Friedrich Engels, *The Condition of the Working Class in England*, Stanford, CA: Stanford University Press, 1968 (first published in 1845), p.144; Jacques Rossiaud, "Prostitution, Sex and Society in French Towns," in Philippe Ariés and André Béjin (eds.), *Western Sexuality*, NY: Barnes & Noble Books, 1997 (first published in 1982), pp.76-94, Pomeroy, *Goddesses, Whores, Wives, and Slaves*, pp.88, 140, 141 and 201, Ishakamusa Barashango, *Afrikan People and European Holidays: A Mental Genocide, Book I*, Philadelphia, PA: Barashango and Associates, 1979, p.22 and Cheikh A. Diop, *The Cultural Unity of Black Africa: The Domains of Matriarchy and of Patriarchy in Classical Antiquity*, London: Karnak House, 1989, p.83.

49. Pomeroy, *Goddesses, Whores, Wives, and Slaves*, p.201.

50. Crawford (Baruti), "The Cultural Continuum," p.19.

51. Wade W. Nobles' research summary gives added texture to this fact (*Africanity and The Black Family: The Development of a Theoretical Model*, Oakland, CA: Black Family Institute, 1985, pp.84-85).

52. Ani, *Yurugu*, p.439.

53. The "Uh-Oh" Report, *The Caribbean Star*, July 2002, p.33. Nonetheless, we must remember that the homosexual factor in this surge is undoubtedly of

significance. Adult European males are more likely to seek to sexually exploit the younger of these males that heterosexual European females. We should also remember that these islands were derogatorily named after the term "caribe" "meaning wild one or cannibal" by Europeans (Del Jones, *The Black Holocaust: Global Genocide*, Philadelphia, PA: Eye of The Storm Communications, Inc., 1992, p.15 and W. Burghardt Turner and Joyce Turner's "Introduction" to Richard B. Moore, *The Name "Negro": Its Origin and Evil Use*, Baltimore, MD: Black Classic Press, 1992 (first published in 1960), p.21).

54. Llaila O. Afrika, *African holistic Health* (3e), Beltsville, MD: Sea Island Information Group, 1989, p.190.

55. Kwame Agyei and Akua Nson Akoto, *The Sankofa Movement: ReAfrikanization and the Reality of War*, DC:)yoko InfoCom Inc, 1999, p.88.

56. Muata Abhaya Ashby, *TemT Tchaas: Egyptian Proverbs*, Miami, FL: Cruzian Mystic Books, 1994.

57. Robert Staples and Leanor Boulin Johnson, *Black Families at the Crossroads*, San Francisco: Jossey-Bass Inc., 1993, pp.77-78.

58. Pomeroy, *Goddesses, Whores, Wives, and Slaves*, pp.87-88.

59. Malik Anwar Aten-Ra, "To Black Greek Fraternities and Sororities: A Message From Your Homosexual Greek Ancestors," *The Naked Truth*, September 4, 1998.

60. Robert C. Sorenson, *Adolescent Sexuality in Contemporary America*, NY: World, 1973.

61. Charshee C. L. McIntyre, *Criminalizing a Race: Free Blacks During Slavery*, Queens, NY: Kayode Publications, Ltd., 1984, pp.179-180.

62. *Fatal Attraction* and *Sleeping with the Enemy* are movies which present this Western phenomenon affecting a reported 8 percent of all women 2 percent of all men in this society during their lifetimes.

63. This is the scientific term for individuals who become sexually excited by having others watch them perform sexual intercourse.

64. Aristophanes, in Maynard Mack, et. al., *The Norton Anthology of World Masterpieces* (5e), Vol.1, NY: W.W. Norton & Company, 1985, pp.779-814.

65. Llaila Afrika, *Nutricide: The Nutritional Destruction of the Black Race*, NY: A&B Publishers Group, 2000, pp.305-306. Also see Pomeroy, *Goddesses, Whores, Wives, and Slaves*, p.8.

66. Pomeroy, *Goddesses, Whores, Wives, and Slaves*, p.192.

67. London: Longman, 1973.

68. *Facing Mt. Kenya*, NY: Vintage Books, 1965, pp.155-156.

69. Williams, *The Destruction of Black Civilization*, p.19.

70. Africa Information Service (ed.), *Return to the Source: Selected Speeches of Amilcar Cabral*, NY: Monthly Review Press, 1973, p.46.

71. Wunyabari O. Maloba, *Mau Mau and Kenya*, Bloomington, IN: Indiana University Press, 1993.

72. *Nightmares & Dreamscapes*, NY: Viking, 1993, pp.215-261, esp. p.243. Stephen King readers, of course, are familiar with the common racist thought that plagues his writing.

73. Akoto and Akoto, *The Sankofa Movement*, p.5.

74. Benjamin Spock and Michael B. Rothenberg, *Doc Spock's Baby and Child Care* NY: Pocket Books, 1985 (first published in 1945), pp.449 and 510 and Betty G. Eisner, *The Unused Potential of Marriage and Sex*, Boston: Little, Brown, 1970, p.222.

75. Afrika, *African holistic Health*, p.190.

76. Ibid, pp.191-192.

77. Afrika, *African holistic Health*, p.189.

78. The November 9, 2000 *20/20* reported this finding from a *Men's Health* magazine study.

79. McLaughlin, *Dirt*, p.70.

80. Michael Bradley provides some excellent pictures, but a limited and curiously misleading discussion as to the source of European's excessive preoccupation with increasing the expanse of their female's buttocks. With reference to his pictures, he notes that

> Some periods of Western history have featured women's dresses which so over-emphasized hips that women could only pass through doors sideways. This development reached its apex about 1780 in Paris with the *grande toilette*, but unnatural emphasis of the hips has been a more or less constant feature in Western fashion from the time of the Minoans until the very recent past. Other periods have so over-emphasized the female buttocks that women could not sit down in their bustles, or so over-emphasized the hip-waist-bust curve that female ribs were actually permanently distorted by corsets.(*The Iceman Inheritance: Prehistoric Sources of Western Man's Racism, Sexism and Aggression*, (NY: Kayode Publications Ltd., 1978, pp.185-187.)

81. Robert K. Barnhart (ed.), *The Barnhart Concise Dictionary of Etymology*, NY: HarperCollins, 1995 (first published in 1988), p.527.

82. The Roman Holidays were only one kind of festival where sexual intercourse was practiced with abandon. There were many others. For example, "total promiscuity was the rule during the [saquaic feasts of Mylitta]. Their religion required the women to prostitute themselves in the temples (sacred places)"Cheikh A. Diop, *The Cultural Unity of Black Africa: The Domains of Matriarchy and of Patriarchy in Classical Antiquity*, London: Karnak House, 1989, p.82)

83. "Make-Out Party!" *Mademoiselle*, August 2000, pp.54-57.

84. McLaughlin, *Dirt*, Engels, *The Condition of the Working Class* and Larry D. Crawford (Mwalimu A. Bomani Baruti), "The Cultural Continuum," in *negroes and other essays*, Atlanta, GA: Ankoben House, 2000, pp.33-74.

85. Crawford (Baruti), "The Cultural Continuum."

86. The "Gonorrhea Update" discusses this in the context of only one STD (*The Atlanta Voice*, September 30 - October 6, 2000, p.3B).

87. *48 Hours*, "It's Just Sex.," 2000.

88. Lent following the Mardi Gras or extreme constraint following extreme license or fasting following gluttony or puritanicalism following liberalism are one in the same cultural pattern of a people who refuse to take blame or responsibility for controlling their actions. This oscillation back and forth from

one extreme to another is the same moralless principle upon which the European Christian church is built. Even when you know better, sin while the sinning is good and then repent and expect forgiveness for the weakness your philosophical and religious experts have conveniently convinced you that you cannot control. External controls rule European morality. Monday through Saturday licentiousness is followed by Sunday morning prayer because the lie of an innate human weakness is so easy for a spiritually weak people to believe.

89. Taylor, *Prehistory of Sex*, pp.172-175.

90. Picture in front of Robert Flacelière (trans. by James Cleugh) *Love in Ancient Greece*, NY: Crown Publishers, Inc., 1962. The act of males having sex with (sodomizing) fowl is called *avisodomy*.

91. Crawford (Baruti), "The Cultural Continuum," p.17.

92. Claud Anderson gives us a taste of these perversions, and their cover up, in *Dirty Little Secrets About Black History, Its Heros, and Other Troublemakers*, Bethesda, MD: PowerNomics Corporation of America, 1997, p.59.

93. These major countries are Argentina, Australia, Azania, the British Isles, India, New Zealand, Russia, Spain, Uruguay and this country.

94. The early stages of this loss resulting from the massive northern urbanization of southern Afrikans during the early years of the 20th Century is summarized in Carole Marks, *Farewell – We're Good and Gone: The Great Migration*, Bloomington, IN: Indiana University Press, 1989, p.173.

95. Taylor, *Prehistory of Sex*, p.249.

96. Afrika, *Nutricide*, p.205.

97. Kwame Agyei Akoto, *Nationbuilding: Theory & Practice in Afrikan Centered Education*, DC: Pan Afrikan World Institute, 1992, p.189.

98. It is worth noting that the word "booty" has been traditionally used by Europeans to name the spoils acquired from military invasion, piracy and physical aggression.

99. Jones, *The Black Holocaust*, p.9.

100. This speciality, where feces (or filth) are eaten to heighten the sexual experience, is specifically termed *coprophilia*. See Afrika, *Nutricide*, pp.390-397, Jones, *The Black Holocaust*, p.9, Cameron, et. Al., ISIS National Random Sexuality Survey, *Nebraska Medical Journal*, 1985, pp.292-299, Family Research Institute, Lincoln, NE and E. Fields, "Is Homosexual Activity Normal?" Marietta, GA.

101. The term "golden shower" has deep roots in the European tradition. In Greek mythology Zeus impregnated Danaë with a golden shower (Pomeroy, *Goddesses, Whores, Wives, and Slaves*, pp.11-12).

102. It is this that is being referred to when adult men ask to be spanked by a woman or male as a sexual intercourse enhancer.

103. If sexual arousal requires the presence of a real amputee, this is called *amputation fetishism*. And if one must imagine him/herself as an amputee to achieve sexual satisfaction, it is called *apotemnophilia*.

104. NY: Dorset Press, 1971.

105. Leon Festinger, *A Theory of Cognitive Dissonance*, Stanford, CA: Stanford University Press, 1957.

106. "Ten Sex Myths Exploded," in Nat Lerhman, *Masters and Johnson Explained*, Rockville Centre, NY: Playboy Paperbacks, 1970, pp.233-234.

107. *Osiris Rising*, Popenquine, West Africa: Per Ankh, 1995, p.118.

108. Oxford: Heinemann, 1974, p.125.

109. And although most of us missed it or laughed it off, homosexuality is present in many of the Blaxploitation movies of the 1970s such as *Blacula* and *Uptown Saturday Night*.

110. Ayi Kwei Armah, *The Healers*, Oxford, England: Heinemann, 1978, p.176.

111. Wilson B. Key's *Subliminal Seduction* looks into what is in and behind this hidden commercial propaganda (NY: A Signet Book, 1974). Also see Afrika, *Nutricide*, pp.304-305. Madasi to Corey Johnson whose research brought together most of the examples of sex, sexual perversion and confusion presented in this paragraph.

112. It should not be necessary to discuss the satanic nature of this European holiday, but for those who have an interest in this or the other European holidays/celebrations see Ishakamusa Barashango, *Afrikan People and European Holidays: A Mental Genocide, Book One*, Philadelphia, PA: Barashango and Associates, 1979 and *Book Two*, 1983.

113. It would also do the reader good to visit Amos N. Wilson's critique of the Afrikan media in *Blueprint for Black Power: A Moral, Political and Economic Imperative for the Twenty-First Century* (Brooklyn, NY: Afrikan World InfoSystems, 1998, pp.234-240).

Chapter 4. Another World

1. *Monster*, NY: Penguin Books, 1993. *Menace to Society, Streetwise* and *Belly* are superb examples of the many movies dramatizing this way of survival.

2. Boston: Little, Brown and Company, 1967.

3. Chicago: The University of Chicago Press, 1976.

4. For some theoretical discussions of the urban plantation, internal colony model see, Robert Blauner, "Internal Colonialism and Ghetto Revolts," *Social Problems*, 16 (Spring 1969), pp.393-408 and *Racial Oppression in America*, NY: Harper and Row, 1972, Kenneth Clark, *Dark Ghetto*, NY: Harper and Row, 1965, Douglas Glasgow, *The Black Underclass*, San Francisco: Jossey-Bass, 1980, Manning Marable, *How Capitalism Underdeveloped Black America*, Boston: South End Press, 1983, William K. Tabb, *The Political Economy of the Black Ghetto*, NY: W.W. Norton, 1970 and Robert Staples, *The Urban Plantation*, Oakland: Black Scholar, 1987.

5. In respect to the confusion artists sing about somehow being reflected in what they sing, it is worth noting that R. Kelly has a history of pedophilic ways. He

has a well founded reputation for acting out his fantasies of having sex with females below the age of consent (Jim Derogatis and Abdon M. Palasch, "City police investigate R&B singer R. Kelly in sex tape," *Chicago Sun Times*, February 8, 2002, Jamie F. Brown, The R. Kelly Tapes, *Sister 2 Sister*, April 2000, pp.6-8 and 10, Lola Ogunnaike, "Caught in the Act," *Vibe*, May 2002, pp.90-98 and Mike Branom, "Judge sets $750,000 bail for R. Kelly in porn case," *Chicago Tribune*, June 6, 2002). R. Kelly, however, is not unique among artists or those responsible for the production and distribution of his music. The acts he is accused of are normal operating procedure among the Europeans he, if guilty, is modeling.

6. R.K. Byers, "A B-Boy Adventure into Hip-Hop's Gay Underground," *The Source*, December 1997, pp.107-108 and 110, *Vibe*, July 2001, pp.97-106 and *The Source*, November 2001, p.52.

7. "Where Was You At."

8. Terry Williams and William Kornblum, "Players and Ho's," in Paul M. Sharp and Barry W. Hancock (eds.), *Juvenile Delinquency: Historical, Theoretical, and Societal Reactions to Youth* (2e), Upper Saddle River, NJ: Prentice Hall, 1998.

9. Sarah B. Pomeroy, *Goddesses, Whores, Wives, and Slaves: Women in Classical Antiquity*, NY: Schocken Books, 1995 (first published in 1975), pp.140-141 and 202.

10. Daniel S. Campagna, "The Economics of Juvenile Prostitution in the USA," *International Children's Rights Monitor*, 1985, p.2, Daniel S. Campagna and Donald L. Poffenberger, *The Sexual Trafficking in Children: An Investigation of the Child Sex Trade*, Dover, MA: Auburn House Publishing Company, 1988, Joan J. Johnson, *Teen Prostitution*, NY: Franklin Watts, 1992 and D. Kelly Weisberg, *Children of the Night: A Study of Adolescent Prostitution*, Lexington, MA: Lexington Books, 1985.

11. March 2001, pp.186-189 and 267.

12. April 2001, pp.138-139.

13. Pp.116-119, esp. p.119.

14. See pages 20, 35, 66-67 and 129.

15. P.29.

16. Burnett W. Gallman, "Benyin-Besiaba: An Afrikan-Centered Evaluation of Homosexuality," InnerVisions: RX For survival For People of African Origin, Columbia, SC: Imhotep Enterprises, 1994, p.16.

17. Jacob H. Carruthers, *Ndw Ntr: Divine Speech: A Historiographical Reflection of African Deep Thought from The Time Of Pharaohs to the Present*, London: Karnak House, 1995, pp.93-95 and Oba T'Shaka, *Return to the African Mother Principle of Male and Female Equality, Volume 1*, Oakland, CA: Pan Afrikan Publishers and Distributors, 1995.

18. Mari Evans, "The Relationship of Childrearing Practices to Chaos and Change in the African American Family," in Carlos Moore, Tanya R. Sanders and Shawna Moore (eds.), *African Presence in the Americas*, Trenton, NJ: Africa World Press, 1995, p.308.

19. Michele Foster, "Educating for Competence in Community and Culture: Exploring the Views of Exemplary African-American Teachers," in Mwalimu J. Shujaa, *Too Much Schooling, Too Little Education: A Paradox of Black Like in White Societies*, Trenton, NJ: Africa World Press, 1994, p.230.

20. Note the discussions of rap/hip hop's positive force by Marimba Ani, "Kuugusa Mtima: The Afrikan 'Aesthetic' and National Consciousness," in Erriel Kofi Addae (Erriel D. Roberson), *To Heal a People: Afrikan Scholars Defining a New Reality*, Columbia, MD: Kujichagulia Press, 1996, p.109, Erriel Kofi Addae, "Nyansa Nnsa Da: Killing The Enemy Within," in Erriel Kofi Addae (Erriel D. Roberson), *To Heal a People: Afrikan Scholars Defining a New Reality*, Columbia, MD: Kujichagulia Press, 1996, pp.86-87 and Erriel D. Roberson (aka. Kofi Addae), *The Maafa & Beyond*, Columbia, MD: Kujichagulia Press, 1995, pp.121-128.

21. Amos N. Wilson, *Black-on-Black Violence: The Psychodynamics of Black Self-Annihilation in Service of White Domination*, NY: Afrikan World InfoSystems, 1990.

22. Ani, "Kuugusa Mtima, pp.110 and 115.

Chapter 5. The Language of Love

1. And with the new move by some highly confused, young and old Afrikans, society is making it acceptable for Europeans to again call us "niggas" to our faces, as a term of endearment. These individuals argue that since Europeans are their closest friends, and they call their closest friends (and all Afrikans in their circles) niggas, that their European friends have every right to call them and the rest of us nigga. Change in this direction will make it illegal for an Afrikan to act/react against any European for calling him (or her) a nigga. We find the mentacidal reasoning behind this insanity in books like Willie H. Richey, *Racism is a Myth*, Dubuque, IA: Kendall/Hunt Publishing Company, 1996, Errol Smith, *37 Things Every Black Man Needs to Know*, Valencia, CA: St. Clair Rene Publishing, 1991 and Randall Kenney, *Nigger*, NY: Pantheon Books, 2002 and movies like "Training Day" where Denzel Washington spends an inordinate amount of time calling his European partner "my nigga." Understanding the eurocentric motivation behind this name calling, it is easy to understand why he received an Oscar award for this but none of his previous, far superior, performances.

2. To this list of extremely misogynistic terminology we must add sorceress and witch which have well known male counterparts. Sorcerer and warlock are their male counterparts, but they do not carry a similar negative connotation. These male labels also imply an ability to unleash an inordinate amount of magical power. Unlike witches and sorceresses, they do not corrupt the lives of those they envy with magical concoctions and curses derived from evil powers higher than themselves. They tend to be the primary source of their own magical

powers. Usually, the only time negative terms for both male and female in the English language carry similar connotations are those which involve demonic beings. In which case, again, males become supervillians that can match and surpass the naturally evil female as in the succubus (a male demon who rapes a sleeping woman). The incubus (a female demon who rapes a sleeping man) is not accorded the power of the succubus. The same applies to the ogre and ogress. Of course, the satyr, a half-man, half-goat modeled after Pan the Greek god of, interestingly enough, shepherds, was also above humans on the divine chain of power, but he had no female counterpart, probably because he was a Greek invention. Satyrs and centaurs were creatures whose uncontrollable sexual urges led them to sexually assault both male and female humans. Satyrs even have a sexual disorder named after them – *satyriasis*. It, and the *Don Juan syndrome*, are used to label individuals who have uncontrollable and insatiable sex drives.

3. "Playa" is an exception to this sex specific terminology. It refers to either males or females, who may or may not be involved with only one other individual, who exhibit an extreme level of disrespect for members of the other sex.

4. Elleni Tedla, *Sankofa: African Thought and Education*, NY: Peter Lang, 1995, p.31.

5. Larry D. Crawford (Mwalimu A. Bomani Baruti), "The Cultural Continuum," in *negroes and other essays*, Atlanta, GA: Ankoben House, 2000, pp.33-74.

6. Ibid, pp.47-48.

7. Amos N. Wilson, *Afrikan-Centered Consciousness versus The New World Order: Garveyism in the Age of Globalism*, NY: Afrikan World InfoSystems, 1999, pp.95-97.

8. One recent excellent example of scientifically explaining away the chaotic nature of European child raising is Ross W. Greene's *The Explosive Child* (NY: HarperCollins Publishers, 1998).

9. We must make a distinction between "rearing" our children and "raising" them. Rearing them is a political act, full of conscious Afrikan intent and clear in the knowledge of being at war with an enemy who is ever present in the lives of our children. Raising them is simply the perfunctory behavior of Afrikans who see this enemy as their friend, protector and sole reference group. As Mari Evans states

> [R]aising is "providing for," while rearing is "responding to." Raising can be satisfied by providing the essentials: food, shelter, clothing and reasonable care. "Rearing" is a carefully thought out process. Rearing begins with a goal and is supported by a clear view of what are facts and what is truth (and the two are not necessarily synonymous). Rearing is complex and requires sacrifice and dedication. It is an ongoing process of "preparation"....Obviously, something *different*, some carefully thought out *process*, some long-range *political* view is present when one has a clear sense of one's reality and, therefore, intends to rear presidents, rulers, or *free men* and *women* ("The Relationship of Childrearing Practices to Chaos and Change in the African American Family," in Carlos Moore, Tanya R. Sanders and Shawna Moore (eds.), *African Presence in the*

Americas, Trenton, NJ: Africa World Press, 1995, p.306).

10. B.F. Skinner, *The Behavior of Organisms*, NY: Appleton-Century, 1938.

11. Ivan P. Pavlov, *Conditioned Reflexes: An Investigation of the Physiological Activity of the Cerebral Cortex*, (F.C. Anrep, trans.) NY: Oxford University Press, 1927.

12. We look at the unethical behavior of a John F. Kennedy, Clarence Thomas, Newt Gingrich or Bill Clinton as if they were unusual or did something that does not naturally fit the Western pattern of corrupted power. All forms of immoral and illegal abuse of power are evident from the upper- to lowermost levels in both the private and public sectors. The Bohemian Grove, located outside San Francisco, is known to exclusively cater to the satanic, pedophilic and otherwise sexually perverted addictions of high ranking government and private officials from around the globe (G. William Domhoff, *The Bohemian Grove and other retreats*, NY: Harper & Row, Publishers, 1974). "When rot is evident at the top nothing below should be surprising" – Wole Soyinka. Some of the better known sexual escapades of FBI agents acting "in the line of duty," as well as individuals the agency had under surveillance, serve as shining examples of this pattern (Ronald Kessler, The FBI, NY: Pocket Books, 1993, pp.75-6, 95, 124, 128-134, 139, 144, 154-155, 170, 176-177, 258-259, 264-266, 269, 272-273, 274, 277, 346, 356 (which addresses Martin L. King, Jr.'s sexual activities), 358, 359, 361, 414-416, 442, 502, 503, 504 and 510). For a very important discussion of this unethical and immoral behavior at the top read John W. DeCamp's *The Franklin Cover-Up: Child Abuse, Satanism, and Murder in Nebraska*, NY: AWT, Incorporated, 1992.

13. Kwame Agyei and Akua Nson Akoto, *The Sankofa Movement: ReAfrikanization and the Reality of War*, DC:)yoko InfoCom Inc, 1999, p.122.

14. Geoffrey Canada's brief but candid comments on this are insightful (*Reaching Up for Manhood*, Boston: Beacon Press, 1998, pp.69-71).

15. *To The Contrary*, May 6, 2001.

16. Larry D. Crawford (Mwalimu A. Bomani Baruti), "Black Capital," in *negroes and other essays*, Atlanta, GA: Ankoben House, 2000, p.101.

17. Malthus' theories can be found in *An Essay on Population* (NY: Augustus Kelley, 1965 (first published in 1798)) which became so popular it was reprinted and sold for several decades afterward. Swift's work, written in 1729, is one of the West's most popular and is often anthologized. It can be found in *The Norton Anthology of World Masterpieces*, NY: W.W. Norton & Company, 1997, pp.2028-2034.

18. See John R. Weeks, *Population: An Introduction to Concepts and Issues* (5e), Belmont, CA: Wadsworth Publishing Company, 1994, pp.36-37 and 47.

19. Chiekh Anta Diop, *Black Africa: The Economic and Cultural Basis for a Federated State*, Chicago: Lawrence Hill Books and Trenton, NJ: Africa World Press, 1987 (first published in 1974), Walter Rodney, *How Europe Underdeveloped Africa*, DC: Howard University Press, 1982, Chinweizu, *The West and the rest of us* and Eric Williams, *Capitalism and Slavery*, (Chapel Hill, NC: University of North Carolina Press, 1994 (first published in 1944).

20. See Ra Un Nefer Amen, *An Afrocentric Guide To A Spiritual Union*, Bronx, NY: Khamit Corp., 1992, p.37.

21. Terence McLaughlin, *Dirt*, NY: Dorset Press, 1971, p.14.

22. A number of organizations cater to those willing to admit to chronic sexual excess. Sexaholics Anonymous, Sex and Love Addicts Anonymous and Sexual Compulsives Anonymous are but a few. Also see Anick Jesdanun, "'Cybersex' addicts estimated at 200,000," *Boston Globe*, March 1, 2000, p.A6.

23. This natural progression is also discussed in Akoto and Akoto, *The Sankofa Movement*, p.147.

24. William Ryan, *Blaming the Victim*, NY: Pantheon Books, 1971, Jeffrey Reiman and *The Rich Get Richer and the Poor Get Prison: Ideology, Class, and Criminal Justice*, (5e), Boston: Allyn and Bacon, 1998 (first published in 1979).

25. Randy Albelda, Nancy Folbre and The Center for Popular Economics, *The War on the Poor: A Defense Manual*, NY: The New Press, 1996, Denny Braun, *The Rich Get Richer: The Rise of Income Inequality in the United States and the World*, Chicago: Nelson-Hall Publishers, 1991, Reiman, *The Rich Get Richer and the Poor Get Prison*, Ron Casanova, *Each One Teach One*, Willimantic, CT: Curbstone Press, 1996, Larry D. Crawford (Mwalimu A. Bomani Baruti), "Black Capital," in *negroes and other essays*, Atlanta, GA: Ankoben House, 2000, pp.99-114, John Hope Franklin, *The Color Line*, Columbia, MO: University of Missouri Press, 1993, pp.19-20, 1998, Edward N. Wolff, *Top Heavy: The Increasing Inequality of Wealth in America and What Can Be Done about It*, NY: The New Press, 1995 and, as reported by *ABC Nightly News* on July 12, 1999, the 200 wealthiest people in the world have more money than the 200 billion poorest.

26. As with virtually every social initiative in the West's highly individualistic society, the motivation that produced this dilemma is selfishness. Although discussing Afrikan women from a eurocentric perspective, E. Franklin Frazier strikes a familiar chord when dealing with a Western woman's decision to have or not to have offspring. "[M]otherhood becomes an obstacle to women who have broken all social bonds and are seeking the satisfaction of individualistic impulses."(E. Franklin Frazier, *The Negro Family in the United States*, Chicago: The University of Chicago Press, 1966 (first published in 1939), p.101). They are fully aware of the causes of their dilemma as well as the extent of their predicament. See Ben J. Wattenberg, "The Population Explosion Is Over," *New York Times Magazine*, November 23, 1997, pp.60-63, John R. Weeks, Population: An Introduction to Concepts and Issues, (5e), Belmont, CA: Wadsworth Publishing Company, 1994 and Keidi Obi Awadu, "Population War...report from the frontline," *The Conscious Rasta Report*, Vol.3, No.2, March 1996.

27. Asa G. Hilliard, III, *SBA: The Reawakening of the African Mind*, Gainesville, FL: Makare Publishing, 1997, pp.25-31, Kathy Russell, Midge Wilson and Ronald Hall, *The Color Complex*, NY: Anchor Books, 1992 Larry D. Crawford (Mwalimu A. Bomani Baruti), "Racism, Colorism and Power," in *negroes and other essays*, Atlanta, GA: Ankoben House, 2000, pp.115-141 and

N. Jamilya Chisolm, "Imitation of Life," *The Source*, October 2002, pp.114-117.
28. Ayi Kwei Armah, *The Healers*, Oxford, England: Heinemann, 1978, p.213. And this dislike was not only physical. It was also economic and political in the sense that in Western patriarchy children meant a greater dependence on abusive men.
29. Lee Miller, *From The Heart*, NY: Alfred A. Knopf, 1995, Chancellor Williams, *The Destruction of Black Civilization: Great Issues of a Race From 4500 B.C. to 2000 A.D.*, Chicago: Third World Press, 1987, Del Jones, *The Black Holocaust: Global Genocide*, Philadelphia: Hikeka Press, 1992, Mark Twain, *King Leopold's Soliloquy*, NY: International Publishers, 1970 (first published in 1905), Jan Carew, *The Rape of Paradise*, Brooklyn, NY: A&B Publishers, 1984 and Erriel Roberson (Kofi Addae), *Reality Revolution: Return to the Way*, Columbia MD: Kujichagulia Press, 1996, pp.55-81. Also see Marimba Ani, *Yurugu: An African-Centered Critique of European Cultural Thought and Behavior*, Trenton, NJ: Africa World Press, 1994, p.409-485.
30. For more global discussions of this anti-Afrikan (anti-people of color) European initiative see Chinweizu, *The West and the rest of us*, Lagos, Nigeria: Pero Press, 1987 (first published in 1975), p.485 and Keidi Obi Awadu, *Population War...report from the frontline*, Long Beach, CA: Conscious Rasta Press, 1996.
31. Nathan Hare and Julia Hare, *The Endangered Black Family: Coping with the Unisexualization and Coming Extinction of the Black Race*, San Francisco, CA: The Black Think Tank, 1984, p.54.
32. Stephanie Armour's "Family-Friendly Work Policies Get Cold Shoulder" makes this point quite well (*USA Today*, April 30, 1999, p.1B).
33. Ibid.
34. Molefi K. Asante, speech given at the African American Student Leadership Conference, Rust College (January 17, 1997).
35. Larry D. Crawford (Mwalimu A. Bomani Baruti), *Excuses, Excuses: The Politics of Interracial Coupling in European Culture*, Atlanta, GA: Ankoben House, 2000, pp.49 and 52-53 and Rosie Milligan, *Why Black Men Choose White Women*, Los Angeles: Milligan Books, 1998, p.78.
36. Dona Marimba Richards, *Let the Circle be Unbroken*, Lawrenceville, NJ: The Red Sea Press, Inc., 1980, p.5. Also published under the same tile by Marimba Ani, NY: Nkonimfo Publications.

Chapter 6. The Games People Play

1. If for no other reason, dogs have earned the devotion of Europeans through their loyal participation in their master's vicious global imperialism. The Belgium's use of German shepherds to police their colonization efforts in Zaire and the use of dogs, whose owners were paid for their services at the wages of an actual conquistador, trained to hunt and kill by ripping out a person's

abdomen by the Spanish during their efforts to tyrannize parts of North and South America and the Caribbean Islands, as well as again the use of German Shepherds to intimidate and attack members of the Civil Rights and Black Power Movements are but a few of the historical examples of why Europeans rightly consider dogs to be their best friends. For a sampling see Lee Miller, *From The Heart*, NY: Alfred A. Knopf, 1995, p.158-159 and Richard B. Moore, *The Name "Negro": Its Origin and Evil Use*, Baltimore, MD: Black Classic Press, 1992 (first published in 1960), p.75.

2. Larry D. Crawford (Mwalimu A. Bomani Baruti), *Excuses, Excuses: The Politics of Interracial Coupling in European Culture*, Atlanta, GA: Ankoben House, 2000, p.43.

3. Herant A. Katchadourian and Donald T. Lunde, *Fundamentals of Human Sexuality*, NY: Holt, 1972, p.26 and W.H. Masters and V.E. Johnson, "Ten Sex Myths Exploded," in Nat Lerhman, *Masters and Johnson Explained*, Rockville Center, NY: Playboy Paperbacks, 1970, pp.231-232. No research since these "scientific" studies of the "sex revolution" has contradicted this natural, species maintaining, fact.

4. Ibid.

5. Pamela Paul, *The Starter Marriage and the Future of Matrimony*, NY: Random House, 2002.

6. Laws that allow for quick and "painless" divorces are also deeply rooted in ancient European culture. See Sarah B. Pomeroy, *Goddesses, Whores, Wives, and Slaves: Women in Classical Antiquity*, NY: Schocken Books, 1995 (first published in 1975), pp.158-160).

7. Ibid, p.69.

8. Amen, *Spiritual Union*, 1992, pp.19-21.

9. Bobby E. Wright, *The Psychopathic Racial Personality and other essays*, Chicago: Third World Press, 1984, p.7.

10. M. Belinda Tucker and Claudia Mitchell-Kernan, "Trends in African American Family Formation: A Theoretical and Statistical Overview," in M. Belinda Tucker and Claudia Mitchell-Kernan (eds.), *The Decline in Marriage Among African Americans*, 1995, p.10 and Shirley Hatchett, Joseph Veroff and Elizabeth Douvan, "Marital Instability Among Black and White Couples in Early Marriage," in M. Belinda Tucker and Claudia Mitchell-Kernan (eds.), *The Decline in Marriage Among African Americans*, 1995, p.177.

11. John Henrik Clarke, *Notes for an African World Revolution: Africans at the Crossroads*, Trenton, NJ: Africa World Press, 1991, p.390.

12. See endnote number 10.

13. U.S. Bureau of the Census, *Marital Status and Living Arrangements*, DC: U.S. Government Printing Office.

14. Steven Barnes and Tananarive Due, "Ready, Set, Love," *BETWeekend*, May 1999, p.12. In addition, the larger percentage of married men, for Afrikans in particular, does not reflect a disproportionate marriage to those outside their race. It reflects the larger number of women relative to the number of men for both groups. In addition, intraracial male-female disparities are not a reflection,

or indication, of the effect of interracial marriages on marital statistics. The number of Afrikans who marry Europeans remains too small to have a meaningful impact. The differences speaks to the larger relative and absolute proportion and number of women than men for Afrikans and Europeans. In such an antagonistic intimate interpersonal climate, it is no wonder that we cannot find gender balance, only the continuation of one sex controlling another.

15. Also see Reynolds Farley and Walter R. Allen, *The Color Line and the Quality of Life in America*, NY: Russell Sage, 1987, p.170.

16. Maulana Karenga, *Introduction to Black Studies*, Los Angeles: Kawaida Publications, 1982, pp.215-216.

17. Ma'at represents the principles of truth, justice, order, righteousness, reciprocity and balance.

18. Kwame Agyei Akoto, *Nationbuilding: Theory & Practice in Afrikan Centered Education*, DC: Pan Afrikan World Institute, 1992, p.28.

19. Jacob H. Carruthers, *Essays in Ancient Egyptian Studies*, Los Angeles: University of Sankore Press, 1984, pp.69-71 and *Intellectual Warfare*, Chicago: Third World Press, 1999, pp.37-42 and 111-112, Cheikh A. Diop, *The Cultural Unity of Black Africa: The Domains of Matriarchy and of Patriarchy in Classical Antiquity*, London: Karnak House, 1989, pp.147-148 and 151-165, Kobi K. K. Kambon, *African/Black Psychology in the American Context: An African-Centered Approach*, Tallahassee, FL: Nubian Nation Publications, 1998, pp.144-147. An excellent description of European myth is found in Edith Hamilton, *Mythology*, NY: Little, Brown & Company, 1940. The following statement by Na'im Akbar makes this point current in the minds of all Europeanized people.

> Many religions, the mass media, contemporary psychologists, and all of the major influences on our thinking have cooperated in convincing us that we are hopeless victims of our evil natures. After several episodes of the current fare on our tv screens, we are convinced without debate that man at his best is basically evil. The majority of these super-violent presentations drive home the message that man's nature makes him prone to violence and destructiveness. Many of the popular religious systems suggest that man is basically evil and that a violent death is the mechanism of man's redemption...The belief that evil, destructive and violent behavior is to be expected, makes us uncomfortably reconcile ourselves to an environment of blood and gore. We permit our children to absorb hours of violent rapes, killings, and sadistic mutilations from the movies and television. Then we wonder: "Why are the children so unmanageable? Why do they like to fight so much?" We erroneously conclude that there is something diabolical in their makeup.(Akbar, *Community of Self*, p53.)

In *Black Spark, White Fire: Did African Explorers Civilize Ancient Europe?* Richard Poe makes the point that Egyptians were the only people around "the pond" who had a good opinion about everlasting life. Also see John S. Mbiti, *Introduction to African Religion* (2e), Oxford, Heinemann, 1991 (first published in 1975), p.124 and George G.M. James:

> Such was the Egyptian theory of salvation, through which the individual was trained to become godlike while on earth, and at the same time qualified for everlasting happiness. This was accomplished through the efforts of the individual, through the cultivation of the Arts and Sciences on the one hand, and

a life of virtue on the other. There was no mediator between man and his salvation, as we find in Christian theory. (*Stolen Legacy*, p.28)

20. Many eurocentric scholars try to Afrikanize this infidelity by placing it in the lap of the Kemetic deity Nut who was wife to Ra, the Sun deity. Because of their confusion over symbolism and the natural connection between heaven and earth, they portray Nut's birth of a child by Set (the Earth) and her relationship with Thoth (the Moon) as sexual and illicit. They interpret it, as they have historically described interpersonal female behavior, as full of licentious promiscuity. But this misinterpretation of Kemetic myth must be seriously questioned because these erroneous claims are based on the commentary of Plutarch, a Greek biographer, and the single-minded sexual interpretation of his work by others. Afrikan myth cannot be correctly interpreted out of a European mind. The dramatic story line given the relations between deities in Afrikan creation stories by patriarchical, misogynistic and sex-focused Europeans, past or present, cannot stand as Afrikan fact.

21. NORC (National Opinion Research Center) reported these numbers to be closer to 21 percent for men and 13 percent for women (*General Social Surveys, 1972-1994*, Chicago: National Opinion Research Center, 1994 and *General Social Surveys, 1972-1996*, Chicago: National Opinion Research Center, 1996).

22. The Editors of *Heart & Soul* magazine, *Heart and Soul's Guide to Love, Relationships and Sex*, Emmaus, PA: Rodale Press, 1994, p.49.

23. Jennifer Graham, "Sitting 'Unpretty,'" *TV Guide*, September 4-10, 1999.

24. This lyric, from the Parliament Funkadelic hit song "Atomic Dog," speaks to the European idea that one has no control over ones drives/urges, that one must necessarily and naturally surrender to the sexual pull factor.

> The volume of external influences such as television, popular music, and other cultural inputs overwhelm us. Bombarded by fashions, foods, and fads, our appetites remain highly aroused. With images of self-indulgence such as adultery, deception, greed and corruption, it becomes difficult to imagine life in any other form. With songs of seduction and easy drug availability, we begin to conclude that these impulses cannot be controlled, but are the inevitable result of living.(Na'im Akbar, *The Community of Self (Revised)*, Tallahassee, FL: Mind Productions & Associates, 1994 (1985), p15.)

25. Historical examples of this truth about the natural relationship of lying to Europeans are provided of Pythagoras (Dean Dudley, *History of the First Council of Nice: A World's Christian Convention, A.D.325 with A Life of Constantine*, Brooklyn, NY: A & B Books Publishers, 1992 (first published in 1922), p.22), Niccolò Machiavelli, *The Prince*, NY: Mentor, 1952 (first published in 1532) and Plato's *The Republic* (as quoted in Erriel D. Roberson (Kofi Addae), *Reality Revolution: Return to the Way*, Columbia, MD: Kujichagulia Press, 1996, p.39).

26. Carruthers, *Intellectual Warfare*, Chicago: Third World Press, 1999, pp.35-42. Although from a European centered perspective, this exploitative relationship is also assumed as natural and/or necessary in Max Weber, *The Protestant Ethic and the Spirit of Capitalism*, NY: Scribners, 1958 (first published in 1904) and Thorstein Veblen, *The Theory of the Leisure Class*, NY: Mentor, 1953 (first published in 1899). By far, this historical idea of exploiting

other's labor beyond Europe's shores and applauding it as the burden or "work" of the superior race in "civilizing" their backward inferiors is most evident in their ideology of having a "Manifest Destiny."

27. Larry D. Crawford (Mwalimu A. Bomani Baruti), "The Truth of Liars" in *negroes and other essays*, Atlanta, GA: Ankoben House, 2000, p.83.
28. A. Hampaté Bâ, "The living tradition," in J. Ki-Zerbo (ed.), *General History of Africa (Vol. I): Methodology and African Prehistory*, Berkeley: University of California Press, 1981, p.172.

Chapter 7. Boys to Boys

1. Alexandre Dumas.

Chapter 8. Fair Game

1. Kwame Agyei and Akua Nson Akoto, *The Sankofa Movement*, DC:)yoko InfoCom Inc, 1999, p.2.
2. Larry D. Crawford (Mwalimu A. Bomani Baruti), "Racism, Colorism and Power," in *negroes and other essays*, Atlanta, GA: Ankoben House, 2000, pp.115-141.
3. Larry D. Crawford (Mwalimu A. Bomani Baruti), *Excuses, Excuses: The Politics of Interracial Coupling in European Culture*, Atlanta, GA: Ankoben House, 2000, pp.108-113.

Chapter 9. A Tradition of Purpose in Order

1. John Henrik Clarke, *Notes for an African World Revolution: Africans at the Crossroads*, Trenton, NJ: Africa World Press, 1991, p.402.
2. Dona Richards, "European Mythology: The Ideology of Progress," in Molefi Kete Asante and Abdulai Vandi (eds.), *Contemporary Black Thought*, Los Angeles, CA: Sage Publications, 1985, p.64.
3. Ibid, p.62.
4. Kobi K. K. Kambon *The African Personality in America: An African-Centered Framework* (Tallahassee, FL: Nubian Nation Publications, 1992, pp.49-59 and *African/Black Psychology in the American Context: An African-Centered Approach*, Tallahassee, FL: Nubian Nation Publications, 1998, pp.307-309.
5. Heru Ahki Seb (Dr. James Murrell), "Afrikan Science, Engineering and Development," in Erriel Kofi Addae (Erriel D. Roberson), *To Heal a People:*

Afrikan Scholars Defining a New Reality, Columbia, MD: Kujichagulia Press, 1996, p.189.

6. Llaila O. Afrika, *African holistic Health* (3e), Beltsville, MD: Sea Island Information Group, 1989, p.190.

7. *Afrocentricity*, Trenton, NJ: Africa World Press, 1988, pp.52-57.

8. Molefi K. Asante, "Black Male and Female Relationships: An Afrocentric Context," in Lawrence Gary (ed.), *Black Men*, Newbury Park, CA: Sage Publications, Inc., 1981, pp.75-82.

9. 1 Samuel, 21:4-5 points this out.

10.   Na'im Akbar, *Natural Psychology and Human Transformation* (Tallahassee, FL: Mind Productions & Associates, Inc., 1995).

INDEX

Index

Index

Index

Index

262

Index

Index

Index

Index

EXCUSES, EXCUSES: The Politics of Interracial Coupling in European Culture

Larry D. Crawford (Mwalimu A. Bomani Baruti)

Many believe racial amalgamation is the final step into racial equality. The free and open mating and mixing of Afrikans and Europeans is supposed to eventually create a social environment where the idea of race itself becomes meaningless. *Excuses, Excuses* attempts to address this belief by exploring ten of the most popular excuses Afrikan males give for pursuing relationships with European females. They include everything from "I just fell in love" to the aggression of Afrikan women to revenge against European men. In this book, the author exposes them for what they are, rationales to conceal and justify mentacide. In that many individuals use the same excuses, the coupling of Afrikans and Europeans is more than a personal choice. It is a social phenomenon which should be explained through an analysis of European cultural imperatives. And this book does just that.

Order Form

NAME: _____

ADDRESS: _____

PHONE NUMBER: _____

E-MAIL: _____

Please send _____ copies of
Excuses, Excuses at $13.00 each: $ _____
Sales tax (GA residents only: 7% (91¢ per copy)): _____
Shipping & handling (see S&H below): _____
TOTAL ENCLOSED: $ _____

S&H: $2 for 1 book and $1 for each additional book.
Discounts available for book orders of 10 or more copies.

Send your check or money order (made payable to LARRY CRAWFORD) to: **Ankoben House, P.O. Box 10786, Atlanta, GA 30310**

negroes and other essays

Larry D. Crawford (Mwalimu A. Bomani Baruti)

"People sense it. They can feel it in the air even though most cannot identify it or touch it. They know something is wrong, has been wrong, terribly wrong. But, whatever it is, it has run its course. It has returned home. For it has nowhere else to go. It can no longer hide behind blaming others. It is afraid. And its fear reacts with terror against anyone and anything within its reach.

Truth always surfaces. It cannot be hidden or Afrikans could not *know* what we know. But to set us free from this terror it must be acted upon. We must become the force of correction or our enslavement becomes more sophisticated and indefinite. Enslavers learn from and correct those mistakes that in the past threatened their reality with revolution from below.

These essays are merely my way of identifying and explaining this enigmatic wrong so it can correctly be dealt with, finally, forever. In the context of the wisdom of those who have earned the right to be called elders and ancestors, we must walk their path if we are to eliminate this chaos from humanity. In this quest, Afrikan warrior scholars must *know* we owe our people, answer only to the Universe and can no longer allow Europeans to spread their destructive confusion. Of this, there can be no doubt."

These eleven essays which speak to the mentality required of this quest include: The New Humanity; Shackles;, The Cultural Continuum; The Truth of Liars; Inner Vision; Black Capital; Racism, Colorism and Power; negroes ; I Am Not Ashamed; Dedication to an Afrikan; Voices in the Tradition of the Afrikan Warrior

---

<u>Order form</u>

NAME: _____

ADDRESS: _____

PHONE NUMBER: _____

E-MAIL: _____

Please send _____ copies of

negroes and other essays at $13.00 each: $ _____

Sales tax (GA residents only: 7% (91¢ per copy)): _____

Shipping & handling (see S&H below): _____

TOTAL ENCLOSED: $ _____

S&H: $2 for 1 book and $1 for each additional book.

Discounts available for book orders of 10 or more copies.

Send your check or money order (made payable to LARRY CRAWFORD) to: **Ankoben House, P.O. Box 10786, Atlanta, GA 30310**

Chess Primer: An Introduction to the Game of Chess
(Revised Second Edition)

Mwalimu A. Bomani Baruti

Our children are special. Of this fact there is no doubt. And, without question, the game of chess helps them realize their potential. This exciting and challenging game makes their minds even more remarkable because it helps improve their ability to think more independently and critically about whatever they encounter in the streets, schools and homes of our community. It causes them to think about consequences....Furthermore, chess is math. It is a game that requires the constant calculation and recalculation of multiple numerical problems at the same time. The leap in thinking that occurs in a child when s/he is required to simultaneously consider the present and possible moves of 32 uniquely moving pieces continuously traversing a 64 square board is truly amazing to witness....[*Chess Primer*] has been specifically designed to help simplify many of the concepts and ideas fundamental to the game of chess so that they can immediately begin to play and test their skills out on each other....Within the introductory chapter [of this revised edition] more historical and culturally centered analysis have been provided for those to whom this was written. More practice and playing tips have been inserted at appropriate points and a list of "Rules to Learn to Win By" is found at the end of Chapter 6. Of equal importance, sets of one-move and two-move checkmate problems have been placed at the end of the text so that novices can begin to systematically practice the art of mating.

Order Form

NAME: _____

ADDRESS: _____

PHONE NUMBER: _____

E-MAIL: _____

Please send _____ copies of

negroes and other essays at $12.95 each: $ _____

Sales tax (GA residents only: 7% (91¢ per copy)): _____

Shipping & handling (see S&H below): _____

TOTAL ENCLOSED: $ _____

S&H: $2 for 1 book and $1 for each additional book.

Discounts available for book orders of 10 or more copies.

Send your check or money order (made payable to LARRY CRAWFORD) to: Ankoben House, P.O. Box 10786, Atlanta, GA 30310